# PARANORMAL REALITIES III

## Keith Johnson

**With**

**Sandra Johnson**

&

Susan Soares (Executive Editor)

**NEAR Publishing**

**WARWICK, RI**

**Paranormal Realities III**

ISBN 978-0-615-96837-7

Cover design by Jeanine Calkin

# Dedication

## A Tribute to Chris Angelo, Paranormal Investigator

The following is a tribute to my friend and fellow paranormal investigator, Chris Angelo. Chris was born in Rhode Island on August 7, 1981. He became a member of The Atlantic Paranormal Society in 2001, which is how he and I first met. Although Chris often worked closely with Brian Harnois as a technical assistant, he also worked closely with me on cases that potentially involved inhuman entities.

Physically, Chris resembled a huskier, younger version of actor Bud Cort ("Harold and Maude" and "M.A.S.H.").

Chris was skilled at interviewing clients and possessed a background in martial arts. His intuitive level was somewhat higher than average, presumably owing to a slight concussion he sustained about two years prior to joining TAPS. He had an uncanny knack for sensing the presence of danger, making him very protective of his fellow investigators. Another attribute Chris possessed was that he could see unusually well in subdued lighting conditions. This sensitivity was medically verified, caused by an abnormal number of color rods in his eyes. If one views a photo of Chris, they will notice that his eyes were an almost unnaturally light shade of blue. I recall the very first paranormal investigation that Chris and I were on together at a private residence in Newport, Rhode Island that was undergoing renovations. We happened to be walking together down a darkened staircase in the mansion-like house and I was surprised that Chris apparently had no need of a flashlight.

I asked him, "Chris, don't you need a flashlight to see in front of you?"

He replied, "Nah, I can see just fine." Naturally, I did require a flashlight to see the steps in front of me, and prevent me from tripping!

Whenever Brian was not on an investigation with us, Chris and I would usually be paired up as a team. I soon learned that Chris had a sense of adventure, and enjoyed exploring on-site locations where there was an element of danger. Although he was by nature very soft-spoken, Chris also had a daredevil side to his personality and shared a subtle sense of humor with myself, Carl, and Chris Finch.

I came to respect another factor of Chris's persona. One evening, when we were at a local coffee shop with several other TAPS members, I happened to have my son Keith Jr. with me. Although Keith is autistic and has difficulty communicating, Chris offered to sit with him for a while and patiently managed to have a normal conversation with him. I was extremely impressed with this, especially since Chris was only 21 years old at the time and had no formal training in dealing with special needs children.

In 2003 Chris enlisted in the Air Force Reserve branch because he felt the need to serve his country, which necessitated him taking a temporary leave of absence from TAPS. However, later that same year, after he'd completed his basic training, Chris expressed an interest in returning to TAPS as often as his military career permitted. In October of 2003, Chris was slated to return to investigating again with TAPS.

My brother Carl and I happened to meet up with Chris in downtown Providence, while waiting in line with him to audition as extras in a movie to be filmed locally. The three of us shared some laughs and enjoyable conversation, despite the blustery wind and raindrops. Chris had neglected to bring a jacket. Chris expressed just how excited he was at the prospect of returning to TAPS, and he promised to join us again soon... if not for the next investigation, then definitely on the one after that.

Our next investigation was scheduled for that weekend which, being Halloween was naturally a busy one for us in TAPS. Founder Jason Hawes and I did a Halloween radio interview on Friday in Taunton Green. The following afternoon, November 1st, Jason, Grant, Brian Harnois, Brian Bell and I were guest speakers at a writers' conference held at the "haunted" Cumberland Monastery. That night, my wife Sandra and I, as well as Brian Harnois, Brian Bell and Kristen Allen conducted an investigation at an apartment in Marlboro, MA. Unfortunately, Chris Angelo had a prior commitment with a friend of his for that evening, but he assured us that he would be making his return to TAPS on the following weekend.

On Monday evening while I was at work, I received a call from a very somber Jason Hawes, informing me that Chris Angelo had been killed instantly late on Saturday night when his friend's car (which Chris was driving) had gone off the road under slick conditions in Smithfield, RI. Chris was 22 years old at the time of his death on November 2nd, 2003.

On September 22nd, 2007, at the Paranormal X convention organized by Raymond Dowaliby, Sandra and my brother Carl and I gave a talk on demonology. At the onset of our presentation, I gave a brief tribute to Chris Angelo and led everyone present in a round of applause for him.

To this day Sandra and I regularly receive inquires about Chris Angelo from people all over the country. And although none of us who knew him personally has ever been contacted by him from the other side – although he did once mention that he would try to contact us should he go before us – Chris will always remain in our thoughts and memories as a cherished friend, as well as a talented paranormal investigator. There will be no forgetting Chris, as the tribute on our site at New England Anomalies Research attests. We prefer to think of Chris as merely being on another temporary leave of absence, and we wholeheartedly believe that we will one day be reunited with him.

**Chris Angelo**

# Introduction

Sandra and I had already been married for some years, and she was familiar with my interest and involvement with paranormal research and exploration. She herself had a moderate interest in the paranormal, and would often watch the more interesting TV programs on the subject. Sandra would also put up with my occasional 'emergency' excursions, when a client would be in need of assistance, often feeling nowhere else to turn. The following day I'd of course share the details of the case with her, usually during breakfast in relaxed surroundings. She also enjoyed hearing my stories of the 'good old days' of my associations with seasoned psychic researchers such as Ed and Lorraine Warren, as well as Ed and Patricia Morgan. On weekend afternoons, Sandra and I would sometimes take our son out for a family outing, perhaps visiting a local historic cemetery or two. Or perhaps we'd embark on a family daytime excursion to an alleged 'haunted' location such as Ram Tail in Foster, RI…always in a pleasant, non-threatening atmosphere, since we'd have our young son with us.

And then one day I happened to be reviewing audio evidence from a recent investigation, which included a recording of me performing a religious cleansing. Sandra suddenly turned to me, and said with a tone of realization to her voice, "I'm living with the Exorcist!"

It was shortly after this that she began taking more of an interest in my research and in the work I was participating in. Now this is not to say that Sandra had never had a paranormal experience in her entire life prior to this time. In fact, her first apparent brush with the paranormal occurred when she was about twenty years of age. It was actually witnessed by a family member while Sandra was sleeping, when a tall, hooded shadow figure was standing over her bed watching her. In fact, the family member did not mention the incident to Sandra until a few days later, for fear of upsetting her.

But now that Sandra was actually beginning to take more of a serious interest in the field of paranormal research, I began requesting her assistance in analyzing various examples of EVP (Electronic Voice Phenomenon) I'd captured on audio recordings during investigations. Although examples of photographic and video evidence were much rarer, she'd assist me with these as well. Sandra's computer experience also came in handy when needed, and before long, her assistance was proving quite valuable. However, it was not only the technical mechanics that appealed to her, but also the fact that she and I shared the same Christian faith, a significant part of the work I was involved with. I shared with my wife many of the things I'd learned over the years on the subjects of angelology and demonology, and how this knowledge could be applied in a practical manner when assisting victims of oppression, and other forms of psychic attack. Because of her newly acquired avid interest in the subject matter, Sandra proved to be both a willing student and a quick learner.

Sandra was eventually invited to become a member of The Atlantic Paranormal Society, or TAPS, an organization which my brother Carl and I had been members of for the past few years. She quickly proved herself to be very adept, using her computer skills to contribute some wonderful improvements on the TAPS website. Not only this, but her talents as a field investigator also rapidly developed. Before long, Sandra became my partner on paranormal investigations, and, what was more, she was also able to assist me on demonic cases.

A little known and underrated fact is that during the year leading up to the advent of the hit TV series Ghost Hunters, Sandra, Brian Harnois and I were very much an inseparable team. The three of us would be out on cases practically each and every weekend. And even when we weren't out on an actual investigation, or involved in a house blessing or a deliverance session, we'd either be getting together over dinner or at least chatting on the phone about our latest paranormal investigations. Of course, we very often investigated with other TAPS team members as well, such as with my brother, Fran Ford, Renee Laverdiere-Smith, Chris Finch, Brian Bell and others. But the main core would always be the trio, the 'three amigos', consisting of Sandra, Brian and myself.

All through this time, there was much talk and negotiations involving our founders going on about the possibility of TAPS doing a weekly TV series. When this eventually manifested into a reality, in the form of the widely popular TV series 'Ghost Hunters' on the SyFy Channel, things changed rapidly, and in many ways unexpectedly for TAPS. The incredibly hectic schedules of filming a weekly television show (not to mention the sudden demands placed upon individual investigators, especially the founders themselves) meant that much of our activities in TAPS suddenly had to revolve around the show itself. It quickly became evident that TAPS had to adapt by dividing into two separate teams, meaning one would have to be available as cast members of the show, and the other would be tending to private cases where the media was not involved. Although my brother and I did participate in several episodes of Ghost Hunters during the first and second seasons, neither of us became regular cast members. Also, it is the nature of the beast, so to speak, that 'couples' are generally thought to detract from the main focus of reality TV shows… unless, of course, the main cast members themselves happen to be a married couple. This pretty much left Sandra out of the picture, as far as us investigating on cases together. It is for that reason that we stayed mainly out of the media, and continued with private cases. Another problem was that since Brian Harnois was now so heavily involved as a regular cast member of Ghost Hunters, he was no longer available to assist us on private non-media TAPS cases.

Throughout the next several months, both Sandra and I kept up our diligent work as TAPS investigators. However, the tremendous success of Ghost Hunters resulted in a rapid influx of cases coming in from all over the country. Because of this incredible surge, the majority of these cases were handed over to our friends in New England Paranormal. Even our close friend and N.E.P. Founder Steve Gonsalves, who Sandra and I had regularly assisted on extreme cases, had suddenly been recruited as a regular cast member on Ghost Hunters.

Eventually, Sandra and I decided we could work best by branching off and forming our own organization. We named our new group New England Anomalies Research, due to the fact that we would be concentrating on cases predominantly within the New England area. NEAR quickly became a success, which eventually resulted in Sandra and I forming our own informal paranormal TV talk show, titled 'Ghosts R N.E.A.R.,'episodes of which are uploaded to our website at www.nearparanormal.com, as well as on YouTube.com. We have also occasionally continued to assist both TAPS and NEP, and other paranormal research teams with cases involving extreme situations.

This book, as with 'Paranormal Realities' and 'Paranormal Realities II', primarily documents my early days of paranormal research and investigation, then segues into some of our adventures with TAPS and NEAR. It is told in my own words, and it is my sincere hope that you the reader will enjoy its content. And like my first two books, it is comprised of many of the stories I have so often verbally related to others while seated in a local coffee shop, or within a lecture hall or classroom settings. Many of my friends and listeners so often suggested to me,

"Keith, why don't you put your experiences into book form?" And I promised them I definitely would. So, with a great deal of encouragement and inspiration, especially from my dear wife Sandra, here is 'Paranormal Realities III'! 9

~ Keith E. Johnson

Nathan Mayer, Sandra Johnson and David Grist taping Ghosts R N.E.A.R.

# Contents

Statue within a haunted cemetery located in Coventry, RI.

# Chapter 1

**Bathsheba's Curse**

Throughout my career in the field of paranormal research, which now spans over four decades, I have investigated a great many diverse locations and situations. Along with investigating freelance, I have also belonged to a number of paranormal investigation organizations, including The Atlantic Paranormal Society (TAPS), and New England Anomalies Research (NEAR), which was founded by my wife Sandra and myself.

However, throughout all these years and the multiple investigations I have been involved with, still one case in particular stands out for me above the others. This is the case involving Carolyn and Roger Perron, their five young daughters and an 18th-Century farm house in Harrisville, Rhode Island. It was also the site of mine and my brother Carl's first residential paranormal investigation and intervention.

At the time I was 18 years old, and was a member of an organization called Parapsychological Investigation and Research Organization (P.I.R.O.) based at Rhode Island College. I'd placed a self-designed ad in a local newspaper regarding our services. Carolyn Perron answered just three weeks later

Officially known as the Dexter Arnold Estate, the Perron family reported some truly terrifying activity in their 237 year old home. Carolyn had been slicing an orange and blood suddenly began oozing from the orange onto the floor. Then on another day, a coat hanger leaped seemingly by itself from off of a coat rack and began viciously assailing Carolyn until it went clattering to the floor. The family also witnessed the large, antiquated radio that would spontaneously start playing by itself... even when unplugged! Curiously, the song that would repeatedly play on this old radio was the end refrain of the Moody Blues song, "Nights in White Satin."

During the course of P.I.R.O.'s investigation, it did not take long for us to discover that this was the real deal, and that genuine, incredible spirit activity was taking place there. And obviously, the Perron family members had to live with this activity on a daily and nightly basis. Although we were a young college-age organization, we assured them we would do all we could to help.

Once we'd investigated and realized the genuine validity of the phenomena taking place, Donna, chairperson of P.I.R.O., contacted our friends Ed and Lorraine Warren and consulted with them, because of their years of experience and valued advice. And in fact, Ed and Lorraine did more than merely consult; they also became personally involved in the case along with us, which we greatly appreciated. For novice investigators, actually working on a case with Ed and Lorraine was the very first time we'd had the opportunity to network with other paranormal investigators of their caliber! Although this was originally intended to be a mutual intervention between P.I.R.O. and the Warrens, Ed and Lorraine soon took over the case, and advised the Perron family that the situation in their home was much too dangerous for any other investigation organization, however well-intentioned that group might be. For the safety of all, they had to handle this case themselves.

In October of 1973, the Warrens returned to further assist the Perron family. Now, it was known that sometime during the late 1700's, an elderly woman named Mrs. John Arnold had hanged herself in the barn that is located on the property. Some years later, a younger woman named Susan Arnold also had hanged herself in the 'birthing room' just outside of Andrea Perron's bedroom. Lorraine, being clairvoyant, began picking up on the presence of a dominant, hostile female spirit within the farmhouse.

"I'm picking up on the presence of a woman who died long ago, but who is still in within this house. Her name is... Bathsheba. And she is mainly responsible for terrorizing this unfortunate family," Lorraine told her husband and the Perron family.

It is on historical record that in the mid-1800's, a woman named Bathsheba Sherman was suspected of killing an infant who she was caring for in the farmhouse, by inserting a sewing needle into the base of the poor infant's skull. Although Bathsheba was never convicted of this crime, she was never able to live down her tarnished reputation in the community, and she died an embittered, cantankerous old woman. And all these many years after, older residents in the town still remembered Bathsheba Sherman and her notorious reputation. There is no historic evidence that Bathsheba Sherman was actually guilty of this crime, nor any evidence that she was ever a practicing witch, as has been rumored.

Following a trying ordeal that continued throughout the better part of a decade, the activity in the farmhouse eventually became somewhat tolerable. At its worst however, Carolyn Perron suffered through episodes of transient spirit possession and other terrifying phenomena that nearly ended her life. Of course, life for the Perron family was not even close to "normal," nor would it even be so for them again. But at least they managed to survive together as a family unit within the Arnold Estate.

Several years after our original investigation, the Perron family reluctantly sold their Harrisville home and relocated out of state. The move however did not completely separate the family from their spiritual connections with the house. In fact, after moving from the house, the members of the Perron family soon realized that some of the activity had actually followed them, and they half-jokingly referred to this as "Bathsheba's Curse," after the main spirit that held absolute dominion in the Harrisville house.

Some thirty-two years after the original events, Sandra and I, along with members of our current organization, New England Anomalies Research visited the Arnold Estate in Harrisville. With the gracious permission of the current homeowners, we also conducted an investigation of the entire house. And as we were determined to find, at least some of the spirits in the house were still active, despite the house having been blessed by Catholic clergy decades before.

Upstairs just outside the den, Sandra was discussing with one of the homeowners some of the activity that he had experienced since living in the house. He had experienced only relatively minor activity, consisting of some unexplained traveling lights, as well as vibrations emanating from various items of furniture he was either sitting or reclining in.

As he concluded his narrative to Sandra, he gave a light laugh and said, "I wish I had more to tell ya."

Of course I'd been standing there recording their conversation on audio tape. When I later reviewed the recording, I heard Jerry's voice saying "I wish I had more to tell ya." This was instantly followed on the recording by an EVP (Electronic Voice Phenomena) harshly whispering, 'Tell her!' At the time of the recording only Sandra, the homeowner and I were in the room.

I captured another clear incident of EVP on my audio recording that evening. While the homeowner's wife was giving us all a tour down in the cellar, Carl indicated our member Russ who was taking readings in a corner, and humorously said, "That's just one of our team members relieving himself." Apparently a spirit presence took exception to this remark and did not appreciate Carl's intended humor. For as soon as I played my recording back, a voice could be heard indignantly commenting, "What?? Don't lie!"


Throughout the years following our original investigation, I had often wondered what became of the Perron family, who I had known all too briefly back in my 18th year but had most certainly made an incredible impression on me. In fact, I included a detailed chapter about the Harrisville case in my first published book, Paranormal Realities.

I especially recalled Andrea, the eldest of the five Perron daughters, who was 15 years old at the time of our original investigation. Being at least somewhat close in age, Andrea and I had developed a rapport with each other. I fondly recalled being at the farmhouse back in August of 1973 when Andrea felt a little uncomfortable about going down into the darkened cellar (which had very little illumination at the time) to grab some preserves, and she'd asked me to accompany her. While down in the cellar, Andrea and I had prayed together and held hands while we did so.

Then, in 2010, I had a sudden idea. Since I'd always wondered how the Perron family was doing, why not try to contact at least one of the family members through Facebook? Of course I initially chose to contact Andrea...and lo and behold, she responded. To my delight, Andrea not only vividly remembered me, but she was just as excited to hear from me as I was to contact her!

Andrea Perron and I soon established a regular communication with each other, and I was absolutely thrilled to learn that she had been hard at work on her own book detailing her family's as well as her own personal experiences from living in the Harrisville farmhouse, in a book titled House of Darkness House of Light. And in fact, this book was actually intended to be the first in a trilogy surrounding the Perron family's personal experiences from ten years of living in a house that was literally "alive with spirits."

In essence, Andrea and I were rekindling our mutual history with that house. I explained to her about our subsequent visit to the Arnold Estate, when I had captured some impressive examples of EVP during NEAR's investigation. Andrea was naturally quite intrigued, although not at all surprised to learn that the spirits in her former home were still somewhat active after all these years.

As Andrea and I continued to communicate, one thing led to another, and before long we arranged for her to visit to Rhode Island. Andrea would be leaving from her home in Georgia and meeting up with her dad Roger and their family friend Manny, who would be documenting highlights of their excursion on video. And of course, Sandra and I invited Andrea to be our personal in-studio guest on our paranormal TV talk show, **Ghosts R N.E.A.R.**

The taping of this episode took place in June of 2011. When we welcomed them into the studio, Andrea's dad Roger was there with her and Manny. It was a wonderful reunion between myself, Roger and Andrea Perron. They instantly took to Sandra like she was part of the family. It was indeed a wonderful pleasure meeting Manny as well.

The taping of this episode of **Ghosts R N.E.A.R.** was an exciting experience, and Andrea proved to be a fascinating guest. She was extremely well-spoken as she explained many of her experiences while growing up in the haunted Arnold Estate as a teenager, and the stigma this sometimes caused for her and her family within the community. She related some of the horrific events that took place within this house, such as the ghostly manifestation of a woman wearing a long Victorian-style dress, with an apparently broken neck and desiccated facial features that had terrified her mother Carolyn, hovering over her bedside just before daybreak one morning. The spirit also uttered a bizarre, very threatening chant to Carolyn, telling her, "I'll drive ye out with fiery brooms. I'll drive ye mad with death and gloom." From this spirit's apparent 18th-Century style of dress and archaic speech - as well as the broken neck, it seemed to have taken on the personification of elderly Mrs. John Arnold, rather than Bathsheba Sherman.

Andrea also talked about finally deciding to share the story of her and her family's ten year experience by writing volume one of House of Darkness House of Light. And during the show, Andrea was kind enough to present Sandra and me with an autographed copy of her book, and sincerely thanked us for our personal efforts in promoting the book project.

Needless to say, the taping of this episode of **Ghosts R N.E.A.R.** with Andrea Perron seemed to fly by all too quickly, and we afterward began discussing plans for future interviews.


While still in Rhode Island, Roger and Andrea visited the Arnold Estate in Harrisville... and it seemed that at least something in the old homestead remembered them. While Roger and Manny were downstairs in the cellar, Roger suddenly had the sensation of being "approached" by an unseen presence, causing him to react visibly. It was a distinct presence that was eerily familiar to him from years past. This was believed to be the entity known to Roger and his family as "Bathsheba"... and Manny caught the moment on video.

Meanwhile, Andrea was upstairs in the kitchen chatting with the current residents, and a journalist from a local publication, interviewing them about some of the supernatural events that had been experienced in the farmhouse over the years. Suddenly, a daughter's instinct caused Andrea to sense that her father may be in some sort of danger, and she abruptly excused herself, heading for the cellar door. An instant later, in full view of everyone, Andrea was physically turned around by an invisible presence and very forcefully slammed against the wall, causing her head to roughly hit the door jam.

As the terrified journalist looked on, all Andrea could manage to do was growl through her teeth, "You leave my father alone!" Instantly the unseen force released her, and she nearly collapsed to the floor.

A moment later, Roger and Manny returned upstairs, and from the look on her father's face, Andrea knew he had experienced an encounter with an otherworldly presence.

Andrea commented, "She did not want my father in the cellar." By "she" Andrea was of course referring to Bathsheba. Immediately after witnessing this, the journalist abruptly excused herself, left the house and never returned.

Months after this incident, Andrea told me, "I hit that door jam so hard, I had a bruise on my spine and the back of my head for three months."

Back in the 1970's, a psychic medium named Mary who was visiting the Perron family with the Ed and Lorraine Warren had told them, "The answer lies buried beneath the bell stones." Could she have possibly been referring to Bathsheba Sherman? In Andrea Perron's opinion, Bathsheba Sherman may not even be buried in the nearby historical cemetery at all, but may in fact have been buried somewhere on the grounds of the farmhouse itself. Because of Bathsheba's reputation, the local church authorities may not have allowed her to be buried on concentrated ground.

In October of 2011 Sandra and I, along with our team members David Grist, Daniel and Jeanine Calkin, Nathan Mayer and Valerie Moskowitz conducted a follow-up investigation at the Harrisville farmhouse at the courtesy of the current residents. We decided to do a follow-up episode for **Ghosts R N.E.A.R.** using footage from this investigation. At Andrea's personal request, we would also attempt to find some answers for her and her family.

While we were there, the homeowners graciously gave us an on-camera tour of the entire house. During our investigation, Sandra, Jeanine and I conducted an on-camera EVP session in the den. At the time the Perron family lived there, this was actually the location of Roger and Carolyn's bedroom, where the horrifying manifestation of the woman with the twisted neck had appeared to Carolyn. We intended to review our recordings later on, as time permitted.

Just before we concluded our investigation that evening, Jeanine videotaped a walk-through of the first and second floors of the house. Weeks later, upon viewing this segment of the episode at her home in Georgia, Carolyn Perron remarked how eerie it was for her to watch this first-person walk-through of her old homestead.

Before leaving that night, we all gathered in the kitchen for some group discussion and evidence review. I happened to capture one significant EVP in particular, in response to a question about the Warren's intervention. One of the current homeowners had asked, "Now Lorraine did the séance thing, correct?"

"Right," I agreed, "Lorraine, Ed and another medium conducted a séance, and then later on, clergy came in and did a blessing of the entire house. Now, that supposedly didn't expel the spirits, it just nullified them."

On the recording, an inhuman sounding voice could suddenly be heard harshly whispering "Did not expel the spirits!" In fact, it sounded exactly like the same spirit voice I had caught on EVP when Sandra and I had been in the house during our previous investigation, in August of 2005.

Just before we left, I said a prayer of protection for all of us there; that in the name of God nothing unholy would be allowed to attach itself to any of us.


Andrea and Roger Perron visited Rhode Island again in October of 2011. This time, Andrea gave a one-woman presentation at The Assembly Theater in Harrisville, her old stomping grounds from her theater days, titled **"The Biggest Chill"**. The presentation took place on Monday evening, October 10th, 2011, which also happened to be Andrea's birthday. I was honored to be asked by Andrea to personally introduce her, and during the introduction I explained to the audience that throughout all my years of paranormal investigation and pursuing the study of demonology, it was the Perron case above the rest that had remained with me the most, and haunted me to this day.

As the audience sat spellbound within the large auditorium, Andrea shared many of the details surrounding House of Darkness House of Light. The low stage lighting cast dramatic shadows as Andrea went through the retelling of her personal story with an air of conviction.

**"The Biggest Chill"** concluded that evening with Andrea inviting a brief discussion with some of the audience members on the reality of paranormal phenomena, followed by a meet and greet. And it was clear from some of the comments a number of the local people in attendance, would definitely be sleeping with the lights on that night!

The following evening, Roger, Andrea and I traveled together to Groton, Connecticut, where we were invited to be guests on the paranormal talk show "NEST Files" hosted by Michael Lee Carroll.

Not surprising, it was eventually decided that the story of the Perron family and their haunted farmhouse in Harrisville, RI, would finally be made into a major motion picture. The premise of the film focuses entirely around Ed and Lorraine Warren's intervention on behalf of the Perrons. Produced by New Line Cinema and directed by James Wan (who also directed the "Saw" and "Insidious" films) the title of the movie is "The Conjuring." The action of the film is appropriately set in the year 1971.

In March of 2012 Lorraine Warren, her son-in-law Tony Spera, Roger and Andrea Perron and a few of Andrea's younger sisters were invited as special guests to visit the set of "The Conjuring", which had just begun production in Georgia. They were treated like royalty by the cast and crew alike. However, this enjoyable occasion was not also without its share of mishap. At one point when everyone was gathered outside, from out of nowhere, a sudden, unexpected gust of wind registering at 60 mph blew past them. This sudden wind overturned table and chairs, and destroyed other property on the set within moments. It then stopped just as abruptly as it began.

What turned out to be an even more bizarre twist of fate, Andrea and her sisters were later to find out that at the exact moment this wind gust occurred, their mother Carolyn had taken a severe fall at home, which had resulted in a broken hip. When Andrea and her sisters rushed to the hospital to visit their mother, Carolyn was heavily sedated... yet she came to just long enough to declare, "It's Bathsheba's curse!" before lapsing back into unconsciousness.

The night after the Perron family left the set of "The Conjuring" a fire mysteriously broke out in the hotel where the cast and crew were staying, forcing everyone to evacuate. Reports of other bizarre things happening on the set during the filming of "The Conjuring" have also been rumored, much of which the cast and crew have refused to publicly discuss.

In July of 2013, with the huge success of "The Conjuring" just released less than a week prior, Andrea again made a public appearance at the Assembly Theater in Harrisville to reprise her one-woman lecture. And just as in 2011, I was again given the honor of Master of Ceremonies, introducing Harrisville's own Andrea Perron. And indeed, as Andrea took the stage, shouts bellowed from the audience of "Our Andrea! Our Andrea!"

On this occasion, two of my former fellow members of P.I.R.O. were present in the audience: Carl and our former case manager, Donna Neufeld. I was proud to introduce them to the audience as well.

Andrea outdid herself that evening, reliving many of the personal details of the Harrisville haunting, and her family's decade-long saga, which no movie adaptation could possibly have captured as accurately as Andrea did during her presentation. Andrea also personally thanked Donna, Carl and I for being the original investigation team at her family's farmhouse those four decades ago, and for alerting our friends Ed and Lorraine Warren to her family's dilemma.

Not unexpectedly, Andrea's presentation was held over that evening, and after her Q & A with the audience was concluded, Andrea received and enthusiastic standing ovation. Even after this, Andrea found herself completely surrounded in the lobby by friends, fans and admirers, and with the assistance of her dad Roger, she rapidly sold out of the copies of her autographed books!


It has always been my personal belief that the dominant spirit in the Perron family's former residence was in reality a demonic spirit that may have been masquerading as Bathsheba Sherman; perhaps one that may have even been oppressing Bathsheba Sherman herself in life, as well as Mrs. John Arnold and Susan Arnold during their lifetimes. It may also have been this very same inhuman spirit that was responsible for victimizing Carolyn Perron while she lived in that house, at one time invading her body and nearly causing her death.

Some speculation has also arisen as to whether the Sherman burial plot located in Harrisville is actually haunted by Bathsheba Sherman. I personally do not believe this to be the case, and perhaps this was somewhat verified (at least for me) when I took Sandra and our son Keith Jr. to visit the Sherman plot on Sunday, July 28th, 2013. Sandra and I were distressed to find that Bathsheba's headstone had recently been heavily vandalized, completely knocked over and broken in pieces. Fortunately the other gravestones, including those of her husband Judson and their children, remained untouched. We took photos of the graves, and I happened to be audio recording our conversation as I explained to Sandra the difference between the foot stones and the small concrete pillars that were placed to support the iron fence surrounding the cemetery.

When Sandra and I later reviewed my audio recording, we could hear my voice explaining the difference between the foot stones and the support stones. Immediately after this, an example of EVP was captured on my audio recording. It was a male voice clearly saying the word "No." And in my experience, it is not all that uncommon to have a negative, or "contrary" comment recorded on audio in a location such as a cemetery where vandalism and desecration have recently taken place. It is not necessarily the restless spirits of the departed that are speaking. Rather, I believe these are negative, inhuman spirits that have been attracted by the negative energy introduced to these locations, i.e., like attracts like.


And so, the story of the Haunting in Harrisville continues, and what the next chapter in this ongoing saga is nobody knows.

Keith Johnson with Andrea Perron

Harrisville Anomaly photo

**Bathsheba Sherman's gravestone**

# Chapter 2

## Vampire's Grave

$A$s the local story goes, in the year 1967, a Coventry, Rhode Island high school teacher allegedly told his class that a 19-year-old woman accused of vampirism, who died in the late 19th Century lies buried in a cemetery located of Route 102. Although he did not give a name, he was almost undoubtedly referring to the grave of Mercy Brown in Exeter. The following Tuesday evening, on Halloween night, several members of this teacher's class set out in search of the "vampire's grave" and traveled in the opposite direction off of Route 102. They eventually wound up at a rather foreboding looking historical cemetery, surrounded by a stone wall, located along Plain Meeting House Road in West Greenwich (WG Historical Cemetery #2). During a diligent search of the headstones, the teenagers came across one in particular, which read: "Nellie L. Vaughn; Daughter of George B. and Ellen; Died in her 19th year, March 31, 1889." The age and the year certainly fit. Further, when the teenagers shone their flashlights on the bottom of the headstone, they unexpectedly read an ominous sounding inscription: "I Am Waiting and Watching For You." Now utterly convinced that they'd found their girl, the students wasted little time in spreading their story around the school…and eventually, the legend of 'Vampire's Grave' spread throughout the entire community, and even beyond.

Unlike Mercy Brown, very little is actually known about the brief life of this unfortunate young woman, whose name was Ellen (Nellie) Louise Vaughn. She was the daughter of George B. Vaughn, a Coventry blacksmith, and Ellen (Knight) Vaughn. The Vaughn family owned a small farm located on Robin Hollow Road in West Greenwich. When Nellie Louise Vaughn died of pneumonia at the age of nineteen, she was buried on the family homestead. However, when the Vaughn family sold their property several months later, Nellie's mother obtained permission to have her body relocated to the then new cemetery on Plain Meeting House Road. According to town records, certainly no indication exists that any vampire mystique was suspected surrounding Nellie L. Vaughn until nearly eighty years after her untimely death! This does, indeed, seem to have been a case of mistaken identity. Unfortunately, over the years, her grave (and indeed the entire cemetery) has become a virtual haven not only for the merely curious, but also for party-goers, cultists and those that are intent on senseless, mindless vandalism. Many claim that Nellie Vaughn herself may have taken exception to her undeserved reputation.

According to "The New England Ghost Files" by Charles T. Robinson, one afternoon some utility workers were busy repairing power lines right outside of this cemetery. Suddenly, one of the utility workers alerted his co-worker beside him.

"Hey… check that out!" he said, motioning in the direction of the cemetery.

Sitting on one of the graves was a young woman dressed in Victorian style clothes, stroking her long dark hair in an agitated manner. On closer observation, however, the young woman actually appeared to be floating a few inches off the ground, rather than sitting. As the two men watched with unbelieving eyes, the ghostly young woman completely vanished from their sight. Of course, the grave she'd been hovering over belonged to Nellie L. Vaughn.

Also according to Charles T. Robinson, in the year 1993 a Coventry resident named Marlene was visiting the cemetery with her husband one afternoon, when her husband suddenly heard a disembodied female voice whisper "I am perfectly pleasant." He then received several superficial scratches on one side of his face, inflicted by an unseen hand. Understandably, Marlene's husband adamantly refused to ever again set foot in this cemetery. Marlene herself claimed that photos she'd taken of Nellie's gravestone, when processed, either didn't come out at all, or came out with the image reversed. Gravestone rubbings of Nellie's headstone also proved to be a problem for Marlene, since peculiar wet spots would suddenly appear, even on dry days.

Marlene's most disturbing experience in the West Greenwich Cemetery was the day she met up with an attractive young woman, who was the only other person present in the cemetery. She was attired in modern clothing, and pleasantly introduced herself to Marlene as a member of a local historical society. However, when their conversation inevitably turned to the subject of Nellie Vaughn, the young woman suddenly and inexplicably became defensive, repeating over and over, "Nellie was never a vampire. Nellie was never a vampire." Suspecting the young woman might be mentally unbalanced, Marlene finally turned and began to walk away. Seconds later, Marlene glanced back to make sure she wasn't being followed... only to see that the young woman, who'd been standing only several feet away, had completely vanished! There was now no trace of her in the otherwise deserted cemetery. Come to think of it, Marlene recalled that she hadn't seen any other vehicles parked anywhere in sight.

As for the inscription on Nellie's headstone, it was most probably intended to mean, "I am waiting and watching for you to join me in Heaven." This is not an uncommon epitaph on many headstones in Plymouth, Massachusetts, denoting a child or a young person who had met an untimely death.

A prevailing legend declares that no grass will grow on Nellie's grave. However, ever since Nellie's headstone has been removed, grass does indeed grow freely over her grave. Since most of the general public is unaware of the exact location of her grave, it is obviously no longer repeatedly being trampled upon.

Because of repeated vandalism, town officials eventually removed Nellie's headstone, which for years had been broken off and propped up against the stone wall near the cemetery entrance. A completely sealed cement vault in the middle of the cemetery, approximately 12 feet by 6 feet by 6 feet, has been vandalized repeatedly, erroneously believing that the body of the 'vampire' Nellie Vaughn is encased inside (a.k.a 'Barnabas Collins'). In actuality, the bodies of two brothers of the Knight family – Nellie's uncles on her mother's side – are contained therein. Ironically, the most likely reason this vault was cemented over in the first place was probably to prevent vandalism!

By far the most disturbing act of desecration within this cemetery took place on Halloween night in 1993, when some nighttime visitors to the moonlit cemetery grounds – obviously out for a thrill – nearly stumbled across a freshly unearthed grave. The coffin had been partially pulled out of the grave, and the upper half of the lid pried open. Inside the coffin was the body of a recently deceased local gentleman, dressed in his fine burial clothes. A pack of cigarettes had been placed in one hand, and a can of beer in the other. Repeated damage has also been done to the small white Baptist church, located just outside of the cemetery entrance. This is the 'Plain Meeting House' from which the street in front of the cemetery derives its name.

Of course, some serious attempts at paranormal investigation have also occurred in this cemetery. However, due to evidence of continued vandalism and even cult activity taking place there, visiting this particular cemetery in West Greenwich after dark is not recommended. The infamous 'red phantom pick-up truck' will seemingly appear out of nowhere and chase away unwelcome nocturnal visitors to the cemetery, often pursuing fleeing vehicles nearly the entire length of Plain Meeting House Road. Unfortunately, this phantom pick-up truck – most likely the brain child of a dedicated member of the local neighborhood crime watch – often fails to arrive in time to prevent the senseless destruction that continues to take place in this cemetery in the dead of night.

One final aspect to the Nellie Vaughn legend has recently surfaced... the rumor that she may have been buried alive. Because Nellie died of an intense fever, she was buried rather quickly following her death to prevent contagion on the family property located on Robin Hollow Road. According to one account, a gentleman passing by the Vaughn family homestead the evening after her burial overheard the sounds of a woman screaming, although he could not locate the exact source of the screams. The following day, this gentleman alerted the local authorities, and returned to the site with the local constable. Together with George Vaughn, they searched the area, but all the three men found were footprints from the night before, on top of the fresh soil covering Nellie's grave. If this account is indeed true, then it remains a matter of speculation whether someone's screams could be heard emanating from within a freshly buried coffin six feet or so underground.

Whenever I myself have visited this cemetery, I undeniably experienced the pervasive feeling of being watched…sometimes accompanied by a peculiar stillness, even on clear days, when birds would normally be chirping in the surrounding wooded area. At other times, out-of-season birds have been both seen darting about the cemetery and heard screeching in the surrounding wooded area. Near twilight time, dim shadowy figures can often be glimpsed moving about the edges of the stone wall which borders the cemetery. Investigators at this cemetery have also had to contend with battery failure in their recording devices, even when the batteries are fresh, and other inexplicable equipment failure.

As a word of caution, however, I would not recommend visiting this cemetery after sunset simply because of numerous reports of cult activity and vandalism. As a result, the area is closely watched at night by local law enforcement, especially around Halloween.

# Chapter 3

## The Ghost of Ram Tail

To this day, some long-time residents of the rural town of Foster, Rhode Island, will boast that their hometown still lays claim to the only "officially" haunted location in the entire state...and perhaps even the entire country, for that matter. It is a well-known fact to these local townsfolk that "The Ghost of Ram Tail" still haunts the lengthy stretch of Ram Tail Road, as well as the ruins of a small, long abandoned community and mill complex located deep within the nearby woods. Today, all that remains of this mill complex, and community, are a series of crumbling foundations, which are difficult to find unless one knows exactly where to search. Still, there are those who will readily attest that the eerie specter of the infamous night watchman, who died by his own hand all those many years ago, still roams the moonlit nights in this area, lantern in hand, his grim and ethereal form forever doomed to wander.

The historic truth behind this tale actually began in the year 1791, when Mr. William Potter relocated from the city of Warwick, Rhode Island, to the northwest town of Foster. With him were his wife Mary and their three children: a firstborn son named Olney, a sweet little girl who was named Mary after her mother, and an infant son also named William. Before long, Mr. Potter became actively involved in local community and town affairs, rapidly establishing himself as one of Foster's most notable citizens. In 1799, industrious William Potter founded a large weaving/fulling mill to clean and process homespun wool, on acreage he had recently acquired from Ezekiel Hopkins. This property also included the site of the already existing Hopkins Mills district and was chosen because of its proximity to the Ponaganset River, which would be used to power the mill. Mr. Potter officially named his new mill building the Foster Woolen Manufactory. However, it also locally became better known by the name of "Ram Tail Mill" perhaps owing to the woolen fleece used in the manufacturing process, which would resemble a ram's tail prior to being trimmed.

Throughout the following decade, Mr. Potter's mill business steadily continued to thrive…so much so, that by the year 1813, William Potter decided to significantly expand his mill operations to include the mechanized spinning of woolen cloth on a grand scale. Soon the Ram Tail Mill was well on its way to becoming a lead source of employment throughout the entire vicinity. It was William Potter's fervent dream, that his own manufactory would become the northwestern Rhode Island equivalent of the unrivaled Slater Mill in Pawtucket. Eventually, Mr. Potter was able to expand his business even further by erecting a few separate, smaller buildings for the manufacturing of additional mill products, which included a blacksmith's shop, a general store, and even a small, self-sufficient housing community of workers and their families, centered around the mill. This small community was also given the colloquial name of Ram Tail.

Also by 1813, William and Mary Potter's eldest son Olney, having now come of age, had taken a young local woman named Orra as his bride. Orra was the daughter of the prominent Col. Hugh and Dorothy Cole, who were neighbors and fast friends of the Potters. Around this same time, William and Mary Potter's daughter Mary, herself now a lovely young woman, had also fallen in love and become engaged to a rather dashing young fellow with the Biblical name of Peleg (meaning "division"). Peleg was a son of James and Rhoda Place Walker, who, besides being upstanding citizens and devout church parishioners in the community, were also close friends with the Potters.

At the time of the marriages of William Potter's two eldest children, the Foster Woolen Manufactory, or Ram Tail Mill, was by far the largest and most productive factory complex of its kind in the entire vicinity. Mr. Potter therefore decided to form a family partnership in the mill operations, to ensure the financial prosperity of the next generation, and to secure the future of the mill complex itself. It was readily agreed upon that William's Potter's eldest son Olney, along with William's son-in-law Peleg, would share an equal partnership in the mill, under the executive ownership of William Potter himself. It was also understood that upon coming of age, young William A. Potter would inherit an equal partnership as well.

The ensuing years indeed proved to be happy and prosperous for the hard working William Potter, Sr. and his family. Mr. Potter also remained extremely active in local politics, and eventually held several prestigious town offices. Indeed, the Potters, Walkers and Coles were well-respected and admired by their fellow citizens in the town of Foster…especially those residents of the little community of Ram Tail, whose livelihoods were so dependent upon the mill operations.

It would often be quite an impressive sight, when William Potter, accompanied by Olney Potter and Peleg Walker, would arrive at the Ram Tail Mill to oversee the operations and conduct official business. The three elegantly attired gentlemen exuded an air of genial authority while commanding respect, as together they stepped out from William Potter's handsome carriage and strode past the large, majestic waterwheel that powered the mill operations with a roar.

By the onset of the 1820's, with his youngest son William having grown into young adulthood, the by-now wealthy Mr. William Potter – also now having acquired the formal title of "Esquire" – decided to bequeath most of the responsibilities of the prosperous mill to his two sons and his son-in-law. Naturally, both Olney Potter and Peleg Walker, being senior partners, took on the job of mentoring young William A. Potter in the practical aspects of supervising the mill operations, and overseeing the laborers in their various duties. William Potter, Sr. could not have been more pleased with the current protocol at his manufactory, secure in the knowledge that the entire production was in competent hands when he was not there to personally manage things.

Nearly two more years passed in this agreeable family arrangement, with the mill business continuing to thrive. However, an unfortunate chain of events was about to unfold, which would cast a terrible blight upon this tranquil setting.

For all outward appearances, the year of 1822 began as a prosperous time for the respectable Potter family. This was also apparently true for Peleg and Mary Walker and their children. In January, Peleg even purchased an additional quarter share of the Foster Woolen Manufactory from his brother-in-law Olney Potter. Shortly after this latest business investment, however, things mysteriously began to go awry for Peleg Walker. For reasons that remain unclear, Peleg suddenly ran into some serious financial trouble, and found himself heavily indebted to his father-in-law, William Potter. Whatever the explanation, Peleg Walker, who for years had enjoyed an enviable lifestyle, now found himself facing financial ruin. In desperation, Peleg turned to his wealthy father-in-law to hopefully work out some sort of arrangement, in which he would eventually be able to pay off his substantial debts. Unfortunately, the only arrangement that William Potter seemed able or willing to offer his son-in-law was a position as night watchman at the Ram Tail Mill.

Peleg's duties as night watchman would include overseeing the deserted mill overnight, as well as periodic patrols of the grounds and inspections of the smaller buildings, for which he would carry a lantern to see his way in the darkness outside. He would also be responsible for taking inventory of whatever stock may have arrived during the daytime. One of Peleg's most important duties came at the end of his shift each morning when, at daybreak, it was his responsibility to ring the mill bell, signaling the workers of Ram Tail Village to a new work day. He would them have to remain until the mill workers began to arrive, much to his humiliation.

Weeks passed in this manner, during which time Peleg became increasingly despondent with his new position. Long, lonely nights spent in solitude gave Peleg ample time to brood over his lot in life. Here he was, at thirty-five-years of age, a former full partner in the business, now working out his "sentence" – or so it must have felt – in the lowly position of a night watchman. In essence, he'd now been reduced to being Squire Potter's lackey! When Peleg was finally forced to sell his remaining financial assets to William Potter in May of 1822, these feelings of failure and frustration became overwhelming. Finally, in desperation, Peleg decided that the only solution was to personally confront his former business partners concerning his situation. After all, not only were they intelligent, reasonable men, but also family, and fellow lodge members. Also, since Peleg himself was the father of William Potter's own grandchildren, perhaps he could persuade the older man to have compassion.

Peleg chose a Saturday afternoon – the 18th of May in 1822 to be exact – to air his grievances with his business associates at the Ram Tail Mill. When Peleg arrived at the main mill building attired in his professional finery, no one thought anything unusual. The men, women and young children of various ages at work in the mill that day were much too busy tending to their assigned labors to take much notice. Both Mr. William Potter himself and his eldest son Olney happened to be present at the mill this particular afternoon. These were precisely the men whom Peleg had come to see. Amidst the hustle and bustle of the noisy mill operations, Peleg approached his two former business partners and requested a private conference with them, to which they acquiesced.

Unfortunately, the interview did not bode well for Peleg. He apparently found his father-in-law and brother-in-law somewhat less than sympathetic to his plight, and was utterly unable to prevail upon them. Before long, tempers began to flare. The shouting eventually ensued, causing the mill workers who were present to momentarily halt their labors and listen. Although the exact content of this heated conversation was not recorded, it is generally assumed to have been over finances. At the conclusion of this confrontation, William Potter, Sr. emerged red-faced and flushed with anger, with his son Olney beside him.

"This conversation is over, young man!" William Potter shouted at his son-in-law Peleg. "There is nothing more to say."

Trembling with rage and defeat, Peleg Walker was then overheard to issue an ominous sounding warning to both the Potters:

"Alright, then. But mark my words, sirs… one of these days, you'll have to take the keys to this mill from a dead man's pocket!" With that, Peleg turned and stormed out of the mill.

William Potter merely stood there glowering for a moment. He then grumbled something under his breath, before sauntering off in the opposite direction. Glancing about, Olney admonished the curious onlookers in the mill to return to their work, before quickly following after his father.

Sometime after sunrise on the following Sunday morning, May 19th, Mary Potter Walker awoke to find that her husband Peleg had not returned home from the mill as usual. As the hours passed, Mary and her children became increasingly concerned. Eventually, some of the men in the community were summoned to investigate. When they arrived at the Ram Tail Mill, they found the doors of the building to be securely locked from the inside. They began knocking at the doors and calling out, but no one answered. To all appearances, the building was completely empty. Where, then, was Peleg Walker? Surely his distraught wife and children were anxiously awaiting an answer at home.

Since no one present had a key to the mill building, one of the men decided to gain access through a side window.

Once inside the darkened interior of the building, the man called out, "Hello? Anyone in here?"

All he heard was the dull echo of his own voice, followed by silence. He paused for a moment, allowing his vision to adjust to the darkness surrounding him. Cautiously taking a few more steps forward, he again called out, "Hello? Mr. Walker, Sir... are you in here?" Again, there was no response.

He was about to turn back, when something caught his attention in the shadows just up ahead of him. Peering into a darkened corner, he could just barely make out what appeared to be a dim, shadowy figure sprawled out upon the floor. To his utter horror, he suddenly realized that he was gazing down at the lifeless body of Peleg Walker, lying in a pool of his own blood. On the floor nearby to his right hand was what appeared to be a long cutting knife.

"Oh, my God!" he cried out in shock, nearly stumbling over backwards. After regaining his balance, he then scrambled back towards the window, screaming.

"Help! Peleg Walker's lyin' dead in here, and it looks like he's sliced his own throat!"

As quickly as possible, the local constable was alerted and summoned to the scene. A short time later, William Potter and his two sons Olney and William also arrived at the mill. Right there in the mill, the corpse of thirty-five-year-old Peleg Walker was hastily examined, and his clothing searched. True to Peleg's oath of the previous afternoon, his personal keys to the mill were found in one of his jacket pockets. No note of any kind was found either on his person or anywhere in the mill. However, since there were no signs of a struggle, the constable quickly attributed the cause of death to suicide, with no further need for an official inquest. The Potters also testified to the constable, regarding Peleg Walker's recently unbalanced state of mind.

The body of Peleg Walker was then hastily covered up with a sheet of canvas. As more and more alarmed and curious residents of the small community of Ram Tail arrived, the constable assigned two of the men standing nearby, to the grim task of carrying out the lifeless body from the mill, and loading it onto a cart.

Later that morning, accompanied by the constable, Olney Potter and his younger brother arrived at the Walker homestead, to deliver the unhappy news to their sister as well as their nieces and nephews.

"Oh, dear God in Heaven," Mary sobbed, collapsing into her brothers' arms. "My poor husband! I've lost my husband!" The Walker children were also inconsolable, at the sudden loss of their father.


Three days later, on May 22nd, 1822, Peleg Walker was laid to rest at the Potter's small family burial ground, located just off of Winsor Road. Because of the scandalous nature of Peleg's untimely end, there was a general atmosphere of foreboding, as the local parson recited the funeral oration. Yet, Peleg Walker had for many years been known as a respectable citizen and businessman. He had come from a well-known and prominent family in the town, and he'd also been an honored member of the local Hamilton Lodge. Therefore, his graveside service was quite dignified, as afforded a gentleman of his standing in the community.

"Ashes to ashes," droned the parson. "Dust to dust."

As Peleg Walker's pine coffin was lowered into the open grave, Squire William Potter and his wife Mary both embraced their trembling, weeping daughter and their four grandchildren in an effort to console them. Perhaps even then, the members of the Potter family who were present hoped in time that Peleg's madness would be forgotten, and that his widow Mary would someday remarry and find happiness. After all, plenty of other suitable young gentlemen lived in the county, who were more emotionally and financially stable than Peleg had been, and who would welcome the chance to marry into the prosperous Potter family.

But alas, such was not to be the case.

On the very evening following Peleg Walker's burial, around midnight, the bell inside of the supposedly empty Ram Tail Mill began furiously ringing, arousing townsfolk from as far away as the Foster/Scituate Turnpike (now Danielson Pike). When curious investigators arrived, the maniacal ringing suddenly ceased. The mill was found to be locked and deserted, with no signs of a forced entry. The following evening, the wild ringing starting up once again in the middle of the night...and as before, the mill was found to be locked and empty. Suspecting that pranksters were somehow gaining clandestine access to the mill, William Potter promptly ordered that the pull rope be taken down. However, the very next night around midnight, the bell once again began ringing by itself, forcing the Potters to have the bell removed altogether. But the problems were just beginning.

One evening a few weeks later, residents in the entire community of Ram Tail were once again awakened in the middle of the night by a loud clattering sound coming from the mill. When investigators rushed to the mill to find out what was happening, they were astonished to find that the entire mill operations – every mechanized loom, drive shaft and spindle - had somehow spontaneously started up in within the darkened, apparently empty building. If this was not enough, the large waterwheel that powered the mill operations was observed to be turning AGAINST the current of the Ponaganset River! This seemingly impossible phenomenon would later be verified by dozens of credible witnesses.

Olney Potter himself was summoned to unlock the main entrance door, allowing workers to enter the building and begin the process of shutting down the entire noisy operations. Accompanied by several of the men, Olney Potter descended into the dark, dank wheel pit, to investigate for himself what could be causing the waterwheel to churn in the opposite direction of the river's flow. However, no logical explanation could be found. And then just as suddenly, it stopped altogether.

Because of these recent inexplicable events, it is not surprising that the Ram Tail Mill now had a reputation of being terribly haunted by the vengeful spirit of Peleg Walker, who had met his demise at his own hand within the mill! Throughout the entire town of Foster, the main topic of conversation inevitably centered on "the ghost of Ram Tail." Many of the mill workers themselves reported feeling very uncomfortable inside the Ram Tail Mill, even in the daytime, saying they sensed they were being watched by unseen eyes. Often, workers would claim to have glimpsed a shadowy figure lurking in the bell tower, even though the mill bell had long since been removed. Some even reported that they had been touched or prodded, only to turn and see no one immediately behind them. Before long, every unexplained mishap or accident occurring in the mill was instantly attributed to Peleg's ghostly antics.

It was not uncommon during this era for entire families to sometimes be employed in mill factories, and the Ram Tail Mill was no exception. Young children were included in some of these families, and these children were now terrified of even setting foot in the "haunted mill," let alone spending an entire workday. Whether they admitted it or not, many of the adult workers were also becoming equally terrified. Eventually, some the workers began leaving their positions at the mill, and a general feeling of trepidation consumed those who remained.

Then one relatively clear, moonlit winter evening, three men who were returning on foot from a local tavern happened to be passing by the deserted Ram Tail Mill. They were sharing lively conversation when one of them noticed something peculiar over at the deserted mill, and alerted his two companions. Over by the darkened mill building was a figure clad completely in white, holding a lantern aloft, walking along the moonlit grounds. The figure was plainly visible, being illuminated by the pale moonlight…or perhaps even possessing a ghostly luminescence of its own. It did not take long for the men to recognize the familiar stride of this mysterious white-clad figure. With a shock, they realized they were now gazing at the eerily recognizable apparition of Peleg Walker himself! He appeared to be carrying on his duties of patrolling the mill grounds, lantern in hand, just as he had during the last few weeks of his life. As the three men stood transfixed to the spot, the ghastly figure turned, strode back to the mill building, and vanished from their sight.

Soon after this latest incident was reported, more and more people began leaving their positions of employment at the Ram Tail Mill factory.

One by one, whole families began moving away from the small community of Ram Tail. Alarmed cries of "There's trouble at the mill again!" had now become all too familiar and no one wanted to work in, or even live near, a "cursed" building that was haunted by a vengeful spirit. Although no further incidents were reported in 1822, the damage to the Ram Tail Mill's reputation had already been done. The Potters were forced to accept the fact that the stigma of the haunting would remain etched in the legacy of both the Ram Tail Mill and community for as long as the two existed. The very name of Ram Tail had become synonymous with that of Peleg Walker, and vice versa.

Several other factors also contributed to the eventual decline of the Ram Tail Mill and community. For one thing, a series of seasonal droughts resulted in a significant decrease in production for the once thriving industry. Ownership of the mill then changed hands in 1831 when William Potter, now elderly, transferred the entire ownership of the dwindling mill business to his two sons. In the year 1837 Mary Potter Walker died at the age of forty-four, having never remarried. She was laid to rest beside her late husband in the family burial ground. In 1843 production at the mill shut down completely, and the little village of Ram Tail ceased to exist as a community. The several buildings that had comprised this small village were soon afterward left to fall into a state of neglect.

The long abandoned Ram Tail Mill building itself caught fire in 1874. Despite the efforts of dozens of volunteers from the nearby Hopkins Mills community, the building was completely destroyed. As the fire consumed the building, those among the onlookers that day swore that, amidst the roaring and crackling of the flames, they could hear the faint pealing of a bell from the upper portion of the empty mill. Perhaps, just perhaps, the Ghost of Ram Tail was tolling his own farewell to the old mill building!

An 1885 census for the town of Foster officially lists the Ram Tail Mill as "haunted." Succeeding generations in Foster have continued to keep the legend alive through oral and written tradition. Despite the fact that all that remains of the mill itself is the crumbling foundation, located along a densely wooded path and difficult to find unless one knows exactly where to look, reports of paranormal activity in the area continue to this day.

Tom D'Agostino, a local author and paranormal investigator, claims to have recorded the unmistakable creaking sound of a hand held lantern passing directly in front of him. This, of course, was the very type of lantern that Peleg Walker would have carried on his rounds. In 1822, Peleg would have used a candle-illuminated lantern, as opposed to a kerosene lantern. Tom and numerous other explorers have also witnessed bluish, glowing orbs of light floating among the trees in this area at night. My brother Carl, among others, has reported hearing the distant tolling of a bell in this area during the evening hours.

On an evening in August of 2005, I along with several other members of New England Anomalies Research (NEAR) conducted an official investigation at the Ram Tail Site. Tom D"Agostino and his wife Arlene accompanied us on this investigation, as well as Denice Jones of Connecticut and author of "The Other Side." Denice's mother Jan Pierce, who frequently assists with investigations and who happens to be somewhat clairvoyant, was in attendance as well. About forty-five minutes into our investigation, Denice's mother announced she had caught a brief glimpse of something – or someone – standing among the dense overgrowth of trees almost directly in front of her. Although it was indistinct, Denice's mother could just barely make out the figure of a tall, thin man dressed in dark clothing, with a rather gaunt expression. She only witnessed this dim figure for a few seconds before it was gone.

Meanwhile, my wife Sandra went to check on the video camera which she'd set on night vision and placed on a tripod in front of the mill foundation. While checking the camera, she heard the sound of footsteps approaching directly behind her.

Naturally assuming it to be either myself or one of the other investigators, Sandra said over her shoulder, "I don't know if I'm getting much of anything tonight."

When no one replied, she turned and saw that no one was standing there. After hesitating only for a second or two, Sandra raised her digital camera and snapped a picture. What appeared in the photo was a segmented light streak brightly illuminated against the dark background. Beginning at the top center of the photo, this segmented light streak appears to have been descending at the moment Sandra snapped the picture. The rounded end tip of this light streak actually appears to be luminescent.

More recently, on a warm July evening, I and several members of NEAR returned to the Ram Tail area in Foster for a subsequent investigation. During the hike along the rough and overgrown path leading to what was once the mill site, one of our members, Kim, glanced behind and saw what appeared to be a figure following along the trail about thirty yards. Since this was obviously no one who was with our group, she alerted Russ who happened to be beside her. When no one answered them, they halted and called out to whoever it was. The strange thing was, although Kim could clearly make out a pair of legs moving towards them in the gathering darkness, she was unable to see anything else. Russ had just called out for one of our other members to pass the searchlight to him when the figure silently darted behind a tree, and did not reappear.

As we continued on along the path, an owl hooted its greeting to us, and a dog could be heard loudly bellowing from somewhere in the far distance. A short time later, after we'd arrived at the site of the Ram Tail Mill foundation, NEAR members Rob and Mike both felt their shirts being tugged, even though no one was close enough to them at the moment to have done so. Rob and Mike also reported to have separately experienced a sudden, cold rush of air against their faces and necks.

The NEAR team also obtained a few examples of Electronic Voice Phenomenon that night. One of the clearer EVPs, captured on audio by team member Kim, seems to be a male voice quietly saying either "Help Peleg" or "Kill Peleg." Another EVP, captured by team member Amie, also sounds like a male voice clearly hissing the word "Bitch."

Just prior to leaving the area that night, we distinctly heard the voices of two men rapidly approaching along the path, and immediately ceased our own conversation to listen. Although we could not decipher exactly what was being said, the voices sounded harsh and angry, as if whoever it was did not like the fact that we were there. We indeed wondered if they were coming to chase us out of the area. Strangely, although we were now in complete darkness, we could see no trace of flashlight beams from our approaching visitors, although they were certainly close enough to do so. And then, to our relief, the voices abruptly faded out, and were not heard by us again that night.

With a touch of humor, Rob asked, "Do you think maybe we scared them off?"

The conclusion seemed to be that what we actually heard were phantom voices, especially since there were no sounds whatsoever of anyone retreating through the brush.

Tragically, Ram Tail was the final paranormal investigation that my brother and his fiancée Laura Casey shared together. Laura unexpectedly passed away in her sleep less than 48 hours later, at the age of thirty-eight.


One can only speculate as to the reality of the Ghost of Ram Tail. It would certainly seem that the ghost (or at least the legend) of Peleg Walker, true to his biblical name, did once cause a great deal of division among the residents of the Ram Tail village. Does the restless spirit of Peleg Walker continue to roam the mill site, re-enacting his duties as night watchman, while reminding the living of his tragic fate? Or is some other mysterious and unknown force at work here?

Some have theorized that the streams of water from the Ponaganset River running through this area, once harnessed to power the Ram Tail Mill operations, continue to serve as a power source for the paranormal phenomena experienced in this area. This too remains a matter of speculation. Whatever conclusions one may draw, the legacy of the Ram Tail Ghost will most probably endure, for as long as the town of Foster continues to exist.

If you should venture to visit the small Potter family lot today (now Foster Historical Cemetery # 38, located off of Winsor Road in Foster), you will find that William Potter's headstone lies cracked and broken near the far left corner of the graveyard, partially covered over by the earth. Much more noticeable is the upright grave marker of Peleg Walker, which stands beside that of his wife Mary Potter Walker, near the center of the lot. Although Peleg's headstone is now covered with a thick growth of moss, a close examination will reveal the words: "Here lies the body of Peleg Walker. Died May 19th, 1822, age 35 years." Inscribed at the bottom of his headstone is a curious, perhaps prophetic epitaph: "Life how short. Eternity how long."

Update: Recently, a search of family genealogy has revealed that my brother Carl and I are directly related to Peleg Walker, through our maternal side of the family; we are also directly related to horror fiction writer H.P. Lovecraft.

**Peleg Walker's gravestone**

# Chapter 4

### TAPS Returns to Skowhegan

(The names of the family involved have been changed to protect their identities.)

It was an early evening in late September of 2001 while I was at my second-shift job, that I received a phone call from my friend and fellow TAPS member Brian Harnois.

"Hey, Keith, it's Brian. I'm sorry to call you up and bother you at work," he apologized.

That's okay, I'm actually on break right now," I said. "So, what's up?"

Brian explained, "Well, I was just contacted by Mandy Kingston in Skowhegan, Maine. It seems that the negative activity in her house has started up again, and she's asking if we can return for another investigation. Of course, she's also desperately hoping for you to come back and perform another blessing."

"Oh, really? What does Jason have to say about this?" I asked.

Brian replied, "He wants to discuss it with everyone at the meeting this Sunday night. But from what he was saying, he's all for going back if the family needs us to."

I responded, "Well, if it's an emergency situation, then I suppose a return trip to Skowhegan is in order."

"Oh, it's definitely an emergency, dude," said Brian. "According to Mandy the family's in desperate need of help, maybe even more so than the last time. And they're really counting on you being there again!"

"Okay… I'll talk it over with Sandra, and then get back to you," I promised him.

After getting off the phone with Brian and returning to work, I contemplated having to leave Sandra and Keith Jr. again for a couple of days, for another trip to Northern Central Maine. This was some time before Sandra had become a member of TAPS. And if the activity had picked up again as Brian had just described, then this would obviously be no ordinary investigation. Just like last time, it would involve a thorough spiritual cleansing of the 26-room 19th Century farmhouse. Not only that, but it would also most likely entail having to confront the same demonic entities, and the situation could potentially present even more dangers than the last time.

That Sunday evening, at our next private meeting of The Atlantic Paranormal Society, we discussed our plans for a return trip to Skowhegan, Maine. TAPS founder Jason Hawes would again be leading the investigation team. Co-founder Grant Wilson would unfortunately not be available, since he, along with his wife Rhianna and their small children, had temporarily relocated to Utah.

It was decided that our return trip would take place on the following Saturday, October 6th, and that we'd be spending the entire weekend there. Besides Jason, the TAPS members returning included Brian, Rich, Andrew and myself. Also joining us for this investigation, who had not been with us the last time, would be members Carl, Stephanie, Theresa and Theresa's boyfriend Eric.

Brian Harnois explained, "That was my first demonic case. That was when I could see the rage and anger that these things have. Because it's true. These things are disgustingly evil."

In a serious tone, Jason said, "Now, I realize that even though Carl wasn't with us the last time, he's had years of experience in dealing with these types of situations. And Brian, Andrew and Rich already know what they're up against in this case. But as for you other three, I want you to know that I certainly won't hold it against you if decide you'd rather stay back on this one."

Theresa, Stephanie and Eric were adamant about not backing out, and all three very much wanted to participate, despite the potential dangers involved. They were also all motivated to help out a family in spiritual crises.

"Good," said Jason. "But still, I want either Carl or Keith close to you three at all times. Most preferably Carl, since Keith will be the one conducting the house cleansing."

Before we concluded our meeting that night, I mentioned to everyone present that I had an example of audio evidence from our initial investigation in Skowhegan, that I desired to share with them, especially the three newer members.

I explained, "This is an EVP I came across while reviewing my recordings, after we'd returned home from Skowhegan the first time. It was recorded upstairs in the house in one of the daughter's bedrooms. You'll be able to hear one of the girl's asking a question and Jason answers it. What you'll hear next is an EVP commenting on what Jason just said."

I switched on my small Panasonic tape recorder, and turned up the volume. One of the Kingston girls could be heard asking why the spirit had scratched her brother Michael, to which Jason responded, "I don't know why it did it to him." A harsh sounding voice could then be heard whispering, "Know why... miracle!"

I rewound and played the recording several more times while turning the volume up at the EVP, so everyone could plainly understand exactly what it was saying. Stephanie, Eric and Theresa were especially astonished. Brian told them, "So, that will give you just a hint of what we'll all be going up against there."

My brother Carl added, "Since this entity on the EVP Keith just played made an intelligent comment on what Jason said, albeit a sarcastic one, then it stands to reason that this is a sentient, intelligent personality speaking on the recording."

Rich Einig said, "And that's of course just one of the entities there. We have no way of knowing exactly how many spirits are actually in that house."

"Yes," I agreed, "and it would really help if we had someone with the spiritual gift of discernment along with us on this trip. But since we don't, we're basically on our own. And if it comes down to it, we may have to rely solely on religious provocation."

Jason also informed us that there just might be someone with the gift of discernment at the house with us. He and Brian had touched base with Mandy the previous day, and she had asked if it would be alright if a "psychic medium" friend of hers stopped by while we were there. Her friend had recently done a walk-through of the house, and had picked up on the presence of several spirits. Her name was Peggy and according to

Mandy, she was a deeply religious woman who simply wanted to share her input while we were conducting our investigation.

Jason added, "Now, if anyone has any objections to a psychic medium being there with us for awhile, just let me know, and I'll inform Mandy that we're simply not comfortable with that."

None of us voiced any objections to a psychic being there, and sharing her impressions with us.

We started out early on the following Saturday morning, October 6th, 2001, in a rented sport utility vehicle, very similar to the one in which we'd made the first trip back in January. However, for those of us who'd made the original trip to Skowhegan, it was a very different experience from driving through treacherous winter conditions like last time. Although the day was overcast, the New England autumn scenery along the way was breathtaking.

During the drive we discussed the case ahead of us, as well as the tragic recent events of September 11th, which had affected the entire nation. However, we also tried to remain as upbeat as possible, knowing from past experience that maintaining a positive attitude was often essential when dealing with what we referred to as a "heavy" case such as this.

As I was taking a turn riding up front with Jason driving, I overheard Andrew saying with a laugh, "I've only got two changes of clothes; I'm not getting all bloodied up this time!"

Carl said, "Yes, Keith was telling me about some of the mishaps you suffered back in January."

Theresa asked, "Why, what happened, Andrew?"

Andrew said, "Well, at one point while we were blessing the house, I had to climb up into the attic to spray some holy water, which really wasn't an attic at all, but rather it was a small crawl space supported by sawed-off logs. So when I was coming out I had to twist my body around into a sitting position and just sort of jump, which caused me to land on the floor in a heap. Not only that, but I wound up with a wooden splinter in my hand about four or five inches long."

"Ohh!" Theresa winced.

"To make matters worse," said Andrew, "the family didn't even have so much as a single band-aid in the entire house. I simply had to pull it out with a pair of tweezers, and then wash it off."In the driver's seat, Jason said, "That's why we've made sure to bring our own first-aid kit with us from now on."

Andrew said, "I also wound up gashing my leg by tripping over something in the snow, while we were on our way out to the barn."

Brian laughed and said, "I guess it just wasn't your weekend, dude!"

Jason also explained to our new people that back in January, novelist Jodi Picoult had traveled from New Hampshire and joined us at the Kingston residence, because she was doing some on-location research with TAPS for her upcoming novel, "Second Glance."

Jason added, "Of course, we had the full permission of the Kingston family for Jodi to be there."

Theresa and Stephanie both remarked about how exciting that must have been.

Along the way the group had a very serious discussion about the activity we'd experienced during our first investigation at the Kingston residence back in January. For example, Rich described to our members who were not with us the last time, about the EVP he'd managed to capture on the audio of his video camera.

"I'd positioned my video camera in one of the upstairs rooms where supposedly a lot of activity occurred, set it on infrared and left it recording with the room lights off," Rich explained. "Well, around two-thirty in the morning we were downstairs in the parlor, taking a short break from our investigation, when suddenly we all heard a door loudly slam from that room upstairs. We knew it was that room because it was the closest one to us at the top of the staircase. So of course we immediately rushed upstairs to check it out, but the room was completely empty with the door still open. And we knew it wasn't any of the family members, because they were all downstairs in the parlor with us. So the next day, we replayed the video footage on the family's large screen TV, and at that exact spot on the recording, just before 2:30 AM, we clearly heard the sound of a door loudly slamming... although on the tape it sounded more metallic, like a locker door slamming... and then seconds later we could hear what sounded like a little girl's voice on the recording saying, 'They're coming.' Then we could hear the sound of our own footsteps coming up the stairs, and about three seconds before we entered the room, a deep, ominous sounding male voice said: "They're here."

"Oh, my God!" said Theresa. "Just listening to you telling us about that gave me chills!"

Rich said, "Of course when we walked through the room we didn't find anyone up there. Although, after we left to go back downstairs we heard a light tapping sound on the recording, as if someone was tapping the edge of a drum. But again, that should give you some idea of what you might expect while we're there."

Carl added, "Then again, very little or nothing at all may happen. It's impossible to predict exactly what will occur."


Needless to say, we made the second trip in at least two hours less time than we had during our previous trip in January. Within fifteen minutes after arriving in the town of Skowhegan, we were pulling into the driveway of the Kingston residence. With the front entrance way of the house now decorated for Halloween, the place looked very different from the snowbound house we'd arrived at back on that January evening nine months ago. Mandy Kingston and her teenage daughter Michelle came outside to greet us.

"Hi guys, it's so great seeing you again!" said Mandy, as Jason and I stepped out from the front of the SUV. "I just wish it was under better circumstances."

Jason said, "Well, at least this time we were able to make the trip in beautiful fall weather, instead of a snowstorm."

We quickly began unpacking our equipment, and Mandy welcomed us all inside. As soon as we entered, Mandy's husband George also welcomed us. George, Mandy and Michelle were especially intrigued to see the resemblance between Carl and myself, being twins.

Suddenly from the nearby kitchen, a voice began squawking: "The bitch is home! The bitch is home!"

Carl, Eric, Theresa and Stephanie glanced around in surprise, as the rest of us laughed. Mandy also laughed and apologized, "I'm sorry. That's just my talking African gray parrot Skippy, who just turned five. Obviously Skippy picked that one up from George." She gave her husband a little nudge, which he acknowledged with an embarrassed nod.

Unfortunately, it was not long before a significant problem developed. Shortly after we'd all settled in, Theresa announced to everyone that she was suddenly feeling overwhelmed by the negative energy she perceived in the house. "I-I'm sorry, but I've got to get out of here," she said. Violently trembling, Theresa first dashed into the kitchen area, before rushing outside.

Mandy was naturally concerned, and asked us, "Is she going to be alright?"

In a frustrated tone of voice, Jason said, "Yeah, I'm sure she'll be fine, once she gets herself under control. In fact, I'm going outside to have a talk with her right now."

Jason then went outside with Theresa and firmly reminded her that the situation she was going into had been thoroughly explained to her ahead of time, and that she had assured everyone she wanted to be involved. Eric also spent some time talking to Theresa and calming her down, until she felt sufficiently collected to come back inside and rejoin us in the parlor.

As soon as Theresa had regained her composure, we all gathered together with the Kingston family to discuss their present situation. Their second youngest teenage daughter Megan also came downstairs and joined us. George and Mandy explained to us that their son Michael, who was now 19, would not be there this time, since he had recently moved in with his girlfriend Chrystal and their baby. Since the activity had picked up in the farmhouse, Michael reasoned that it might be safer for all three of them if they moved out. Also, George and Mandy's eldest daughter Melissa was out with friends, and was not expected to return until sometime late that evening.

Our interview then commenced. According to the family, things were initially fine after our last visit back in January. The blessing we'd done seemed to have had a very positive effect, because not only did the paranormal activity completely cease, but everyone experienced a feeling of peace and calm within the house, which had never been that prevalent before. And things had remained that way in the house for a good several months afterward.

In fact, it was only in the last month and a half that they'd noticed the activity returning. At first only subtle indications became noticeable, such as household items disappearing and showing up again in odd places, and the uncanny feeling of being watched, especially whenever one of the family members happened to be alone in any of the rooms. Mandy herself felt particularly affected in the cellar, and would only venture down there when absolutely necessary.

And then the knockings resumed within the walls and at the sides of the house. As before, they would usually hear three distinct raps.

Addressing me, Mandy said, "I remember what you told me before, about the three knockings possibly being an insult to the Holy Trinity."

I asked, "Has there been any other explicit anti-religious activity?"

Mandy's daughter Megan answered, "Oh, yes! Tell them about the crosses, Mom."

Mandy said, "Well, it seems we can't keep any crosses on the walls on the first and second floors anymore, because in the morning we always find them turned upside down. So we had to take all of the crosses down into the cellar."

Carl asked, "And do you also find them turned upside down in the cellar?"

Mandy said, "No, because we don't have them hung down there. Maybe we should have, just to see if it would happen down there too."

Michelle said, "And the landlord's saying we kids are on drugs, and that we watch too many scary movies."

Mandy confirmed, "Yes, we told the landlord what's been going on here, but she hasn't been very understanding or sympathetic."

Michelle said, "I haven't touched any drugs. I mean, I'm only fourteen. I'm not gonna do that stuff."

George Kingston added, "That landlord's a bitch anyway."

George's comment was enough to set Skippy off again in the kitchen. "The bitch is home! The bitch is home!" he squawked.

"Ah, be quiet!" George called back.

Once again, we all shared a brief laugh.

Jason then asked, "Is there anything that anyone else would like to add?"

Megan said, "Awhile ago, my sister Melissa's boyfriend was visiting and he saw an apparition upstairs in the hallway, in between the bathroom and the in-laws room. It was like an old guy in a rocking chair holding my nephew, playing with him and rocking. My sister's boyfriend's eyes just swelled up with tears, because it was his grandfather."

Theresa asked "He was certain that it was his grandfather?"

"Oh yes, he got a good look at him, and he recognized him right away," said Megan. "So my sister's boyfriend hasn't been back here since."

George's friend Preston was somewhat of an eccentric character, who came around from time to time to visit with George and the family, sometimes staying overnight. But during one of his recent stays Preston had been downstairs in the cellar when he'd suddenly been overcome with a choking sensation. The experience had terrified him so much that he'd fled the house, and had not been back since.

Rich asked, "How have things been in the in-laws room upstairs?"

Mandy said, "It's been pretty quiet up there since the last time you were here, thank goodness."

I asked, "Have there been any more instances of pictures being turned over by themselves?"

"No, not that I know of," said Mandy.

I directed the next question at Michelle and Megan. "How about any more visits from the 'Indian spirit' you were seeing upstairs?"

Michelle perked up and said, "Oh, one time my sister Melissa woke up and saw what looked like a shadow spirit in her bedroom! It was right after Preston left that last time."

Megan added, "And the next night after she told us, all three of us got together in Melissa's bedroom and asked the Indian spirit to appear to us, but it never did."

Carl and Jason and I shared a quick glance with each other.

Mandy added that she and her daughters had been feeling very uneasy whenever they were out in the barn. Mandy explained, "It's always like somebody's right over your shoulder watching you in the whole time, just like in the cellar. And if we stay for any length of time, we start feeling sick and dizzy."

Andrew asked, "How about you, George? Do you ever feel anything unusual in the barn?"

"Nah," George replied. "I'm out there a lot, and I never feel anything strange. But I'll tell ya, our dog Blue won't go near the barn for some reason."

Near the end of the interview, I asked Mandy and George, "By the way, have you been attending church at all as a family, like we discussed last time we were here?"

"No, I'm afraid we haven't gotten around to it," Mandy said somewhat apologetically. "I remember you recommended that it might help."

I said, "Well, like I mentioned last time, it wouldn't necessarily have to be every single week. It would mainly be a positive reinforcement, especially going together as a family."

"I know, we should really make an effort to start doing that," said Mandy.

Jason then mentioned to Mandy, "Now, I understand that you're expecting a friend of yours to arrive sometime this afternoon, who wants to assist with the investigation, is that correct?"

Mandy said, "Oh, yes, my psychic medium friend Peggy! In fact, she should be arriving shortly. I hope you don't mind if she takes part in the investigation for awhile."

Jason said, "No, we all agreed that it shouldn't be a problem, as long as Peggy understands that we have our own method of investigating, and that Keith will be leading the house cleansing."

Sounding relieved, Mandy said, "Oh, good. She promised that she won't be in your way, and that she only wants to assist."

Carl said, "As a matter of fact, it might be interesting to get her impressions."

Mandy also explained that Peggy had already done a walk-through of the house that past week, and that she'd picked up on two spirits in particular – a man and a woman that were haunting the cellar.

That afternoon Mandy's friend Peggy did arrive and was delighted to be introduced to us. She was a tall, middle-aged woman with a confident demeanor, who explained that she was not only a psychic medium but a certified hypnotist as well.

Peggy told us, "It's such an honor to get to work with a professional investigation team such as you people. And I promise not to be intrusive, I simply wish to observe and to share whatever impressions I may pick up on."

Jason said, "You're more than welcome to join us during our investigation. And of course, you understand that we mainly investigate by using scientific methods and recording devices to try and capture evidence."

"I understand completely, and I'm sure that we'll work very well together," said Peggy.

We split up into two separate teams for a walk-through of the entire household and the property. Peggy was in the same group as me, along with Brian, Stephanie and Rich. Mandy's daughter Michelle accompanied us.

We began by perusing the grounds outside. When we came to the chicken coop, Brian reminded me, "Hey, Keith, you remember the last time we were here, and we found those freeze-dried chickens half buried in the snow?"

"Oh yes, I remember," I said. "How could I possibly forget?"

Fortunately, no trace of the chicken carcasses remained.

When we arrived at the barn, Peggy announced to us that she was picking up on some sort of hostile presence. "It's almost as if something doesn't want us being in here," she said. "It's telling us to leave."

We took photos and audio recordings, and although Rich did get a few unaccounted-for spikes on his Electro Magnetic Field detector, the rest of us experienced nothing unusual while we were in there. Still, I made certain not to stand directly underneath any loose boards, recalling the near miss that had happened to Bill Washell of Maine Paranormal while he was in the barn.


Back inside the main house itself, we met up with our fellow investigators to compare notes. The only anomalous readings that Jason's group captured were in the in-laws room upstairs, and these were only very slight.

Andrew Graham said, "Frankly I experienced nothing unusual this time. With the possible exception of the in-laws room, the place seems devoid of any paranormal activity so far."

In preparation for the night ahead of us, we obtained two of the small crucifixes from the cellar and hung one on a wall of the in-laws room upstairs, with a digital video camera trained on it in case it moved. We hung the second one in the parlor where it would be in plain view of anyone who was in there.

We then decided to begin the spiritual house clearing upstairs on the second floor, with myself leading the team up the staircase like the last time. In the interests of the family's safety, Peggy, Eric, Stephanie and Theresa remained downstairs with them, in case activity picked up on the first floor.

Assisted by Carl, Brian and Andrew, I went through each of the rooms on the first floor, reading Scripture passages and praying for the expulsion of any negative forces. Rich was of course videotaping the entire procedure. However, unlike the last time we were here back in January, we head no growling sounds emanating from the walls or other extraneous phenomena.

As each room was cleansed, I also asked for the protection of angelic spirits, to keep at bay any negativity that may try to re-enter. Both Carl and Brian thoroughly anointed each door and window with blessed water, to spiritually seal the separate rooms.

This time we also made certain that instead of having Andrew actually climb into the attic crawl space, he would only reach in to spray some holy water, while properly supported on a sturdy chair!


When we came back downstairs, Mandy and her family were pleased to hear that the entire second floor blessing went smoothly and without incident, including the in-laws room. Brian said, "Even the cross stayed in place on the wall."

Sounding relieved, Mandy said, "Thank God for that! The cross down here didn't move at all either."

We next decided to take care of the first floor, and afterward conclude the blessing of the house with the cellar. Once again, just like the second floor, the blessing of the first floor rooms went completely without incident.

Jason said, "It does seem to be a lot quieter here that the last time. But that doesn't mean that things won't start up once Keith starts blessing the cellar, since whatever is here might be hiding out down there. So let's all stay alert and focused, okay?"

We all agreed.

This time, both Jason and Carl would be taking a turn remaining upstairs with the family, for the family's protection. Since Peggy had previously picked up on the presence of two active spirits in the cellar, she would be coming downstairs with us and assisting with the blessing.

"Okay, let's rock and roll," said Brian.


Once we were actually in the cellar, we all agreed that the atmosphere down there was somewhat thick and uncomfortable. Brian was wearing his white Red Sox baseball hat on backwards with a small headlamp secured to the front with a headband, which caused him to resemble a coal miner.

As we explored the area, Brian mentioned to me, "Dude... have you noticed that the deer head we found last time isn't down here anymore?"

"Yes, I did notice its conspicuous absence," I said.

Peggy asked, "What, there was a deer head down here?"

Andrew explained, "Yeah, it was here when the family first moved in, so they didn't even know how long it had been here."

Brian said, "That thing was disgusting! It was just lying on the floor, and it didn't even have any eyes or anything, just empty eye sockets!"

I added, "We weren't even sure if a previous tenant had intended it for mounting, or if it was being used for ritualistic purposes."

Peggy said that from the negative feeling she was getting, it was quite possible that profane worship ceremonies had taken place here within the confines of the cellar. Perhaps even animals had been sacrificed here.

We had only been down in the cellar for perhaps less than ten minutes, when Peggy's intuitive abilities began picking up on at least two spirits that dwelt within the dark recesses of the cellar. These were the ones she had discerned during her recent visit, and their names were Mary Stuart and Jacob. According to Peggy, they were both historic personages who had once lived in this house.

Rich was getting some random EMF fluctuations, which were most likely caused by the outdated electrical wiring within the cellar. As we entered the main section of the cellar - the section of the cellar that Melissa Kingston referred to as "the dungeon" - Rich switched on his digital video camera and began taking footage, while I was recording audio with my analog tape recorder.

Peggy then attempted a communication session with the spirits who were present, particularly the spirit of Mary Stuart.

"Mary?" she asked. "Mary Stuart, I've come back. Are you going to let us help you? Or is there another spirit present here with us? Mary, if you are truly here, show us a sign of your presence. We need you to communicate with us so that we can help you. Why are you here, Mary?"

Peggy paused for a moment before continuing.

"Please Mary, we've come to help you. Please, give us a sign. Give me a sign so that we can help you. We come with love. We've come to help you. Please, Mary. It's alright. Just you and I, Mary. Just you and I and friends."

When no response was forthcoming, Peggy became somewhat frustrated and said quietly to us, "She's not coming out at all." Peggy then tried changing her line of questioning.

"Who are you? If there is a spirit in this room, then please let us know. Is Jacob here?"

Stephanie suggested, "Try Mary again."

Peggy said, "Mary, we know you are frightened, but there is no reason for you to be. We've come to help you."

Andrew asked, "Rich, are you picking up anything on video?"

Rich replied, "That's a negative, Andrew. At least nothing significant. You know, dust particles orbs flying up in the air, because we're still moving around."

Peggy then suddenly glanced around and said, "Oh, we've got something else down here, too."

I asked her, "What are you feeling?"

"Pain," she replied. "I always know when we have an entity that isn't any good, because I feel pain."

We then heard a slight sighing sound within the room. Brian asked Rich, who was standing next to him, "Did you hear that?"

"Yeah," said Rich.

"Where did it come from?" asked Brian.

"It sounded like it was coming from all around the room," said Rich.

Eric suddenly stumbled forward slightly. Peggy asked, "Are you alright?"

Appearing more startled than frightened, Eric said, "Yes, but... something just touched me from behind."

"That was freaky, dude!" Brian told Eric.

As a matter of caution, I said, "In the name of Jesus Christ, may we be under the protection of holy angels."

Peggy was now clearly becoming impatient for a spirit to manifest itself visually. In an authoritative voice she said, "Show your presence to us! We know you're here. You have come to see us, now show us your presence. In the name of Jesus Christ, we demand that you come out of the shadows and show us your presence!"

There was suddenly a noticeable change in temperature within the section of the cellar we were in. But instead of becoming cooler this time, the temperature actually seemed to be rising. Brian asked the rest of us, "Does anyone feel it getting warmer in here?"

Peggy said, "Yes, it's getting very warm in here."

Brian's eyes were now starting to water. "Something's definitely going on down here," he said. "I can feel it."

Peggy suddenly said, "Wow! My holy water just started to bubble."

We all took a closer look, and sure enough we could see what appeared to be a slight bubbling taking place within the small glass vial. Theresa and Stephanie both gasped at the sight of it.

I said, "If you are an unholy spirit, in the name of Jesus Christ, on the authority of His shed blood, give us a sign."

We waited in silence for several seconds, before Peggy announced, "There, over in the corner. I just saw three blue lights appear, forming a V." We looked, but whatever Peggy had seen was already gone.

The room suddenly began turning noticeably cooler, so much so that both Brian and Peggy said that the bottles of holy water they each held now felt like they were freezing.

Peggy began shouting. "In the name of Jesus Christ and all that is holy, we demand to know your name! Tell us your name! If you hide in the shadows, then you are a coward to us!"

It became obvious that Peggy was anticipating no less than a full-bodied apparition to materialize directly in front of us, and to audibly tell us its name.

Brian did alert our attention to what he said was a shadowy, humanoid figure on one of the cellar walls. It was observed by Brian, Rich and

Peggy. But by the time the rest of us turned to look, it was already gone. According to Brian, it quickly flitted by along the wall for about two seconds before vanishing from sight.

While I continued with the blessing of the entire cellar, Brian and Theresa assisted me by wedging themselves up into a crawl space together and liberally spraying holy water.

When the remainder of the blessing had been completed, I said "In the name of Jesus Christ, we ask for a sign of departure, of any negative or unholy spirits."

Peggy gave a sharp gasp, and exclaimed, "Oh! When Keith said that, I just saw a few sparks shoot out from the wooden cross I'm holding!"

Unfortunately, this anomaly was not picked up by Rich's video camera. Brian then radioed upstairs. "Jason, we're about to wrap things up down here," he said. "But I'll tell ya, Jason, we've been experiencing activity down here! In fact, I almost wound up calling you and Carl for back-up."

On the other end, Jason's static-sounding voice said, "Well, you can explain it to us in detail when you come back upstairs."

"Copy that," said Brian. "We're on our way back up right now.

As soon as we were back upstairs, everyone gathered around us, anxious to know exactly what we had experienced downstairs.

Brian and Peggy excitedly told about the sudden temperature changes and the holy water that suddenly started to bubble. To Mandy and her two daughter's relief, I informed her that the cellar had now been completely blessed.

I also mentioned that we noticed that the desiccated dear head was no longer down there on the cellar floor.

Michelle told us, "Yeah, my mom finally insisted that my dad get rid of that awful thing once and for all. So he pitched it out in the trash."

"Just as well," Brian commented. "That thing really gave me the heebie-jeebies last time."

Since it was now well past midnight, we decided to hold off on the blessing of the barn until the following morning, instead of fumbling around in the darkness. Peggy would be staying overnight as well because she wished to participate in the blessing of the barn. Mandy set up a separate room for her downstairs.

The rest of us were making preparations for what rooms we were going to bed down for the night in, when Mandy's eldest daughter Megan arrived back home from a night out with some of her friends. However, because they had just returned from partying throughout most of the evening, Megan and at least four of her friends were quite intoxicated, and Megan was requesting that her mother allow them to crash at the farmhouse for the night, in the interest of their safety.

Needless to say, we soon found ourselves doubling up in cramped quarters within the upstairs rooms. As for myself, I wound up sharing a section of one of the cold, hard upstairs bedroom floors with Theresa, with one blanket between us. Soon after Theresa had dosed off, she turned over in her sleep and pulled the blanket off of me. I did not bother retrieving my half of the blanket, and instead rolled myself into a fetal position in a useless attempt to gain some warmth. After all, this was northern Maine in October.


The next morning after Mandy had served us a light but delicious breakfast, it was time for us to conduct the blessing of the barn before leaving. Accompanied by Peggy, the TAPS team ventured outside into the crisp October morning air. Peggy suddenly gasped, apparently startled by something she saw on the front porch. However, it turned out to only be a harmless "Chucky" doll, which the Kingston family had put out on the porch as part of their Halloween display. Laughing with embarrassment, Peggy told us, "That Chucky doll has got to go!"

Since Brian himself had a personal trepidation of dolls, he uncomfortably edged around it and said, "Get that thing away from me."

With Michelle Kingston accompanying us, we then ventured out to the barn and entered in through the front. Because sections of the floor were littered with broken glass and sheet metal, plus two antiquated Volkswagen bug vehicles parked there, we had to be very careful while maneuvering around in the subdued lighting within the barn's interior. After I had recited an invocation along with Scripture passages, and asked in the name of God that the barn be cleansed from anything unholy or oppressive, Peggy took out her small vial of holy water and removed the cork stopper. She then went to throw some holy water, but surprisingly nothing came out from the bottle.

"That's funny," Peggy said. "Nothing's coming out." She gave the bottle a more forceful shake, but again nothing came out.

Brian asked, "What the heck? What have you got in there?"

Peggy replied, "Just regular holy water, but for some reason I can't seem to get it to come out. It seems to have gelled at the bottom."

My brother Carl commented, "Perhaps something in here doesn't want the holy water to be dispersed."

"It would seem that way, wouldn't it?" asked Peggy. She held it out for us to inspect. Brian and I both took turns examining the bottle and its contents. The bottle was over half full, and because the water was a bit cloudy, most likely salt crystals had been added to it. Brian and I each took turns shaking the bottle with our thumbs over the stopper, and it certainly seemed diluted enough. Peggy gave it a third try, and this time the water came out freely.


When the blessing of the barn was completed, we came back inside for a final conference with the Kingston family. Since Peggy had to get back home, she said her good-byes to us and Mandy, and again emphasized what a wonderful opportunity it was getting to work with TAPS.

We then gathered in the parlor with Mandy, Michelle and Melissa. Unfortunately, George Kingston had been called into work for the morning, and Megan had left with her friends again, and was therefore unable to join us. Speaking to Melissa and Michelle in particular, we made a point of addressing the dangers of attempting to communicate with any spirits in the house.

Jason told the girls, "I wish that your sister Megan was also here with us right now, to listen to what I'm telling you. Considering the history of this house, especially the possibility of satanic worship, it could be very dangerous communicating with the spirits in this house. They could take this as an open invitation to attach themselves to you, even the so-called 'friendly' spirits. I certainly would never invite a spirit to come home and play with my children. And Keith and Carl will both tell you the same thing."

"That's absolutely correct," I agreed. "There are parasitic spirits that are experts at masquerading as friendly 'spirit guides', when in reality it could be a ruse to gain permission to enter."

Carl added, "The best way to counteract this negative spirit activity you've been experiencing here is to cut off its feeding source, so to speak. Certain types of entities seem to intentionally generate fear and other negative emotions in people, because they tend to feed off of negative energy."

Each of the Kingston family members said that they understood and agreed that they would make more of an effort to maintain a positive atmosphere within their house. Mandy then embraced each of us, and tearfully thanked us for our intervention on their behalf. We also thanked her for the hospitality she'd shown to us throughout the weekend.

It certainly looked like a perfect day for our trip back home. Just before we left, however, Jason made the discovery that nearly $80.00 was missing from his wallet. Mandy was frantic when she found out, and immediately launched into a search of the entire house, assisted by her two daughters. However, no trace of the missing cash turned up.

Although Mandy was desperately apologetic, Jason told her not to worry about it. The only two possible explanations were that it was either a paranormal occurrence, or more likely, one of Michelle's intoxicated friends was responsible for rifling through Jason's personal belongings sometime during the night. In either case, there was very little likelihood that Jason would recover his missing cash.

Before leaving the area, we of course stopped at The Purple Cow restaurant for a late brunch. While there, we discussed what we'd experienced at the Kingston farmhouse and drew what conclusions we could.

Andrew said to Jason, "That's a shame about the money missing from your wallet. How much was it?"

"Close to eighty dollars," said Jason. "But I'm just going to have to chalk that up as a loss."

Stephanie mused, "I wonder what the outcome of this will be, now that the farmhouse has been completely blessed for a second time."

Jason shrugged and said, "That depends to a large extent on the Kingston's themselves. Right, Keith?"

"Exactly," I agreed. "Just like we advised them last time, they'll have to work together as a family unit to keep the activity from coming back. Entities seem to feed off of the energy produced by negative emotions. And the family should be counteracting this by creating a positive atmosphere within their home."

Carl said, "I have to concur with Keith on this. There certainly was negativity in the house last night. For example, I couldn't help overhearing a few of Melissa's friends discussing with each other about how they were going to 'snuff' someone. I was surprised that anyone still uses that term!"

Rich agreed, "That certainly didn't help the family's situation at all. I understand that Mandy didn't want to let her daughter's friends drive home drunk. But hopefully they won't be congregating there on a regular basis."

Andrew added, "We'll just have to see how long the positive effect of Keith's blessing lasts this time."


Shortly after returning home from our second visit in Skowhegan, TAPS conducted an evidence review. Although Rich found no anomalies on the video footage he had taken, something unusual did show up on one of the photographs taken in the barn. The digital photograph was taken by Theresa inside the barn just before I had begun doing the blessing. But for some unknown reason, the image came out in reverse. Not only that, but although Brian and my brother Carl distinctly recalled standing behind me at that moment, they both somehow appeared in the photograph. In fact, just a moment before the picture was taken, Brian had announced that he was feeling a bit dizzy and off balance. Unfortunately, this digital photograph was subsequently lost.

A review of my own audio recordings revealed only one example of EVP. It was recorded when we were in the Kingston's cellar, and the psychic medium Peggy was demanding a sign from whatever spirit may have been present. At one point Peggy had exclaimed, "Show us a sign of your presence!" A whispering voice quietly but firmly responded, "No."

Over the ensuing years, TAPS maintained a sporadic communication with Mandy Kingston. Although the paranormal activity within the farmhouse never returned full force after our second house cleansing, the family did wind up moving away from the Skowhegan farmhouse a few years later. Mandy Kingston and her husband George eventually split up, and Mandy and her three daughters relocated back to Massachusetts.

Several years after they had moved, Mandy's daughter Melissa bore Mandy a grandson, who at an early age began showing signs of being sensitive to the presence of spirits. Mandy herself began independently investigating the paranormal, to try and assist people who were being frightened by spirit phenomena as she and her family had.

It is also Mandy's wish to someday purchase their old farmhouse in Skowhegan, Maine, and move back into it with her family.

# Chapter 5

## What's That in the Woods?

**A** genuine Bigfoot sighting in little Rhode Island?? Yes, we have them here too, although the reports have admittedly been few and far between. A Bigfoot sighting took place in 1978 when a Charleston resident who was out driving with her eight-year-old son allegedly crossed paths with a towering man-like creature that was covered with snowy-white fur. But this occurrence was not the only one to hit the record books.

According to Shawn Robbins, his encounter took place when he was just twelve years old, out bicycle riding on a Saturday afternoon with his cousin Chris. They were riding their bikes along Seven Mile Road near the Cranston border, aligned by woods on either side. At one point the two of them stopped to rest for a moment. While chatting, they heard a crunching sound in the wooded area to their right. Glancing in that direction, they both saw a black shape plodding along in the nearby woods, slowly making its way through the brush.

"Hey, what's that in the woods?" Shawn whispered to Chris.

"Don't know. Can't get a good enough look at it," Chris whispered back.

Because overhanging leaves and branches mostly obscured it, they could not get a clear view of the slowly moving creature. But whatever it was, it appeared to be at least the size of a large, full-grown man. Chris and Shawn began quietly speculating whether it might simply be someone wearing dark clothing, or maybe even a foraging black bear. In either case, both Chris and Shawn were at first ready to bid a hasty retreat on their bikes.

As the thing, whatever it was, moved a little closer, the two boys observed that it appeared to be walking upright, but with a peculiar sort of lumbering gait. It was somewhat stoop-shouldered and seemed to be disoriented.

Chris whispered, "Do you suppose it's some drunk guy, tripping around in the woods?"

"Either that, or maybe he's hurt," said Shawn. "Maybe we should see if he needs help or something, y'think?"

Chris agreed, and the two boys began calling out to him, asking if he was alright. The figure paused momentarily, but made no attempt to respond. Shawn decided to take the initiative and investigate, since he was the slightly older of the two. After getting off his bicycle, he cautiously took a few steps towards the dark figure to get a closer look. His own footsteps were crunching on acorns and snapping twigs, causing more noise than he wished.

Still on his bicycle, Chris whispered from behind, "Shawn, what do you see??"

"Shhhh!" Shawn hushed his younger cousin.

Scarcely a moment later, the dark figure suddenly turned towards Shawn and stepped forward from out of the brush, allowing Shawn for the first time to get a clear view of it. Shawn instantly found himself frozen in shock. In front of him, now only three or four yards away, stood a tall, seemingly ape-like creature, basically in the shape of an upright human, but covered in what appeared to be coarse dark hair. Because the creature was no longer slouched, Shawn estimated its height to be at least a good six feet or more. Chris obviously also saw it, because he let out a terrified scream.

Shawn suddenly regained the use of his legs, and bolted out of the woods – scrambling up the small embankment with his feet slipping on acorns - back to where his bicycle and his younger cousin Chris were waiting. Close behind him, Shawn could hear the heavy tread of the creature and for perhaps a split second, he wondered if this was his final moment alive. Luckily his survival instincts fully kicked in, and an instant later he had hopped on his bike and was peddling away as fast as he could alongside Chris. Shawn took a quick look back, and saw that the tall hairy ape-man was thankfully not perusing them, but was merely looking at them as if out of curiosity. A second glance confirmed that the creature had now vanished from sight.

To this day, all Shawn Robbins remembers about the face of the creature from that close encounter, is that it appeared somewhat ape-like, and that the face and eyes were dark in color. He still hesitates to make any definite conclusion as to what he and his cousin Chris had encountered that day in the woods alongside Seven Mile Road.

"Could it have been something like an actual Bigfoot?" he wonders. "I don't know exactly, because Chris and I didn't stay around long enough to get that good a look at it. But I do remember that it was at least six feet tall. And it didn't really chase after us. In fact, I think that if it had wanted to catch us, it would have, so I don't think it actually meant us any harm."

Renowned Bigfoot researcher Don Keating, after hearing Shawn's story, does not doubt his sincerity, nor does my brother Carl Johnson. In fact, although Shawn's sighting seems to have been an isolated, one-time encounter of its kind in this particular rural area of Rhode Island, Carl's friend Dina Palazini had an encounter with a Bigfoot, or Sasquatch-like creature in 1983, in the Cumberland area.

Tower Hill Road in Cumberland, RI is a narrow, winding road near to Diamond Hill State Park and the Woonsocket City line. It was dusk as Dina and three friends, all of them in their teens at the time, were riding in an open-top convertible on this stretch of road, when they decided to pull over and park for a while. Dina was seated in the back of the vehicle. She and her friends had been chatting for a few minutes, discussing where they wanted to go next that evening, when Dina suddenly became aware of an inexplicable sensation of being watched. She could also smell something acrid, what she described as smelling like urine or a musky "animal scent". She turned and beheld a sight that would stay with her as a vivid memory for many years to come. A hulking, broad-shouldered, biped creature, covered with matted dark brown fur or hair, with a strangely human-like face loomed over her. She, and her three teenaged companions screamed upon seeing the creature, and the driver of the convertible nearly broke off the key in his car's ignition, frantically starting the engine and peeling out of that space. Speeding down the road, the teens hailed down a cruising Cumberland Police officer to alert him about the "monster or something" they'd just witnessed! Dina also recalled that the fur-covered creature was naked, and obviously of the male gender.

A lady who has chosen to remain anonymous described having a similar experience along this same stretch of road in Cumberland, in 1989. She recalled encountering what appeared to be a huge, hair-covered creature, with characteristics both simian and human. This creature terrified her as it emerged from the woods' edge, and ferociously banged its fists on the hood of her car.

These experiences, combined with other reports suggesting a possible Sasquatch presence in Rhode Island, have inspired both Carl Johnson and Dina Palazini to cofound the 'Big Rhodey Research Project.' The term 'Big Rhodey' is Carl's personal spin on Rhode Island's nickname of "Little Rhodey". They and their team members dedicate much of their free time to researching possible evidence of this elusive local creature, and they also welcome and encourage submissions of eyewitness reports.

In September of 2011, the cast and crew of Animal Planet's TV series 'Finding Bigfoot' visited Rhode Island to film an episode for Season Two of their show. Members of the Big Rhodey Research Project participated in this episode. On Monday, September 19th of that year, the 'Finding Bigfoot' crew also hosted a Town Meeting held at the East Greenwich Town Hall to discuss Bigfoot sightings within the Ocean State. I attended this meeting and found it very surprising just how many Rhode Island residents turned out to share their personal stories of Bigfoot encounters!

The episode aired on Sunday, January 8th, 2012 and was appropriately titled "Big Rhodey."

And so, in Rhode Island as well every other state of the USA with the exception of Hawaii, reports of encounters between humans and large hairy ape-like creatures with human characteristics continue to surface annually. Of course, until either a nearly complete carcass or a live specimen is produced, the existence of these creatures cannot be fully authenticated. Let us hope that if and when this undeniable proof is finally forthcoming, it is not the result of violence or bloodshed.

TAPS member Chris Finch surrounded by plasma lights

# Chapter 6

## The House Infestation

(The names of the family members involved in this case have been altered to protect their personal privacy.)

**A**lthough Sandra and I had branched off from The Atlantic Paranormal Society and founded New England Anomalies Research in 2004, we of course have always maintained friendly relationship with TAPS and its members; many of whom are close personal friends of ours. We are also sometimes called in to assist on TAPS cases, especially those that may possibly involve inhuman spirits. The following case was investigated by the TAPS home team, and was not filmed as part of the Ghost Hunters TV series. It took place in 2006, approximately two years after Sandra and I had founded NEAR.

Due to the nature of the reports TAPS Case Manager Kristyn Gartland had received from the clients, she'd personally contacted Sandra and I requesting our assistance. We assured Kristyn that we'd do all we could to help.

Over the phone, Kristyn told us, "I knew that I could count on you guys. This particular case is in Dracut, Massachusetts. It involves an elderly woman who lives by herself in an older house. And although she has family members who check in on her at least twice a day, she likes the independence of living alone in her own home."

Accompanying Sandra and I on this particular case would be Lisa Dowaliby, Paula Donovan and Michael King, who at the time were all members of the TAPS Home Team. Lisa and Paula were both great people with professional backgrounds. Although this was our first time meeting Michael, he certainly seemed to be a like-minded individual with a professional attitude. We were all anticipating an enjoyable investigation for that evening.

When the four of us arrived at the Victorian-style two-story house in Dracut early on the scheduled Saturday evening, four members of the client's family were present, including the eldest son and his wife, and the younger son and his wife. We were then introduced to the client herself, a charming New England lady named Mary, who was in her early 70's the actual homeowner. The two sons explained that recently Mary, though very independent, had been feeling very uneasy while being in the house alone, because of unexplained noises and the feeling of an unseen presence within the house.

Paula asked Mary, "What kind of unexplained noises have you been hearing?"

Mary replied, "Well, my family doesn't like going down into the cellar anymore, especially since Todd had something happen to him down there. And I can't get up and down the cellar stairs like I used to. But up here, well, I've been hearing all sorts of bangs and noises, against the walls and the windows."

All throughout our interview, we happened to detect a distinctive odor of rodent urine, which was obviously wafting up from the basement through a grating in the hallway floor. Out of politeness we refrained from mentioning it right away in front of the homeowner, although right away we suspected that this could be a serious health issue that obviously needed looking into.

Since the rest of the family members would be leaving shortly, we decided to continue our interview with Mary after they left.

Addressing the eldest son, whose name was Todd, Lisa said, "Now, Todd, I know I've spoken to you over the phone, about what you had described happened to you downstairs. And I was wondering if you would be so kind as to relay to my fellow team members exactly what you experienced."

Todd told us, "I'll say the same story the same way. Basically, I was downstairs picking up wood, placing it into a bag to bring upstairs for firewood. And I suddenly started getting the feeling that I wasn't alone down there, that someone had their eyes upon me. Now, I've gotten that feeling before down there, but this time it was very intense. I kept looking around, but I couldn't see anyone or anything down there with me. And so I just started bending over and picking up some more wood from the wood pile. Then all of a sudden, without warning I just felt my brain almost exploding with electricity. It was as if my head was suddenly ablaze, and I felt as if I didn't get out of there right away, I might not make it out alive!"

I asked, "Why do you think this happened to you, Todd?"

Todd replied, "I don't know, but I got the impression that something definitely didn't want me down there in the cellar. So I haven't been down there ever since."

When we questioned the other family members, none of them had an experience like this. Todd's brother John had never experienced anything unusual in the cellar, although he admittedly did not like spending a great deal of time down there. Neither Todd or John's wives really liked being in the cellar either, and John's wife refused to venture down there at all anymore, alone or otherwise, because she didn't like the feeling she got being down there.

Paula asked, "Todd, I have to ask, do you have any history of seizures?"

"No, none that I'm aware of," he said. "Certainly I've never had a problem before, except for that one time recently in the cellar."

Paula said, "Okay, so, we were explaining what each one of us do, and you remember me saying that I'm more on the technical side - the cultural and historical side. My qualifications are old building structures. Also, since you happen to be of the Catholic faith, we were wondering if you might like to have Sandra and Keith go through the house and perform a blessing of each room before we leave tonight. They have a lot of experience."

I explained, "Basically, Sandra and I handle the spiritual and religious aspects. And if you would feel more comfortable with a religious cleansing or blessing of the house, we usually conclude with that."

Mary and her family members all agreed that this would be a good idea.

The eldest son Todd then thanked us for coming out to help, and said, "We're actually gonna get going now, but we'll be back in a couple of hours, to see how everything went with your investigation. I don't know if you'll find anything."

Lisa said, "Well, we'll continue the interview with your mom, and then we'll conduct our own investigation throughout the house, and then we'll let you know if we find anything."

Paula added, "It may take a while to go over whatever data we collect, such as our video and audio recordings, but we'll certainly let you know later on if we do find anything."

The family members again expressed their gratitude, and then made their departure.


Once the other family members had left, we continued our interview with the homeowner, Mary, who turned out to be a charming woman in her early 70's. Lisa asked her, "You're the owner of this home, correct?"

"I am, yes," replied Mary. "I've been living here the better part of my life, because it's been my family home for three generations."

Mary told us there were three rooms upstairs which she jokingly referred to as "The Three Bears," explaining, "There's a little room, a middle room and a big room."

Paula asked, "And your bedroom is upstairs?"

"Yes, it is," said Mary. "And then there's the doggone stairs I have to climb. I'd like to get one of those seats you sit on, that you could ride right up to the next floor. You know what I mean?"

Sandra said, "Yes, they look like they'd be fun to ride."

Although Mary did not give us an actual tour of the house, she did verbally describe the layout of the entire house to us. Mary told us that there was a stove in the basement that burned both oil and wood, and also that there was a wood pile in the basement.

Michael asked her, "How long has it been since you yourself have been down in the basement?"

Mary replied, "Oh, not for a couple of months now. I don't get down there too often, because my knee joints make it difficult for me to maneuver stairs. In fact, it's usually my sons who go down there when they're here, if anything needs to be done in the basement, like tending to the stove in the wintertime. But of course, Todd doesn't even like to go down there anymore."

As an afterthought, Mary looked at Sandra and added, "By the way, I also have a refrigerator down in the basement that's in perfect working order, just in case you're interested."

Sandra smiled pleasantly and told her, "We're not in the market for a refrigerator at this moment. But we appreciate the offer."

Paula asked, "So, Mary, could you elaborate a little more about what's been disturbing you here? Especially while you're alone."

Mary said, "Well, for one thing, I keep hearing a banging sound against the wall right in this room, and I'm sure it's a ghost doing it, because I'm always alone when it happens."

Michael asked, "How often does the banging sound happen, Mary?"

"Oh, it usually happens at least two or three times a night," said Mary.

I asked her, "Do the knockings happen in any particular numerical pattern, like, say, two or three times in a row?"

"No, I don't think so," said Mary. "There will usually be just one knock at a time."

To me, this made any demonic aspect less likely, since the demonic calling card will usually be three knocks in a row.

Paula asked, "What else has been bothering you while you're alone here, Mary?"

Indicating the wall windows, Mary said, "Well, almost every night I hear sounds outside of these windows, as if someone's trying to get in. I don't know if it's ghosts or real people in the neighborhood, but I know that someone's trying to get in. So I've nailed them shut."

I asked, "Do you ever call the police when you hear people at your window?"

Mary replied, "Oh, no, I haven't yet, but if it keeps up, maybe I should."

I asked, "Haven't you told your family about this, Mary, if you think that people are trying to break into your house at night?"

"Yes, I've told them about it," said Mary. "And they told me I should call the police right away next time I hear those noises. And like I said, I'm not even sure whether it's ghosts or people at the windows."

During this part of our interview, Lisa had been seated in a parlor rocking chair, contentedly rocking back and forth. But when she rose, the chair rocked backward, causing the headrest of the chair to bump the wall behind her.

Mary instantly flinched and exclaimed, "Oh! That's the sound of the ghost banging on the wall that I've been hearing!"

We all glanced at each other, and Lisa explained, "No, Mary, that was just the headrest of your rocking chair banging against the wall when I got up. See?"

Lisa demonstrated with the chair, and instantly produced the same exact sound.

"Oh... I guess it is the chair that's been making that sound after all," Mary agreed.

Paula said, "Well, it looks that you now have one less thing to worry about, Mary. You see, we always try to find a rational explanation first before jumping to a supernatural conclusion."

With a light laugh, Mary said, "Yes, I guess that is at least one less thing I have to worry about."


After concluding our interview with Mary, the six of us began our investigation of the house itself. Although we found no anomalous readings in any of the rooms upstairs, we did discover what appeared to be a serious mold infestation in the first floor bathroom, and to a lesser extent the second floor bathroom.

Inspecting it closely in the first floor bathroom, Michael said, "This is definitely black mold, which can be very toxic."

Paula added, "And not only can it cause illnesses, but prolonged exposure could also cause hallucinations. And these people have certainly had prolonged exposure, especially Mary."

Lisa said, "Guys, this is something we should definitely bring to her family's attention, as soon as they arrive back." The rest of us of course agreed with her.

But if we were concerned about the mold problem in the bathrooms, it paled in comparison to what we were to find in the cellar. As mentioned, we'd been aware of the distinctive odor of rodent urine wafting up through a grating in the hallway during our interview. However, once we went downstairs into the cellar itself, the stench was almost overpowering. We certainly did not need to be professional exterminators to realize that the cellar had a serious rodent infestation.

Another discovery that nearly knocked us for a loop was the fact that a thick growth of white mold was growing out in patches on the cellar walls. Some of it actually resembled cotton candy.

Lisa and I looked at each other in astonishment, and she said, "I think it's entirely possible that Mary may be at risk for hantavirus, which is caused by exposure to rodent urine and droppings."

I said, "And I'm wondering if all the mold down here is what caused Mary's son to have that episode."

While we were taking various readings in the cellar, Sandra noticed a distinct clicking sound that seemed to be emanating from a woodpile that was over in a far corner.

She brought this to my attention, saying, "Whatever is making that clicking sound, it sounds as though the woodpile is alive!"

Listening, I could tell that this was no exaggeration on Sandra's part. And on closer inspection, it became obvious that the woodpile was indeed heavily infested with living organisms... termites!

Michael was equally shocked when we brought him over to listen to just how actively the woodpile was infested with termites.

Wide-eyed, Joe commented, "We've definitely got to alert the client's family about these conditions. If something isn't done soon, then it's obviously only going to get worse."

At the other side of the cellar near the staircase, Lisa began finding numerous rodent tracks. She also began smelling the distinctive scent of decay, and soon discovered a mouse carcass that at first seemed to be alive. However on closer inspection, the small carcass was actually writhing with maggots, which at first made it appear to be moving.

Lisa finally said, "Okay, this is enough. We've got to let Mary know that the main problem in her house isn't ghosts; it's vermin!"

Sandra added, "And then, as soon as her family returns, we've got to sit down with them and alert them as to what conditions their mother is living in."

"Amen to that," said Paula.


When we did go back upstairs and explain our findings to Mary, she was initially somewhat reluctant to believe that the conditions in her house were as severe as we described. Apparently, she had grown so accustomed to the odor of rodent urine emanating through the hallway grating that she was not even aware of it. As politely as possible, we tried to convince her that something had to be done about the rodent problem in the cellar, as well as the termite infested wood pile. However, Mary still remained unconvinced, stating that she had never seen any evidence of mice in the cellar, and that she had never heard any clicking sounds coming from the woodpile, although she was admittedly somewhat hard of hearing.

Lisa told her, "Mary, I happen to be a veterinary technician, and I know what I'm talking about. And I'm telling you that there is undeniable evidence of both insect and rodent infestations in your cellar, to the point that these are obvious health hazards. We're simply concerned about you living here alone, and we certainly wouldn't want you to wind up getting sick."

Although Mary was of course very pleasant about it, she still insisted that we were simply being overly concerned. Finally, Lisa felt that the only way to convince Mary of the seriousness of the problem would be to show her some actual evidence. After excusing herself, Lisa went back downstairs and momentarily returned with the maggot infested mouse carcass resting in an aluminum paint roller tray.

"I'm sorry, Mary, I really don't mean to be overly graphic," Lisa apologized. "But I just want to make you aware of the reality of this problem."

It was only after seeing the desiccated mouse carcass for herself that Mary finally seemed to acknowledge what Lisa was explaining to her.

When Mary's family returned a couple of hours later, we sat down with them in the parlor, and specifically informed them about the problems we'd discovered within the house during the course of our investigation.

Paula explained, "The black mold that we found in both the upstairs and the downstairs bathrooms can be an extreme health hazard, especially through prolonged exposure."

Lisa also showed them the mouse carcass she'd found in the cellar, and said, "I'm sure you must have noticed the heavy odor of rodent urine wafting up through the grating in the hallway. And from the numerous mouse tracks I found in certain areas as well as this dead mouse, there's obviously a heavy rodent population down there."

Sandra and Michael also informed them about the infestation of termites that we'd discovered in the woodpile downstairs.

The eldest son Todd shook his head and said, "Gee, I knew that there were some problems in this house, but I really had no idea things had gotten this bad. You see, we're only here for a limited amount of time each day and each night because Mom likes to keep her independence."

Todd's younger brother John said to him, "Yeah, Mom does like being able to live independently, as long as she can basically maintain this house." Turning to his mother, he added, "But I have to agree, Mom, that there are some very serious problems here that need to be taken care of, if you're going to be able to go on living here."

Both John's and Todd's wives agreed that their mother-in-law was obviously living in some very unwholesome conditions. Todd's wife said, "I knew there was a bad smell in here, and I sometimes even started feeling a little sick myself if I'm here for very long."

Mary also agreed with our assessment, and acknowledged that these were very serious conditions that needed taking care of. Looking at us with a smile, she asked, "So, you didn't find any evidence of any actual ghosts in this house?" The rest of the family also waited anxiously for our reply.

Lisa explained, "Well, so far we haven't come across any evidence of actual paranormal activity here, but of course we have to go over our recordings that we'd made."

Michael told them, "We'll certainly let you know if we find any evidence such as Electronic Voice Phenomena, or anything unusual we may have captured on video. I did log some rather high readings in the cellar, but I think that may have been due to the older electrical wiring that's sheathed in a plastic coating."

"Oh, I see," said Todd. "Thank you for bringing that to our attention too."

Of course, we emphasized that we were by no means professional exterminators or house inspectors. We were merely a small group of concerned individuals looking assist in any way we could.


Before we left, Sandra and I did perform a house blessing throughout all the rooms of the house. Although our group investigation had thus far yielded no evidence of any paranormal activity, let alone anything that may have been demonic in nature, the homeowner Mary was devoutly religious, and the house blessing we performed proved to be very reassuring for her. Paula, Lisa and Michael accompanied Sandra and me throughout the house and continued taking readings as we thoroughly blessed each room, including the attic and the cellar.

Mary and her family thoroughly thanked us for all the time and effort we'd put into the investigation we'd conducted.

Todd emphasized, "Again, we knew there were problems in this house, but we didn't realized just how bad things had gotten here. Thank you so much for bringing these things to our attention. You people have certainly gone above and beyond just performing a ghost hunt, which was all we originally expected."

Mary also thanked Sandra and me for the religious blessing we'd conducted throughout her entire house. We assured her that we'd be keeping her in our prayers, and let her know that we'd also prayed for angelic protection on her behalf.


Perhaps not altogether surprising, our evidence review of the house in Dracut revealed no paranormal activity whatsoever. We attributed Mary's "ghost noises" that she was hearing outside of her windows to the wind and possibly voices of people passing by at night from the nearby street.

Before leaving the house that evening we did check the outside of the house, and concluded this could be a logical explanation, just like the thumping of the rocking chair against the parlor wall that Mary had mistaken for a spirit.

However, although we found no evidence of anything paranormal, we did manage to significantly help out our client, Mary. We did remain in touch with her, and within two weeks after our visit, some major changes had begun to take place within her home. Her sons called in a professional exterminator to take care of the rodent and insect infestations, and the mold problem was addressed as well. Also, Mary's family arranged to have lengthier visits with her, and to assist her more in the upkeep of her house.

At our suggestion, Mary's eldest son Todd had told us that he was going to make an appointment with his primary care physician to discuss the mysterious episode he had personally experienced within the cellar, if only to rule out any physical malady. We wondered if his physician might even recommend that Todd see a neurologist. Although we do not know if Todd followed through with this, at least he apparently experienced no more episodes of this type after his mother's house was cleaned up.

Also not surprisingly, after our investigation and intervention on the family's behalf, Mary's "spirit infestation" within her house seemed to have cleared up as well. With her family visiting with her more regularly, Mary was no longer attributing each and every noise she heard to a spirit manifestation. In fact, she now hardly seemed to be aware of these noises at all, or at least she was no longer complaining about them.

And after Lisa, Paula, Michael, Sandra and I had submitted our final report on the Dracut case to The Atlantic Paranormal Society, we all agreed that this served as a perfect example of just how positive an impact an alert paranormal investigation team can have upon a situation, especially involving a family. Working together as a team, each one of us contributed to this investigation with our field of experience and were able to offer positive solutions to our client and her family.

# Chapter 7

### "Gonna Get You, Kitties!"

**A**fter Sandra and I had branched off from TAPS and founded New England Anomalies Research, we still often received requests from other paranormal groups to assist them on cases where religious intervention was required. Most often we'd find ourselves working with groups who were already very familiar with us, such as TAPS and New England Paranormal. It has always been a pleasure for Sandra and me to have the opportunity to work together again with our familiar friends in TAPS and NEP, as well as getting to meet and work with new people.

Reminiscing back on a case we assisted New England Paranormal with in April of 2005 I found it particularly intriguing, mainly because of a rather curious example of Electronic Voice Phenomena captured by one of the team members during our investigation.

Sandra and I were initially contacted by our friend Mike Dion of NEP, whom we'd previously joined on numerous co-investigations and paranormal classes over the previous few years. This particular investigation involved a woman located in New Hampshire, who was allegedly experiencing paranormal activity in her home. According to the client, the activity in her home was initially tolerable, and consisted mainly of household objects being misplaced and turning up in unusual places, including her younger children's toys, sudden cold spots in certain rooms within the house and the eerie feeling of being watched.

Her two young daughters were being badly frightened by strange disembodied voices within the house, along with occasional glimpses of a spectral figure. Also, her teenage son had recently been scratched on his neck while upstairs in his bedroom, by what he described as feeling like invisible claws. Needless to say, the client, whose name was Cheryl, was now becoming very anxious for some sort of intervention on behalf of her children and herself.

Because of our experience in dealing with extreme negative paranormal activity, and we have performed religious house blessings, Mike asked Sandra and me to assist him on this case. We of course agreed and Mike scheduled the trip to New Hampshire for the following weekend. Joining us for this excursion would be a few other members of NEP as well as Kristyn Gartland, a former client who had just recently begun working with TAPS. Although our friend and fellow investigator Steve Gonsalves was the founder of NEP, he unfortunately would not be joining us because of filming obligations with the new televisions series "Ghost Hunters."

After meeting up at Mike Dion's house in Chicopee, MA, Kristyn gave Sandra and me each an affectionate hug, and told us, "It's so great to see you guys again! And I'm so excited to actually be investigating with you, instead of being a client for a change."

Sandra said, "We're certainly glad to be investigating with you too, Kristyn. It'll be a great experience, whether we find something there or not."

We then formed a train of vehicles, with Mike in the lead, and Sandra and I riding with Mike. Along the way Mike told us, "I really appreciate you guys coming with us on this case. Cheryl, who's a single mother, is becoming very fearful about living in her house, especially since her teenage son was recently assaulted by something he couldn't see. In fact, both her sons are even feeling uncomfortable about sleeping in their own bedrooms now. She also has a four-year old daughter who says she's seen a strange man in the bathroom."

Sandra asked Mike, "Does she herself have any opinion about what could be causing this activity?"

Mike replied, "All I know is that Cheryl says it's a very old farmhouse she lives in, dating back to the 1800's, and that if things keep progressing the way they are, she'll have no choice but to move out, even though she can't really afford to."

I said, "Well, we've brought along our house blessing accoutrements. And I've also asked for special prayers for tonight from our church co-pastors, Dr.'s Dan and Reppa Cottrell. They're a husband and wife team."

Mike said, "That's good, because if things are as bad as Cheryl says they are, we'll need all the prayers we can get!"

As we continued driving along, Mike also mentioned our mutual friend Dustin Pari, who had become an investigator with TAPS several months earlier.

"I see that Dustin's also recently become the newest cast member on 'Ghost Hunters.'" Mike mentioned.

"Yes he has," confirmed Sandra. "In fact, it was actually Keith who gave him a personal reference to become a member of TAPS."

"Really?" asked Mike. "No kidding!"

"Actually, Dustin asked me if I could possibly give him a personal reference to Jason and Grant. And since I was very impressed with Dustin's qualifications, I contacted Jason and Grant myself on Dustin's behalf, to make sure his application wouldn't be overlooked among so many others." I explained.

"Well, I'm sure Dustin really appreciated that," said Mike.

About an hour later, we arrived at a long, isolated country lane in a rural New Hampshire town, and eventually came to the client's residence. It was indeed an antiquated two-story farm house, complete with an old, large shed out in back.

"Well, this is the place," Mike said after everyone had parked and gotten out of their cars. "I guess we can start unloading our equipment, and then I'll let the client know we're here."

Sandra and I accompanied Mike to the front door, which was answered by homeowner Cheryl Worthington.

Mike pleasantly announced, "Hi, it's Mike Dion from New England Paranormal."

"Oh," said Cheryl. "Come on in, Mike."

"Thank you," said Mike as the three of us stepped in. He then introduced us. "This is Keith and Sandra Johnson from New England Anomalies Research, and I asked them to join us on the investigation tonight. I believe I've mentioned them to you before. They handle extreme cases, so I was hoping they may be able to help with your situation."

"Yes, very nice to meet you, Keith and Sandra," said Cheryl. "I'm sure glad you're here."

Sandra and I both told Cheryl it was nice to meet her as well.

The rest of the team entered, and Mike introduced each one to Cheryl. Our hostess then invited us all to make ourselves comfortable in the parlor. Some of us switched on our audio recorders as Mike began interviewing Cheryl.

It turned out that the farmhouse was well over a century old. Needless to say, multiple families had lived there over the years, and the house had certainly seen its share of births, deaths and marriages, back in an era when generations of family members lived their entire lives in the same location. Cheryl herself had lived there for a number of years, and now, as a single parent raising her four children, she was forced to deal with the added stress of an unseen presence sharing the farmhouse with them.

Mike asked Cheryl if she knew of anything regarding the history of the farmhouse that may be relevant to the paranormal activity they'd been experiencing. Cheryl replied that local rumors circulated of some sort of tragic deaths under mysterious circumstances occurring in this house, although she'd been unable to verify the facts at the town hall. According to local legend, her house happened to be built upon grounds that once included an ancient Indian sacred site and burial ground, but again, she'd been unable to verify this. At any rate, the house was rumored to be haunted by locals in the community.

"Other kids are coming up to my kids at school and telling them, 'Oh, you live in that old haunted farmhouse. That must be pretty spooky living there.'" Cheryl revealed.

Cheryl also informed us that her two sons had occasionally invited friends to sleep over, but most that had done so were reluctant to do so again.

Mike then asked Cheryl if she would relate some of the activity she'd been experiencing in her house, especially recently.

Cheryl replied, "Well, as I mentioned over the phone, it's been picking up lately. We've always had the feeling that some sort of invisible presence shared this house with us. You know, things would be moved around mysteriously. But recently, we've been hearing mumbling going on inside empty rooms, but when we look inside these rooms, no one's in there. But recently, while I was alone in one of the upstairs bedrooms, I had the feeling that someone was with me, watching me. And as I mentioned to Mike over the phone, just the other day, we had dishes falling off of the kitchen counter by themselves, and smashing onto the floor. And these dishes had been neatly and securely stacked."

Cheryl's two sons, sixteen-year-old Josh and his younger brother Nathan had just joined us in the parlor. When Cheryl encouraged Josh to share with us about how he'd been slapped by an unseen hand, he sounded somewhat self-conscious as he explained, "I was upstairs alone in my bedroom one night last week, and I was lying on my bed listening to my Walkman, just chillin' out with my hand behind my head like I usually do... when all of a sudden, it was like an invisible hand just slapped me across the face. So I went into the bathroom and looked in the mirror, and there was a big red welt on my face where I was slapped."

Cheryl added, "Josh came downstairs immediately after and showed me where he was slapped. Sure enough, there was a big red welt right on the poor kid's face!"

I asked, "Josh, which side of your face were you slapped on?"

"On the left side," Josh answered.

Cheryl asked, "Is that significant?"

I explained, "Well, it could be, since certain types of activity may follow certain patterns."

"Oh, I see," said Cheryl.

She also explained that her 14-year-old son Nathan was now afraid to sleep in his own bed, and the family had heard a low voice telling them to "get out." Cheryl asked us, "But, what do you all think about what we've told you so far? What's going on here in this house?"

Mike said, "Well, perhaps it might be better to wait until we complete our investigation and review our evidence, before we draw a conclusion. However, as I've mentioned, we've brought Keith and Sandra Johnson along with us, and they'll be willing to conduct a house blessing before we leave tonight. They've been very successful in other cases we've been on with them, in lessening the activity."

Cheryl looked at Sandra and me and managed to sound somewhat cheerful as she said, "Well, I sure hope you can do something to remedy our situation. Nathan feels uncomfortable even sleeping in his own bedroom now, and Jessica is getting really scared lately."

"We'll do our best," said Sandra. "And while there are of course no guarantees, you should see a noticeable difference."

"That's all we can ask for," said Cheryl.


We next followed Cheryl as she gave us a tour of the entire farmhouse. She showed us the kitchen, where the stack of dishes had fallen from the counter with no explanation, and the bathroom where the baby saw a man standing after she'd had her bath.

Upstairs, her son Josh's room seemed like a typical teenage boy's room, complete with a drum set, wall posters, etc. Yet for Josh himself, the room had now become a place of unease, where he actually dreaded falling asleep for fear of another assault by an unseen presence. Cheryl then led us through the next room, her son Nathan's bedroom, where Nathan had felt something standing next to him by his drum set. While we were in this room, Cheryl suddenly claimed that she could feel an unseen watching her that very moment, and that she was anxious to get out of there. She told us, "Oh, someone either doesn't like me being in here right now, or they don't like you guys being in here!" Cheryl showed us that the hair on her arms now stood on end, and she was visibly trembling.


Following a complete tour of the house as well as the outer shed, we decided to begin the investigation segment of our visit. It was decided that Mike and Kristyn and the others would investigate the upstairs portion of the house, while Sandra and I, along with NEP member Cliff Williams would be responsible for the downstairs area.

After establishing our baseline downstairs, Sandra, Cliff and I took EMF and temperature readings throughout each of the first floor rooms, but found nothing unusual. In the kitchen area, Cheryl showed us the spot on the floor where her dishes had fallen from out of the cupboard.

"The dishes simply couldn't have slipped off by themselves," Cheryl reiterated. "They weren't anywhere near the edge. But all of a sudden we heard this this tremendous crash, and I came running out here and found them smashed all over the floor. I just can't see any way they could have fallen over by themselves."

We ourselves closely inspected the counter, which certainly seemed sturdy and level enough. The three of us even tried stacking some dishes and jumping up and down together, with no noticeable results. However, when Cliff moved the stack of dishes closer to the edge of the shelf, and we repeated the experiment, we did notice that the dishes did rattle slightly forward. Although our results were far from significant, we decided that it was just barely possible that a stack of dishes may have fallen with repeated heavy vibrations, if left close enough to the edge. Unlikely, but possible. But from what Cheryl had described, the neatly stacked dishes had apparently gone flying off from the counter with a tremendous crash, as if they'd been forcefully ejected.

After Cheryl went to tend to her 4-year-old blonde-haired little girl, Sandra and Cliff and I decided to conduct a communication session within the downstairs bathroom, since that was where her youngest daughter had reportedly seen a strange man taking a bath. It was a fairly large bathroom, so we would not actually be crowded together in there.

With my hand held audio recorder recording, the three of us began taking turns asking general questions.

Cliff asked, "Is there an entity present here?" After a brief pause he added, "If so, could you make your presence known to us?"

Sandra asked, "How long have you been here in this house?"

The questioning went on in this manner for several minutes, with such questions as, "Are you male? Or are you female? Are you the one who slapped Michael? Why are you frightening this family? Do you need our help?"

I then asked a question of a somewhat religious nature: "Do you see angels where you are?" I paused and asked, "Are you human spirit?"

After about fifteen minutes, Sandra, Cliff and I decided to take a break with the questions and conduct a brief evidence review. Although there were no noticeable verbal responses to our questions on my audio recordings, I did find a possible response to two of my questions. When I asked, "Do you see angels where you are?" the question was followed by a distinctive, single tap on the recording.

The three of us glanced at each other. Cliff asked us, "Did you just hear that?"

Sandra replied, "Yes... I wonder if that tap was in response to Keith's question?"

We then listened further. Again, we detected no responses to our questions, until it came to my question, "Are you a human spirit?" This question was answered by another distinctive tap.

Cliff said, "Hmmm... we may have some definite communication here, which would indicate an intelligent presence."

At my suggestion, we attempted some further questioning, attempting to establish a "knock once for yes, twice for no" pattern of communication. Unfortunately, we were unable to obtain any further results in this manner. The knock responses therefore remained inconclusive.

Sandra, Cliff and I had just finished up our own EVP session, when we were radioed by Mike from upstairs. "Just wondering, how you guys are doing down there?" Mike asked.

Cliff replied into the radio, "We just wrapped up an EVP session in the downstairs bathroom. How about you guys?"

Mike said, "We've actually just captured something quite interesting in Josh's bedroom. In fact, I think you guys should come up here, right now."

By the tone of Mike's voice, we could tell that he had certainly found something of interest. "Copy that, we're on our way up, Mike," said Cliff.

The three of us arrived upstairs in less than thirty seconds, anxious to know what Mike and his team had captured. Kristyn's face was flushed, and she was hyperventilating as she said, "Guys, you've just gotta listen to what we just got on our recording!"

Mike informed us, "It's what seems to be an EVP, but I'll let you three take a listen before we say anything more about it."

Mike then switched on his digital audio recorder and instructed us to listen carefully. What we heard was some muffled background conversation, followed by a clearly audible female voice saying, "Gonna get you, kitties."

We all glanced at each other, and then back at Mike, who was smiling in anticipation of our response. I asked, "Was that voice you just played the actual EVP?"

"Yes, that was it!" Mike said excitedly. "I'll play it again for you."

As Mike replayed the recording, we once again clearly heard a female voice saying in a sing-song manner, "Gonna get you, kitties." This was followed by the voice of one of the investigators in the room, asking the spirits if it liked the cats which the family owned.

Mike explained to us, "That question was asked right after the EVP. So, I don't know whether the spirit was anticipating the question ahead of time, or what."

"It's certainly incredibly clear," said Sandra. "In fact, I thought it was someone in the room speaking at first."

Kristyn said, "That's exactly what I would have thought, if I hadn't been right here in the room!"

Mike then suggested that we wrap up our EVP session, and return downstairs. He also told us, "Before Keith and Sandra begin the blessing of the house, I'd like to share our finding so far with Cheryl, especially the EVP we just captured."


Back downstairs, Cheryl asked, "Well? Did you find any spirits in the house?" Although there was a touch of humor to Cheryl's question, the trepidation in her voice was also apparent.

Mike told her, "Well, of course we have to spend at least several hours reviewing all of the data we've collected this evening. But we did conduct a brief evidence review while were upstairs in Josh's bedroom, and we think we may have captured a very interesting EVP. In fact, I can play it to you now, if you'd like to listen to it."

After quickly glancing around to make certain that none of her youngest children were within listening distance, Cheryl said anxiously, "Yes, I'd very much like to hear what you've recorded."

Mike switched on his audio recorder, and played the EVP of a clear female voice saying, "Gonna get you, kitties."

Cheryl's eyes widened, and she gasped before asking, "Could you please play that again?"

"Sure," said Mike. He played the EVP again for her.

"Gonna get you, kitties."

Suddenly, Cheryl broke down sobbing.

Sandra asked, "What is it, Cheryl, what's wrong??"

Cheryl replied, "Oh, my God, it's saying it's gonna get my kids! That's what it's saying, isn't it?"

Mike quickly replied, "Oh, no-no-no, Cheryl, it might not be saying that at all! In fact, we think it's actually saying, 'Gonna get you, 'kitties'', referring to the cats in the house. There was actually one of them in the upstairs bedroom with us when we captured that EVP, and immediately afterward we'd asked, 'Do you like cats?' So the spirit may have even been anticipating our question."

"I hope that's what it means," Cheryl said with a sniffle.


We were now ready to commence with the blessing of the farmhouse, which would be conducted by Sandra and myself. Accompanied by a few other team members who were recording data, we began in the basement, and worked our way upstairs to the first floor rooms. While we were in the kitchen area, Cheryl approached us, and with tears in her eyes said, "I hope this will do something to get rid of whatever is here, because I've got goose bumps going up my arm right now!"

Sandra said soothingly, "Cheryl, the blessing we're performing is very thorough, and it should be effective in neutralizing whatever negative entities may be here."

I added, "Yes, we're going through the entire house, and we're paying particular attention to the children's rooms."

Cheryl expressed her gratitude to all of us, for trying to help her and her family.

We next went upstairs and conducted a thorough spiritual cleansing in each of the upstairs rooms, paying special attention to Josh's bedroom where he'd been assaulted by an unseen hand. We of course also included the attic space in our blessing.

Once the entire farmhouse had been blessed, we ventured outside as a group, where Cheryl's two sons Josh and Nathan led us through the shed. Sandra and I made certain to thoroughly bless the shed as well, both inside and out.


We returned inside and informed Cheryl that the religious cleansing of her entire property, including the farmhouse and the outer shed, had been completed. She was extremely grateful for our intervention, and thanked us for making the trip to her house to help her and her family.

Kristyn said, "Remember that we're only a phone call or an e-mail away if you need to contact us, Cheryl. And I want to know that I can personally vouch for the effectiveness the blessing that Keith and Sandra performed. They are very faithful people, and they'd successfully helped me before. You see, before I became a member of TAPS, I was also a victim of spirit infestation."

"Is that so?" Cheryl asked with wonder in her voice. "I hadn't realized that, Kristyn."

"Yes," said Kristyn. "I was dealing with more than one spirit in my apartment, and my young son was being terrified as well. Thankfully I had people to turn to, who believed me and were able to help me."

After we'd packed up all our equipment, I said a final closing prayer of protection for Cheryl and her children, and we were ready to depart. Cheryl gave each of us a hug, and promised to be in touch, to let us know how things were going for her after the blessing we'd performed.

Then, just as we were leaving, Cheryl's 13-year-old daughter Jessica came running over to Sandra and threw her arms around her in a big, affectionate hug. "Thank you so much for being here," she told Sandra.

Mike Dion, Sandra and I did remain in touch with Cheryl Worthington over the next week, and according to her everything was going well for her and her children at the farmhouse since our visit there. It was not until the second week following our visit that we heard from Cheryl that some minor activity had begun to return, such as various unexplained knockings here and there, but it was not nearly as severe as it was before.

During a phone conversation Mike advised her, "Just as Sandra and Keith said, there may be a slight resurgence of activity, but if you follow through by taking the proper precautions, and not feeding into it, then it should gradually taper off until it stops altogether."

Again, Cheryl was extremely grateful, and thanked Mike and the rest of us for keeping in touch with her and for caring how she and her children were doing.

As for Cheryl's feeling of her hair standing on end while she was in her son Nathan's room, Mike mentioned to us and the other team members that his EMF detector had registered slight fluctuations in both of the boys' bedrooms, especially near some electrical appliances such as the alarm clocks. However, while this may have explained some of the uncomfortable feelings the family was experiencing in these rooms, it did not account for Josh being slapped by what felt like an invisible hand, or the EVP recorded in Josh's bedroom clearly saying "Gonna get you, kitties."

Shortly after Mike and Kristyn submitted their report of our investigation of the Worthington case to TAPS Headquarters, it was selected by Pilgrim Films to be included as an episode of the hit SyFy TV series "Ghost Hunters." This second investigation of the Worthington farmhouse, filmed for the series, took place on May 27-28, 2005. In this episode, Jason Hawes and Grant Wilson introduced Dave Tango, an investigator from the New Jersey branch of TAPS.

This time, Steve Gonsalves was available to participate in the investigation. And because of Mike Dion's familiarity with the case from having led the initial investigation, he was also selected to participate in this episode.

While the TAPS team was at the Worthington farmhouse, team members Andy Andrews and Dave Tango attempted to recreate the dishes falling in the kitchen, and concluded that the countertop itself was a bit loose, which might have caused the dishes to fall to the floor.

Cheryl Worthingtons' eldest son, Josh, explained on camera to the TAPS crew about the incident when he was suddenly slapped in the face while he'd been listening to CDs.

Shortly after this, while Grant was inside of Nathan's bedroom, he announced that he'd suddenly been hit on the back of his leg by part of the drum set. Steve Gonsalves and Mike Dion also experienced some significant battery draining with their equipment during the investigation, as is sometimes the case when investigating paranormal phenomena.

Before leaving the Worthington farmhouse that night, the TAPS team entered Cheryl's teenage son Nathan's bedroom once again and attempted to find a logical explanation as to why Grant was apparently 'attacked' by Nathan's drum set. They even attempted to recreat the incident, but without success. Meanwhile, upstairs in Cheryl's bedroom, Mike Dion and Dustin Pari believed they heard a feminine coughing. They conducted a brief EVP session and asked the spirit a series of questions, but received no response.

During the evidence analysis of the TAPS investigation, Steve and Dave showed Jason and Grant a section of video footage taken in the kitchen at the Worthington house that appeared to be something moving. However, they eventually dismissed this as floating dust particles, rather than an actual anomaly.

Also, during their evidence review, one slight but significant mix-up occurred. While analyzing the audio evidence, somehow Mike Dion's EVP of a female voice saying, "Gonna get you, kitties" that was captured upstairs during our first investigation, was mixed up with the audio evidence from the second investigation. As a result, Jason and Grant mistakenly dismissed it as being Cheryl's voice, although Cheryl was not even present at the time the EVP was captured. But I figured this needed clarifying.

When the evidence analysis was done, Jason and Grant advised Cheryl that in their opinion, genuine paranormal activity was taking place in her home. However, they did not feel that she and her family were in an immediate danger, and were hopeful that the situation would eventually resolve itself, although perhaps not easily. They also encouraged Cheryl to give them a call if they could be of any further assistance.

Sandra and I kept in contact with Cheryl Worthington, on and off, throughout the following year. Although the activity in the New Hampshire farmhouse had initially lessened after our spiritual cleansing, it seemed to have started up again some months later, and Cheryl and her family did eventually wind up moving out of her New Hampshire farmhouse to a location in the mid-west. Fortunately, none of the paranormal activity they'd experienced at the farmhouse seemed to have followed them to their new home.

Shortly after their move, I received an e-mail from Cheryl that touched Sandra and me deeply, and I would like to include a small portion of it here:

*Keith ~ What a pleasure to hear from you. We often think about you and your lovely wife. As for us, we have left New Hampshire. The house was just too much to handle and it devastated the kids. It took a year to get the baby comfortable in a house again. Josh never did move back to his room, and refused to go back in to pack when we moved. Josh now sleeps better and is happy here. We have friends that say the new people that live in that house are having problems like we did. They tell kids at school that their house is haunted.*

*You and your wife are lovely people and I wish you all the best. We are fans and talk about you to many people. We have an awesome church family here and the kids are in youth groups and doing well. Your wife made a huge impression on Jessica (the thirteen-year-old) and she still prays for you at night when she goes to bed.*

*I wish God's Blessings on your wife and son. Thank you for contacting me. May God Bless you!*

*Sincerely,*

*Cheryl Burger -Worthington*

# Chapter 8

## The Joseph H. Ladd Center

Back in the early days of The Atlantic Paranormal Society, at a time when TAPS was a relatively new organization, we of course made the rounds of investigating local historic cemeteries and abandoned buildings, especially those with a reputation for being haunted. One place of particular interest to us was the Joseph H. Ladd Center, located in Exeter, Rhode Island.

The Ladd School, as it is most commonly referred to today, possesses quite a morbid history, to say the least. Founded in 1907, its original name was "Rhode Island School for the Feeble Minded." In the early years of this institution, the inmates lived in small cottages, with a girl's dormitory being erected in 1909. The institution began as a farm colony where the residents performed menial tasks such as preparing food, mending clothing and working in the fields. By 1917 the connotation of "Rhode Island School for the Feeble Minded" was considered inappropriate, and the name was changed to the Exeter School. Nearly four decades later, on June 1, 1956, Dr. Joseph H. Ladd retired as the director of the center, which was now named after him.

Although, in its heyday, the Joseph H. Ladd School was considered to be a top notch facility in the humane treatment of the mentally ill, problems soon began to surface. For one thing, as early as 1928, overcrowding had already become a significant issue. Stories of patient neglect and abuse were rapidly becoming associated with the institution. When compared with modern standards, some would even label the conditions there as being barbaric. Reports soon surfaced of patients having teeth pulled without any local anesthetics to save money. Water torture was also said to have been commonly used as a treatment for the mentally ill patients.

Residents were denied their basic human rights and stripped of their dignity. In fact, the inmates were quite often used as "human guinea pigs" to practice experimental therapies on, without their consent. Stories spread of enforced "sterilizations" being routinely carried out, as well as lobotomies and other irreversible surgical procedures being performed that would render the patient in a vegetative state.

Despite these reported conditions, the Joseph H. Ladd Center functioned as a prominent institution for the mentally and emotionally challenged in Rhode Island for the better part of a century. In the 1960s the facility housed over 1,000 patients. By the 1970's, however, as state inspections exposed the reality of these reports of patient neglect and abuse, a string of human rights lawsuits were begun by some of the families of these patients. The years of the Ladd School were soon numbered, as private assistance homes were considered as alternatives. The hospital itself was ordered closed in 1982. In 1986 human rights activists sought to permanently close the entire facility and by 1994 the State of Rhode Island officially closed the doors of the Joseph H. Ladd Center for good. Dr. Joseph H. Ladd, M.D. died on May 12, 1974, and is buried in Quidnessett Cemetery, North Kingston, RI.

At the time of the Ladd Center's closing, ten buildings still remained across the expanse of the property. These buildings were comprised of classrooms, dormitories, a crematorium, a recreation building, a chapel, operating rooms, a dental clinic, a community building with its own greenhouse, an x-ray room, a morgue, and most imposingly, a six-story cylindrical-shaped infirmary, containing a padded cell within.

Not only was much of the original furniture left behind, but many of the dental records and incident reports concerning patients were left scattered about the rooms of the buildings. Strangely, some of these official documents were found to be dated up to 1987, despite the fact that the hospital section was ordered closed in 1982.


Even while the Ladd Center was still in operation, rumors circled among staff of the place being haunted. For example, the doors of an elevator in at least one of the main buildings was said to open and close at all hours of the day and night, as if it had a mind of its own. Repairs to this elevator reportedly did nothing to alleviate this problem. Staff at the Ladd Center also claimed to overhear phantom footsteps and muffled voices emanating from empty rooms and deserted hallways, especially after hours. After a while, it became difficult to find enough staff willing to work the night shifts.

Over the ensuing years since its closing, the Ladd Center became increasingly popular as a fascinating place for local paranormal groups to investigate. The Atlantic Paranormal Society was among the earliest to begin investigating at this location. Fairly regularly, when we did not have a pressing client investigation on a weekend night, several members of TAPS would meet up and explore the grounds and the deserted buildings that comprised the remainder of the Ladd Center.

During the course of our many investigations, we often came across evidence of some of the appalling conditions the residents of the Ladd Center were forced to endure. Some of this evidence was downright disturbing. For example, not only were patient's dental records still strewn haphazardly about some of the rooms, but we also occasionally came across unopened personal letters from some of the residents, presumably addressed to their families, that were never mailed.

In the mortuary house, a metal slab still remained intact, complete with a groove on one side to allow for the drainage of blood and other bodily fluids. Also, in one of the empty rooms in the infirmary, an ominous looking table stood, complete with restraints, upon which patients were presumably restrained while undergoing such treatments as electroshock therapy.

Not surprisingly, we also experienced a fair amount of paranormal activity while investigating at the Ladd Center. Quite often, approaching footsteps could be heard echoing along the darkened hallways, which would suddenly cease just before they reached an investigator. A flashlight pointed in the direction of the footsteps would inevitably reveal nothing. TAPS member Richard Einig was the first to experience this phenomenon, and often reported that he was being "tracked" by an unseen presence behind him while in the deserted buildings.

One thing we soon became aware of while investigating the Ladd Center was that battery-powered equipment such as cameras and tape recorders would routinely fail, even if the batteries were fresh, so most of our recorded evidence had to be captured near the very beginning of our investigations. However, our batteries would often automatically "recharge" themselves as soon as we left the grounds. We soon learned not to discard them without checking first.

TAPS investigators repeatedly experienced instances of being touched by no one who was nearby, and at least one instance of a female investigator having her hair tugged by what felt like an invisible hand. In fact, TAPS identified so muc threatening activity that team member Chris Angelo regularly began bringing along an aikido fighting staff during investigations at the Ladd Center. Since Chris happened to be proficient in martial arts, when paired with Christopher Finch, who also possessed defense skills, the team at least felt relatively safe in case of a chance encounter with physical intruders!

During one nocturnal investigation, TAPS member Heather Droulet was carrying a hand held digital recorder through the deserted buildings, recording audio for any possible examples of EVP. And she was not to be disappointed. As soon as she and the other members went back outside, Heather began listening to some of the audio she had just recorded.

Although she had not asked any specific questions at that point in the recording, a low, clearly male voice was suddenly heard to say suggestively, "My pleasure!"

The eerie tone of the EVP literally sent shivers up Heather's spine. She informed the other members that she'd had quite enough investigating for the night, and that she was anxious to leave.

During one particularly memorable visit on a moonlit evening in January of 2001, nationally acclaimed author Jodi Picoult was doing research for her book "Second Glance," and had contacted TAPS asking if she might be allowed to accompany us to some allegedly local "haunted" spots in rural Rhode Island. Jason Hawes, Grant Wilson and I agreed to take Jodi on a visit to the Ladd Center in Exeter. The atmosphere at the abandoned institution that night was nothing short of incredible, for not only were the abandoned buildings illuminated by a brilliant full moon, but a mist had risen over the grounds.

Growing more nervous by the minute as we escorted her along the mist-enshrouded grounds while relating some of the macabre history of the Ladd Center, Jodi asked us what the chances were of us encountering any actual paranormal activity here. Almost instantly, I alerted her attention to a nearby oak tree where the energy in the area was so high that sparkling balls of light were traveling up the tree trunk in a swirling motion. Almost as if on cue, a pack of coyotes suddenly began eerily howling together in the distance.

Now visibly trembling, Jodi told us, "Okay, guys, I think I've experienced enough of this place tonight, and I'm ready to move on!"

Because of its growing reputation for paranormal activity, an increasing number of investigation groups soon began converging upon the Ladd Center. And although The Atlantic Paranormal Society usually refrained from posting on the Internet about our visits to the Ladd Center, other local groups soon began posting more and more frequently about the phenomena they had experienced. For example, one group reported a camera being repeatedly knocked out of a woman's hand by an unseen force while in one of the abandoned buildings. Other groups began including examples of light streaks they'd captured in photographs, as well as their own EVP recordings taken at the Ladd Center. One thing that all investigation groups reported in common was the undeniable feeling of being watched while investigating the complex.

Unfortunately, all this added attention the Ladd Center was now getting resulted in local law enforcement cracking down on people trespassing on the grounds and prowling through the dilapidated buildings. A minor controversy even developed around this, eventually making its way on to one of the local TV news stations.

Being apprehended by law enforcement was not the least of the dangers associated with investigating this abandoned complex. The structures themselves were becoming increasingly unsafe from years of neglect and disrepair. I personally know of one recent local investigator who was there investigating with his girlfriend, and she fell through the floor stepping on a loose floorboard. She wound up spending the night in the Emergency Room with a broken wrist. Aside from the physical dangers of the property, another significant danger arose when would-be investigators suddenly were attacked and robbed of both money and equipment. Thieves reportedly armed with weapons and adept at striking in the dark were intentionally lying-in-wait within the dark recesses of the buildings for unsuspecting victims.

For over two decades, officials have talked of leveling the remaining buildings that once comprised the Joseph H. Ladd Center and developing the 331-acre parcel of land into condominiums. Other options for the property have included new Exeter school being built on this property, as well as a walking trail, a research and technology park, and perhaps even a golf course. But at least for now, this location is still known as the foreboding Ladd School, or Ladd Center, with its horrific history and rich reputation as being one of Rhode Island's most haunted locations.

And although the Joseph H. Ladd Center is still strictly off-limits to the general public, special permission to access the property can occasionally be granted by the proper authorities. For example, the Rhode Island Film Commission was recently able to pull enough strings to allow local filmmaker and producer Michael Corrente into the Ladd Center, to use it as the backdrop for his film "Blackmask" directed by Marcus Nispel. Obviously walk-in paranormal investigators are not allowed on the premises, and camera surveillance is now regularly kept there both day and night.

Is the Ladd Center truly haunted? Yes, I feel it most definitely is, and this is based on my own personal experiences there as well as the combined experiences of close personal acquaintances of mine.

However, to me, the Joseph H. Ladd Center is much more than a place of paranormal interest. Having personally known some of the actual residents and employees who lived and worked there, and having heard their stories, the Ladd Center for me will always remain an echoing testimony to the unfortunate and long forgotten souls of this former institution, so many of whom endured years of neglect, profound suffering and lonely isolation. Seeing the unopened, unmailed envelopes addressed to families strewn about the floor, is what I found to be especially heartbreaking. And I regard the memory of these people with the utmost respect and dignity.

**Rich Einig investigates at Ladd School**

# Chapter 9

### The Legend of Sarah Tillinghast
### A Vampire Tale

(The following story is based upon actual accounts.)

**O**n a fine day in late spring, a prosperous Pine Hill farmer stood surveying his expansive orchards, now in full, healthy bloom. A smile of satisfaction crossed his face, for, come autumn, his orchards would most certainly produce a bountiful harvest. As he stood gazing out over his orchards, a sudden stiff breeze picked up from his left. The forcefulness of this breeze rapidly increased, indicating that a storm might well be brewing. Thick dark clouds soon began billowing overhead. The farmer naturally became concerned that a frozen rain of hail might begin to fall, thereby threatening the survival of the tender shoots. Even if he were to quickly alert the farm hands, they simply had no way to protectively cover all these apple and peach trees in time. The storm was approaching way too fast. Distressed, the farmer was about to turn and head back towards the main house, when he was suddenly stopped by the sound of his daughter Sarah's voice calling to him.

"Papa…Papa…"

Squinting against the specks of dirt and sand that were now assaulting his face, the farmer called back to her.

"Sarah? Sarah, where are you, child?"

"Papa… Papa," Sarah again called out, her voice sounding strangely hollow and distant.

Thinking his daughter Sarah might be in trouble, the farmer became desperate to find her. He'd begun to move forward, when his nostrils were suddenly assaulted by a sickening-sweet odor of decay, seeming as if it were carried on the stiff breeze. Again, he could hear Sarah's lost voice pathetically calling out to him.

"Papa….oh, Papa…"

The stench of decay being carried on the breeze quickly intensified, until the farmer felt as though he might retch. Placing his right hand over his nostrils, he turned to his left, from where the overpowering stench was coming. He could scarcely believe what his eyes beheld. To his utter horror, he saw that the entire section of orchard trees to his left were now bent, withered and in a deplorable condition, with the once budding fruit now turned into a putrefying mess. And yet, glancing to his right, the farmer observed that the orchard trees to his right remained completely healthy. He looked back at the decayed and wilted trees on the other side of his orchard, and it was then that he realized this was the direction his daughter Sarah's voice had been coming from! The farmer froze with paralyzing dread, unable to explain what was happening around him. Somehow he knew that his beloved daughter Sarah was in terrible danger, and yet he was unable to reach out to her. Had one of the desiccated tree branches fallen on her, having been blown down by the gusting wind?

"Sarah!" he again called out in helpless desperation. "For the love of God, where are you, girl??"

In response, the farmer could hear the sudden shrill whistling of the wind, mingled with Sarah's high-pitched, heartrending scream, becoming gradually louder and louder, until he thought his own heart would burst with despair.

"SARAH!" he shouted one last time, groping forward against the fetid wind with his arms outstretched.


Stukeley suddenly awoke from his nightmare with a start, covered in a cold sweat, his entire body trembling. But that's all it had been, a nightmare. Here he was safe in his own bed, with the first silvery light of dawn peeping through the curtains of his bedroom window. He turned to glance over at the form of his wife Honor, slumbering peacefully beside him, just barely visible in the darkened bedroom. She stirred slightly as a rooster began to crow from the hen house nearby. Soon she would be fully awake, and busily setting about preparing their morning meal, among a dozen or so of her other morning tasks.

Rousing himself from his bed, Stukeley quietly removed his bedclothes and donning his shirt and trousers, before venturing to the outbuilding and beginning his own morning chores.

It was shortly before 9:00 AM, and Stukeley Tillinghast had been steadily occupied with various farm chores for the past four hours, when he and everyone else outside were alerted to the sound of the dinner bell ringing. Stukeley and his two young sons who'd been working closely with him set down their farming implements, and began making their way towards the main house. While walking along the pathway, Stukeley once again paused to glance out past the fields to his bountiful peach and apple orchards, of course fully in bloom. His 16-year-old son Andris had been noticing his father's preoccupation with the orchards all throughout the morning. Although his father's concern over the orchard was in itself nothing unusual, he seemed almost obsessive this morning, even though the blossoms were obviously full and healthy. Despite his curiosity, Andris knew better than to risk asking his father what the matter was. He and his siblings had always been sternly taught to respect the privacy of their elders. Instead, he merely shared a shrug with his younger brother James, before continuing on his way.

Stukeley passed most of the morning meal hour in brooding silence. While the rest of his family ate heartily, Stukeley barely touched his food, spending most of the time staring straight ahead. It was only when his lovely young daughter Sarah, 21 years of age, came briskly into the dining quarters to join them that his attention perked. Although Sarah herself did not appear to take particular notice, with her flaxen locks cascading over her shoulders and flashing her bright white smile, her father repeatedly cast glances in her direction, although he said nothing. How much she resembled her mother in younger years, Stukeley silently mused. With all the noisy hustle and bustle of this large family seated at the dining board, it was only Honor Tillinghast who noticed just how preoccupied her husband appeared to be this particular morning. He seemed especially concerned over their daughter Sarah for some reason. However, she deemed it best to wait until she could speak with her husband in private, before commenting on the matter.

It was only when the rest of the family was filing out of the dining area, and Stukeley himself was rising to return to his chores, that Honor detained him by saying, "Husband, I would speak with you a moment."

"Very well," he said without emotion, resuming his seat.

When they were finally alone in the room, Honor asked her husband what was concerning him this particular morning, upon which Stukeley unburdened the details of his disturbing dream to her. Honor was rather relieved to learn that the cause for her husband's preoccupation this morning was merely the result of a dream. She did her best to assure him that this dream, however disturbing, was merely the result of his concern over the upcoming harvest. To placate his wife, Stukeley agreed with her, although he remained somewhat unconvinced.

Thus far, life had been fortunate for Stukeley Tillinghast. In the year 1762, having attained the age of 20, he had fallen deeply in love with a beautiful young woman from West Greenwich, Rhode Island, named Honor Hopkins, daughter of Judge Samuel Hopkins and Honor Brown Hopkins. Later that same year, Stukeley and 17-year-old Honor were wed, and over the next two decades, their marriage had produced no less than fourteen healthy children. On acreage given to him by his father, Pardon Tillinghast, Stukeley cultivated expansive orchards of peach and apple trees. The Tillinghast farmstead was located in the Pine Hill section of Exeter, and it was mainly from the harvest of his orchards that Stukeley supported his large family. Stukeley was also a well-respected citizen of the community, and a prominent member of the Exeter Grange. Because of the long, snuff colored overcoat that he so often wore had become his recognizable trademark, Stukeley was affectionately nicknamed "Snuffy Stuke" by the townspeople.

It was now the year 1799, and Stukeley felt especially blessed. All of his fourteen children had survived the usual childhood diseases as well as the ravages of the Revolutionary War. Some of them were by now married and living on nearby farmsteads, busily raising families of their own and tending to their farms. Several of the children, however, still lived at home, and assisted their parents with maintaining the large Tillinghast farm and orchards. And from all appearances, this year's harvest promised to be a bountiful one indeed. The only thing troubling Stukeley was the strange and disturbing dream he'd experienced in the wee hours that morning that awakened with a start. Why had he dreamed so vividly of exactly half of his orchards withering into decay, and why had he so clearly heard the voice of his dear daughter Sarah, desperately calling out to him?

Sarah was the eldest of the daughters still living at home, although she would soon be married and leaving the homestead. Admittedly, there had always been something rather special about Sarah. A precocious yet loving and devoted child, Sarah was well aware of her personal attractiveness from an early age, and had always enjoyed the attention she received from others. Not surprisingly, Sarah had grown into a beautiful young woman, and was adored by her younger siblings still living at home, to whom she so lovingly assisted her mother in nurturing. Many a young man in the community would often visit the Tillinghast farm with the double intention of stocking up on produce, as well as having an excuse to visit with "Snuffy Stuke's" alluring daughter Sarah. Stukeley himself did not mind the attention Sarah received, since it was certainly good for business...and his lovely daughter knew just how to blush or to bat an eye in just the right manner.

"Ah...how much she is the image of her mother," Stukeley often thought.

However, as fine as Sarah's manners and feminine charms were, she was also quite adept at matching most of her brothers in tending to whatever chores were required, making her indispensable around the farm. Yes, it would be a shame to lose her several months from now, when she'd be married and moving away. Yet it was, of course, Sarah's own happiness that was most important.

Stukeley eventually convinced himself that his concern about Sarah's eventual departure from home, combined with his usual concern over the orchards, were the true causes of his nightmarish dream. Honor had been right after all. Stukeley had nothing to worry about.


Scarcely a fortnight later, Sarah developed a rather persistent cough that first became evident while she was reading Biblical verses to some of her younger siblings, shortly before bedtime. She excused herself early and retired to bed. The following day around mid-morning, while assisting her mother with various household chores, Sarah became rather flushed and short of breath. Concerned, knowing her daughter's usual boundless energy, Honor asked her, "Are you not well, child? You appear to be out of sorts."

With a smile, Sarah replied, "I'm merely a bit tired, Mama, after not sleeping well last night. I hope my coughing did not keep you and Papa awake."

Honor quickly felt Sarah's forehead, and found her to be slightly feverish. "You're decidedly warm, dear. I fear you are coming down with something, most likely a cold because of the damp weather we've been having. I want you to be excused from your chores and return to your room to rest, while I brew you some broth."

Despite Sarah's protests, her mother became insistent that Sarah retire to her bed. Reluctantly, Sarah finally agreed, with an exasperated, "Yes, Mama."

By late afternoon, Sarah appeared to be feeling much better, and was granted permission to return to helping her mother with chores. She ate well at supper with the rest of her family. When evening came, however, her cough returned, once again cutting short her reading of Scripture to her younger brothers and her sister prior to bedtime prayers.

Over the next several days, Sarah's condition worsened, with frequent bouts of coughing and sneezing. She slept fitfully if at all, and when sleep did come to Sarah, disturbing dreams often troubled her. A peculiar change seemed to come over her personality as well. Although Sarah had always been pleasant and respectful to others, if a bit strong-willed at times, she was now becoming increasingly belligerent and quarrelsome. She even became somewhat combative when her mother or others were tending to her, totally contrary to her normally sweet disposition.

Alarmed that his daughter's condition was not improving with the usual home remedies, Stukeley Tillinghast instructed one of the farmhands to make a trip into the village to summon the local country physician, who readily agreed to pay a visit out to the Pine Hill farmstead. Sarah was fortunately cooperative with the family doctor, who had cared for every member of the large family over the years at one time or another. Following a thorough examination of Sarah, the physician informed Stukeley and Honor that their cherished daughter was suffering from a severe cold and possible throat infection. He warned them that if Sarah was not careful, the congestion could settle in her lungs and possibly even develop into pneumonia. The doctor prescribed plenty of bed rest and fluids for Sarah, avoiding all possible drafts in her room to prevent any airborne miasma. He drew a small amount of blood from her before leaving, and her upcoming natural cycle should further help to purge her body of toxicity, and align the humors. In the meantime, Sarah was to refrain from having visits from anyone outside the family whom was not caring for her, including her young suitor. Stukeley and Honor readily agreed, and gratefully compensated their physician friend with currency, combined with a small amount of produce.

Sarah's large family, and indeed many folks in the community were greatly relieved when Sarah began to show marked signs of recovery. It seemed that the local doc's prescription of bed rest and temporary isolation, combined with two more sessions of bloodletting, had taken a positive effect. In fact, by the end of that month, Sarah had recovered sufficiently to be able to leave her sick bed, and begin once again assisting her mother with household chores. At the next meeting of local farmers at the Exeter Grange, everyone present made certain to congratulate their friend "Snuffy Stuke" on the recovery of his beautiful daughter from her illness.

Within another two weeks, Sarah was well enough to receive visits from other family members and a few close friends, including her handsome young suitor. Sarah was also understandably becoming a bit stir-crazy, and was eager to get out of the house, if only to tend to her own small flower garden and some minor outside chores around the farm. Although somewhat reluctant, Honor finally gave into her daughter's pleadings. Honor granted Sarah permission to tend her flower garden, with the stern warning that she was not to overexert herself, and was to return inside and rest the moment she began to become fatigued.

With her brilliant smile, Sarah happily agreed. "I will, Mama, I promise," she said, before quickly going to gather her gardening tools.

Before long, it seemed as though Sarah's full strength had returned. She was the picture of health and vitality, and when not tending to her garden and household chores, Sarah would be busily planning the details of her upcoming wedding with the assistance of her mother. In the evenings before bedtime she resumed her readings of the Holy Scriptures to her younger sister Ruth and her three younger brothers, Andris, Clark and James.

But then one afternoon, Sarah returned inside after tending to her flower garden appearing more out of breath than usual and with her complexion noticeably flushed. Honor gave her a sharp reprimand, saying, "I warned you not to overtax yourself outside! Now look how you've tired yourself, after you've so recently been sick."

Catching her breath, Sarah said, "I-I'm sorry, Mama. But I only wanted my flower bed to be in prime condition, after I'm wed and no longer here to tend to it."

"You know that your sister Ruth will be here to tend to it for you," said Honor. "Now I want you to return to your room and rest before evening meal."

Sarah protested, saying that she was just a little tired and wanted to help in preparing the evening meal, but her mother was insistent that she immediately go to her room to rest.

That night Sarah's cough returned, along with her troubling dreams. The following morning, although she rose from bed and dressed herself, she was in a weakened state. Throughout the day she continued to cough up phlegm, with traces of bright red blood in her sputum.

Instead of sending out one of the farmhands, Stukeley took his open carriage and rode to the doctor's house himself. Fortunately the doctor was home, and being a good personal friend of Stukeley and Honor, he agreed to make the trip out to the Tillinghast farm immediately.

After a lengthy examination of Sarah, the country physician emerged from her room with a grim countenance. Taking her parents aside, he explained to them in private that Sarah did not appear to be suffering from a relapse of her severe cold. Rather, it seemed that something of an even more serious nature was now afflicting their beautiful daughter. The diagnosis was "consumption." Stukeley, holding his wife closely, asked what could be done. The physician replied that there was little he could do, aside from continuing to purge Sarah's circulatory system of some of the affliction. In the meantime, Sarah was young and possessed of a strong constitution. She might recover on her own, providing that she be given plenty of rest, and under no circumstances should she be allowed to overexert herself. Just as before, during her confinement, Sarah was to have no visitors outside of her immediate family.

"I'm so sorry," the physician quietly added. "I'm so dreadfully, dreadfully sorry."

Stukeley and Honor thanked him for all that he'd done. Before leaving, their physician friend promised to stop by on at least once every fortnight, to check on Sarah's condition.

Despite her weakening condition and her persistent cough, Sarah did her best to maintain a pleasant disposition around her family, especially her younger siblings. She also attempted to assist with the household upkeep as much as her mother allowed, even if it was only tidying up the house a bit and making her own bed. Ruth also dutifully tended to Sarah's cherished flower garden, while Sarah gratefully watched from her window. And although Sarah was prohibited from receiving visitors, she kept in touch almost daily with her suitor, Ronald, through letters, assuring him that she was doing her best to return to health, by dutifully following the directions of her mother and her physician. After all, the date of their impending marriage was soon to arrive, and Sarah was determined not to be sick in bed for her own wedding day! At least twice each week, Ronald would come to the farm to inquire after Sarah's health, at which time either Andris, Ruth or James would be given the pleasurable duty of passing their sister's letters to him. Sarah would then come to the window of her bedroom, where they would lovingly smile and wave to each other... and if they thought no one was looking (which was rare), they'd also mouth words of love and blow a few kisses to each other.

Also as promised, the county physician continued to make regular visits to the Tillinghast farmstead, during which he would monitor Sarah's condition, and administer small doses of opiates to help her sleep. But nothing the doctor or anyone else did seemed to improve her health. As the weeks passed Sarah's condition steadily continued to deteriorate, until she was finally confined to bed, unable to even sit up long enough to observe the progress of her flower garden, or to briefly greet her young man from the window.

And then, just over one month following the onset of her relapse, Sarah slipped into an unresponsive state. Hours later, she passed from this life.

It seemed as though the entire community had gone into mourning along with the Tillinghast clan, over the loss of their beautiful and beloved Sarah. Just weeks shy of her wedding, which was sadly now never to take place, Sarah was laid to rest in a small lot which had been cleared at the edge of the family property. Her father, with the aid of a few farm hands, had constructed a simple yet sturdy pine coffin for Sarah. Many family members, friends and neighbors of the Tillinghasts attended the funeral. Ronald, who was to marry Sarah before year's end, tearfully and lovingly placed a bouquet of flowers upon his would-be bride's pine coffin, before she was lowered into the earth. Each of Sarah's thirteen siblings then tenderly tossed a small handful of earth into the grave ere it was covered over.     The presiding clergyman intoned, "Thus we commit the body of our beloved daughter Sarah Tillinghast to the earth, in the sure and certain hope of the resurrection, and the life of the world to come. Ashes to ashes… dust to dust."

Both Stukeley and Honor Tillinghast were at first inconsolable at the loss of their beautiful and cherished daughter. The realization that Sarah would no longer be with them was almost too much for them to bear. And yet, they had to be strong for the other surviving children, and set an example for them of their Christian faith. They  also had the farm to maintain, and harvest time would be arriving in just over two months.


As the weeks passed, 19-year-old Ruth Tillinghast continued to lovingly maintain Sarah's small, yet beautiful flower garden, which was enclosed by a small white fence. She had also assumed her late sister's duty of reading Biblical selections before bedtime to her two younger brothers, Andris and James. Not much longer than a month had elapsed following Sarah's death, when Ruth herself began appearing somewhat feverish and short of breath. She tired easily, and became increasingly withdrawn. Understandingly concerned, her mother asked her what was wrong and if she was not feeling well. With a forced smile, Ruth replied that she was simply not sleeping well because of the recent muggy nights. However, it soon became apparent that something more serious was troubling her.

One morning in particular, when Ruth had hardly touched her morning meal and appeared particularly troubled in spirit, Honor sat down with her daughter privately after the others had left the house, and insisted on knowing what was wrong. Reluctantly, Ruth explained to her, "I've been having much trouble sleeping at night, Mama. Sarah has been coming into my bedroom every night, and keeping me awake."

"Sarah?" Honor gasped in shock. She then smiled sadly, and said, "Ruth, we all miss our dear Sarah. It's not surprising that you should dream of her at night, especially since you and Sarah were always so close."

But Ruth became insistent. "No, Mama, I do not dream of Sarah, I see Sarah! She comes into my bedroom at night, and tells me how lonely she is. And then she sits on me, and makes my body hurt."

Honor had heard enough. "Hush up! I'll not endure anymore of this nonsense talk about our sweet Sarah, who has left us to be with her Lord in Heaven. It is because you miss Sarah so, that you dream of her, and that is all."

Tears began to spill down Ruth's cheeks, because of the harsh reprimand she'd just received. With tears filling her own eyes, Honor softened her tone. "Child, I can tell that you are not feeling well, and have not been yourself lately." After gently placing a hand on Ruth's cheek, she added, "You are also warmer than you should be. I want you to be off to your room right now, to get some rest. I will make you some broth for when you awake. And no more talk of Sarah. Agreed?"

"Yes, Mama," said Ruth, wiping her eyes and obediently rising from her chair.

Ruth did seem to feel better after napping for some hours. The following morning, however, Ruth seemed even more restless than she had before. Judging from the dark circles underneath her eyes, combined with her listless manner, she was obviously suffering from sleep deprivation. Worse yet, the poor young woman had now developed a persistent, hacking cough, disturbingly reminiscent of Sarah's. As the day wore on, Ruth again became feverish, and took to bed.

The local physician was again quickly summoned to the Tillinghast farmstead. And, after a thorough examination of 19-year-old Ruth, he once again had unfortunate news for Stukeley and Honor. It seemed that Ruth was also suffering from "consumption," the same illness that had recently claimed Sarah. Before leaving, the good doctor let a small amount of blood from her, and recommended that she be made as comfortable as possible, with plenty of bed rest and fluids.

However, Ruth's health rapidly declined. Her cough worsened, causing her to spit up bright red blood from her hemorrhaging lungs. All throughout her malady, Ruth continued to complain of painful, nightly visits from her recently deceased sister Sarah. The doctor attributed these nightly visits to "hallucinations" brought on by Ruth's frequent high fevers at night. Honor even began spending some hours with Ruth in her bedroom during the night, to comfort her and prove to her daughter that Sarah was indeed not coming into her room. All through these long hours, Honor would keep vigil while lovingly tending to her daughter, as Ruth pathetically coughed and alternated between chills and fevers.

One evening Ruth's eyes suddenly widened in terror as she gasped, while gazing at something beyond her mother. Honor quickly grasped onto her daughter's shoulders and asked, "What is it, child?"

In a hoarse whisper, Ruth weakly replied, "Sarah… she was just at my window."

Instantly, Honor glanced over at the bedroom window, but could see nothing. Nonetheless she called out, "Husband!"

Having been awake for some hours himself, Stukeley immediately leaped from his own bed and rushed into Ruth's bedroom. "What is it?" he asked breathlessly.

All Honor needed to do was to nod to him in the direction of Ruth's bedroom window. Instantly recognizing this signal, Stukeley wasted no time in throwing on his long brown overcoat over his nightshirt, grabbing his nearby musket from off the wall, and rushing out of the front door, taking one of the hound dogs along with him. Desperate to protect his family from harm, Stukeley stealthily made his way around the entire house in search of any possible intruders which might be lurking in the darkness, his loaded musket at the ready. And although Stukeley Tillinghast was not normally a man given to fancy, his heart was now in his throat, in the advent that he should actually be confronted by the spectral image of his deceased daughter Sarah.

Half an hour elapsed before Stukeley and his hunting dog returned from patrolling the grounds of his farmstead. Quietly entering Ruth's bedroom once again, he saw his wife seated beside the bed, tenderly wiping the perspiration from their daughter's face with a cloth. Honor glanced over her shoulder and glanced at him questioningly. In response, Stukeley silently shook his head no. Honor smiled tiredly in relief, and then turned her attention back to Ruth, who had finally drifted off into a deep sleep.

Ruth died the following day, and was soon laid to rest beside her sister Sarah in the small family burial yard. Stukeley bitterly lamented the fact that Sarah's grave was not yet even adorned with a stone marker, and now another of his children was being buried here. Because of the downpour which took place on the morning of Ruth's funeral, not as many folks tuned out to see her lowered into the earth, as had attended Sarah's graveside funeral. Among those gathered together in the pouring rain for Ruth's funeral, her elder sister Hannah, now married and living on a nearby farm, seemed to be the most effected of all the other brothers and sisters. Hannah wept uncontrollably in the arms of her parents, before her husband Joseph helped her back into their waiting carriage, while attempting to shield her from the drenching rain.

As difficult as it was for Stukeley and Honor, their orchards and farm, which provided their livelihood, still required much work, and the harvest was fast approaching. The livestock also required feeding and tending to, and the hired farmhands were few. Life had to continue, despite the recent loss of both Sarah and Ruth.

But the mysterious illness was soon to strike the Tillinghast clan again. Only this time, it was not confined to the Pine Hill farmstead. One afternoon soon after Ruth had been laid to rest, while Stukeley was busily pressing cider with his sons and some of the farmhands, he was surprised by an unexpected visit from Joseph, who was the devoted husband of Stukeley's 27- year-old daughter, Hannah. Stukeley at first attempted to appear in good spirits as he welcomed his son-in-law. However, the expression of gravity on the young man's face and in his tone of voice indicated that something was greatly troubling him, as he asked to speak with his father-in-law in private.

"Of course, Joseph," said Stukeley, growing concerned. Stukeley immediately led Joseph to the main house, where Honor served them both some apple wine. As they sat in the dining area, Stukeley asked,

"What is wrong, Joseph? Has something happened at your farm? Is Hannah alright?"

Joseph quickly explained that Hannah had caught a chill from the torrential rains during Ruth's recent funeral, and as a result had developed a rather severe cold. In fact, she was now becoming feverish and suffering from night sweats. But there was something more. Hannah was also experiencing disturbing dreams at night; terrible dreams involving her late sister Sarah. Stukeley felt his blood run cold upon hearing this. After sharing a look with his wife Honor, he asked Joseph what Hannah said about these dreams involving Sarah. Joseph replied that all Hannah would say was that she repeatedly dreamed of Sarah being at her window, and beckoning to her.

While Honor hastily began readying herself to accompany Joseph back to his farmhouse, to help care for her ailing daughter, Stukeley assured Joseph that Hannah's nightmares about her late sister Sarah were simply the result of her feverish condition.

But while Hannah's condition eventually began to stabilize, young Andris Tillinghast – now 17 years of age – also began showing signs of the same malady. Although Andris had always been healthy and strong, he suddenly developed the all too familiar cough, and became increasingly weakened, until he was no longer able to tend to his chores about the farm. Not only that, but Andris also began complaining of nocturnal visits from his deceased sister Sarah, who reportedly crept into his room in the dead of night and knocked the breath out of him by sitting upon his chest. Stukeley and Honor were beside themselves with despair, as the country doctor apologetically offered no hope of a cure for the wasting disease that was suddenly claiming their children.

The harvest came and went, with the orchards of the Tillinghast farm producing a bountiful crop. Some of the older offspring who were married with families and farms of their own, including Stukeley Tillinghast, Jr., had come to lend a hand on their parent's farm during the harvest season. And yet, this bountiful harvest was in dread contrast to the malady torturing the Tillinghast family. Although "Snuffy Stuke's" friends in the village greatly sympathized with his plight, they offered little in the way of a solution. Some came to him with well-meaning advice regarding home remedies, anything from applying copious amounts of "goose grease" to bathing in frigid water, to the topical application of sulfur, to continual prayer and fasting. But Honor herself was well-schooled in home remedies, passed down through generations of the Hopkins family, and nothing thus far had worked. Even their physician friend's medicines and occasional bloodletting had proven completely ineffectual. But one thing was for certain; Stukeley Tillinghast was determined not to have to bury anymore of his children!

Stukeley also sought spiritual advice by consulting with his local minister. This well-meaning, kindhearted clergyman did his best to console Stukeley, assuring him that it was not necessarily sin on their part that brought this calamity down upon his family. Rather, God had His own mysterious reasons. The minister also opened up the Good Book and shared with Stukeley the familiar example of Job. Tearfully, Stukeley confided to the clergyman about how his afflicted children were claiming to be visited nightly by their departed sister Sarah. But, like the physician, the well-intentioned minister assured him that these visions were merely the result of feverish imaginations, and nothing more. After all, living in the age of enlightenment, such superstitious beliefs as the dead returning in spectral form were best cast aside. Stukeley again thanked the minister for his time, and further demonstrated his appreciation by leaving a bushel of apples and a jug of cider for the venerable clergyman.

Unlike Hannah, Andris' decline was rapid, as the disease had taken a particularly aggressive hold on him. He complained of his sister Sarah having visited him once again during the cover of night, and of her sitting upon his body and causing him great discomfort. Andris soon began coughing up bloody phlegm both day and evening as his lungs continued to hemorrhage, until he was much too exhausted to fight for his life any longer. One dark and moonless night, scantly a month after the onset of his illness, the poor lad weakly declared to his parents that he was ready for Sarah to take him with her. With a look of peaceful resignation in his eyes, Andris then quietly slipped away.

On the evening of the day Andris had been laid to rest beside his two sisters, as Stukeley and Honor were secluded in their bedroom, Honor sobbed in her husband's arms. "What have we done to deserve this?" she asked tearfully. "What mortal sin must we have committed, that our children are being taken from us?"

"We have done nothing to deserve this," Stukeley assured his wife, recalling what their minister had told him. "Other families suffer the loss of children. We can only pray that no more of ours will be taken from us."

Looking up at him with tear-stained eyes, Honor asked, "But why Sarah? How could our beautiful daughter be causing this to happen?"

Stukeley was resolute as he faced his wife and said, "It is not Sarah who is doing this. Just as the doctor and the Parson said, it is simply the result of nightmares, brought about by feverish minds."

Wiping her eyes, Honor slowly nodded in agreement. "You are right, my husband," she said, sounding as though she were trying to convince herself.


But Stukeley himself was not inwardly convinced, although he hid this fact from Honor and from the rest of his family. As much as it defied everything he'd always believed in, as well as what his own clergyman grandfather had taught him, Stukeley had also begun to contemplate the terrifying possibility that Sarah was returning from the grave. But, why? What could possibly cause such a macabre and horrifying thing to occur? Stukeley knew that he needed an answer, before another one of his children was taken from him. As it was, the health of his daughter Hannah was now precarious. And although she lived with her husband on a farm in West Greenwich, Hannah also claimed to have been visited by Sarah in the dead of night. The effort of the country doctor had proven completely ineffectual, and the well-meaning clergyman had no definable answers either.

In desperation, Stukeley turned to friends and neighbors for any possible solution. At a gathering of his friends and fellow grange members, he poured out his heart, confiding to them about how each of his ailing children claimed to have been visited by their late sister Sarah, who'd been the first to die. Stukeley also told his trusted friends about the dream he'd experienced prior to Sarah's death, in which he'd heard Sarah's voice calling to him upon the wind, and then turned to discover that precisely half of his orchard had withered and died, while the other half remained healthy. His friends unanimously interpreted this dream to portend the immanent deaths of exactly half of his family, being symbolized by the orchard that represented his livelihood. Stukeley himself had wondered if this could be the meaning of his dream, and he now contemplated it with dread.

One man among this company of friends, an elder member of the Exeter Grange named Jeremiah, offered what seemed to be a ray of hope. While puffing away on his clay pipe, he explained to Stukeley and to the others that he had knowledge of a similar situation, which had taken place in the town of Cumberland. Eagerly, Stukeley pressed old Jeremiah for further details.

"Well, Snuffy Stuke," said Jeremiah in his gravelly voice, "a few years back I had some business in Cumberland. And while I was there, I heard tell of a fellow by the name of Staples, who sought permission by the town officials there to exhume the body of his deceased daughter. It seems Mr. Staples was intending to 'try an experiment' to save the life of his second daughter, who was wasting away and near death herself."

Jeremiah went on to relate that, while he did not know whether or not Mr. Staples' "experiment" had proven successful, he'd also heard of two other instances of this practice, which had taken place in Vermont several years back. In both cases, the unearthing of recently deceased family members had revealed the "culprit" who was returning from the grave in spectral form to thrive upon the living while they slept. Stukeley and the others sat there aghast, as Jeremiah explained that the remedy involved removing the heart from the dead body, and then burning it… thereby freeing the spirit of the dearly departed, which had been held captive within the body.

Finally finding his voice once again, Stukeley asked the older gentleman, "But, once the bodies have been unearthed… how does one know for certain which one is the 'culprit?'"

"Oh, you'll know, Snuffy," old Jeremiah slyly replied with a nod. "When your eyes behold that terrible sight, trust me, there will be no doubt." Jeremiah then resumed puffing away on his clay pipe.


Stukeley Tillinghast returned home in a downcast frame of mind. How could he possibly carry through with the ghastly remedy that old Jeremiah has suggested to him? The thought of digging up the bodies of his dear children was utterly repulsive. And how could he possibly bring himself to even suggest such a horrid thing to his dear wife Honor? No… this was a course he was not yet willing to take.


Late that same afternoon, Honor Tillinghast arrived home in her son-in-law Joseph's carriage, following a visit to the smaller Hoxie farm in West Greenwich. She had spent most of the entire day caring for her ailing daughter Hannah, and was now fairly exhausted herself. After arriving inside her home, Honor wearily began preparing for the evening meal.

Honor ate sparingly that evening, and appeared more fatigued than usual. Naturally concerned for his wife, Stukeley asked her if she were not feeling well. Honor forced a feeble smile, explaining to her husband that she was simply tired after a day spent at the Hoxie farm caring for Hannah, whose health was fortunately much improved. With a smile of his own, Stukeley reached across the eating board and lightly touched her hand. He also insisted that she retire early to bed, assuring her that he and the children would tend to all the remaining chores. Honor thanked him, agreeing that she did need a good night's rest.

However, it soon became apparent that Honor was suffering from more than simple exhaustion. The months of caring for her ailing children had finally taken their toll on the poor woman, and weakened her resistance. Within a few days Honor herself was taken with a fever. Stukeley once again desperately summoned the country physician for help. Although the good doctor could not yet say for certain if this was the onset of consumption, he advised his friend Stukeley to prepare for the worse. In the meantime, he promised to monitor Honor's condition as diligently as his practice permitted. The doctor also prescribed lots of bed rest, the avoidance of drafts, and a small periodic amount of bloodletting with his much-used supply of leeches, to help restore her humors.


One evening, Honor was lying awake, feeling feverish and exhausted. Lying beside her, Stukeley was now snoring evenly, greatly exhausted following the harvest season combined with the caring of his ailing family. And now, Honor felt as though she had become an additional burden to him. As a tear streamed down her cheek, Honor gave a deep sigh, and eventually managed to drift off into an uneasy sleep.

It was not long, however, before Honor was awakened, by exactly what she was uncertain. Not knowing what time of the night it was, she glanced around the semi-darkened bedroom, to see a sliver of moonlight streaming across the floor through an opening in the window curtain. But Honor had the eerie feeling that something else was inside the room, and that she was being watched. She then saw a figure silently emerge from the shadows. Thinking it might perhaps be her son James or one of the other children, she was about to call out. The figure then floated forward, moving into the shaft of moonlight. Honor could scarcely believe what she was seeing. With a shock, she recognized the ghastly image of her deceased daughter Sarah, standing there cloaked in her white burial shroud. Sarah's lips parted, and her voiced whispered, "Maaamaaa...."

'"Oh, dear God!" Honor gasped, now realizing that what the other afflicted children had been saying was true. Sarah was indeed rising from her grave at night, and preying upon her brothers and sisters! Horrified, Honor was about to call to her husband, who was still slumbering beside her. She'd opened her mouth to do so, when in an instant Sarah was somehow suddenly upon her, caressing her face while seated partway on her abdomen. Honor could feel the weight of Sarah's body upon her, causing her to gasp for breath. She wanted to struggle against her, but found herself powerless to do so, as her daughter firmly held her in place.

Sarah's own breath was chill, as she smiled down at her mother's face and whispered to her, "Don't be afraid, Mama. I've been so cold and lonely, and I've missed you so. Please, Mama... come to be with me, always."

Although she was initially terrified, Honor could now feel her fear beginning to ebb. The sensation of Sarah's cool hands upon her face even became comforting. Finding her voice, she whispered back with tears streaming from her eyes, "I've missed you too, my sweet Sarah. I've missed you so... terribly... you do not know..."

"Shhhhhh," Sarah soothingly hushed her. Slowly and rhythmically, Sarah then began rocking the weight of her own body back and forth on her mother's abdomen, gradually sliding up to her chest area as she did do. "Ooohhhhh," Sarah moaned in obvious delight, closing her eyes and tilting her head slightly backwards. "Soon, Mama... very soon," she whispered.

Honor submissively lay there, no longer even desiring to resist at all, as she felt the warmth of her body draining into Sarah's. After all, she had given life to Sarah from her own body, and now her dear daughter again needed her to give her life. Gently closing her own eyes, Honor slowly drifted off into unconsciousness.


Stukeley awoke at the crowing of the rooster, and was pleased to find Honor still sleeping, breathing peacefully and evenly beside him in the bed. Reaching over and lightly touching her cheek, he was also relieved to find that her skin felt noticeably cooler, indicating that her fever seemed to have ebbed. Glancing down at her, he smiled at how lovely she still appeared, despite the recent tragedies she'd been forced to endure, now coupled with her own illness. It promised to be a cold and damp November morning, and Stukeley hated having to rise and move away from her. However, it was best to allow his dear wife all the rest she needed. Besides, multitude of chores needed tending to. With a weary sigh, he forced himself to rise and throw on his clothes, before making his way outside for his morning necessities.

While Stukeley was busily tending to chores with two of the farmhands that morning, James took him by surprise by approaching him and saying somewhat sheepishly, "Happy birthday, Pa."

Stukeley was somewhat taken aback. With all that had been happening, it hadn't yet dawned on him that today was his 58th birthday. Although it now hardly mattered at all to him, Stukeley forced himself to smile, and said to James, "Why, thank you, son. You know, I hadn't even thought of it, until you just reminded me."

James briefly smiled back at him. The handsome youth then lowered his eyes, and awkwardly walked away. While leaning upon the shovel he held, Stukeley realized how hard this moment must have been for James, with all that had taken place over the last several months. The loss of James' two older sisters and his favorite brother had been especially difficult for him. Stukeley appreciated the birthday wish, knowing James had made the effort to do so despite the heaviness weighing on his young heart.

When Stukeley arrived back inside the main house, he found the morning meal already prepared by his children. Honor was dressed and seated at the long wooden dining board, with a heavy shawl wrapped about her shoulders for warmth. Stukeley took his seat beside her, and inquired how she was feeling today. She replied that she was feeling somewhat better, and was no longer feverish… although Stukeley could tell that she was more uncomfortable that she was letting on, and that her breathing was somewhat labored. Weakly, she smiled and wished him a pleasant birthday. Stukeley waved his hand in dismissal in an attempt at levity, and remarked that he was now another year older yet none-the-more wiser.

As evening approached, Stukeley returned from the village with James in the large horse drawn wagon, following an afternoon spent marketing their abundant produce. After bringing in the empty baskets and crates, and depositing what produce remained in the storage shed, he and James rejoined the rest of the family for the last meal of the day. Stukeley was concerned that Honor seemed to have completely lost her appetite. He was further dismayed by the fact that she appeared especially jittery and distracted, glancing about nervously at the slightest noise. When one of the older hound dogs sauntered into the dining room to take his usual spot in front of the fireplace, Honor nearly fell out of her seat.

Stukeley quickly reached an arm out to steady her, smiled, and asked, "Are you expecting callers this evening, my wife?"

"Callers?" she asked in a somewhat disturbed manner. Then, realizing that her husband had only been speaking lightly, Honor replied, "No… no one. It's almost evening, that is all."

Stukeley found her statement somewhat curious, but attributed it to her recent fever. "Doctor's orders, you must oft to bed early," he reminded her. "The rest of us will again tend to all the evening chores."

Before retiring to bed himself that night, Stukeley momentarily glanced at his own reflection in the tarnished looking glass. Although he remained broad shouldered and robust, his face had become deeply lined with sorrow, and his graying beard now gave him a grizzled appearance. He certainly felt every one of his 58 years. Thank the Lord he had his loving wife and remaining children to comfort him.

Stukeley entered his bedroom to find Honor still lying awake in bed, staring at the window with her head and shoulder propped up by her pillow. When he inquired why she was not yet asleep, she at first did not answer. He asked her a second time. In a despondent manner, Honor responded by saying, "There will be no moon tonight, will there?"

Stukeley looked at her, puzzled. "No," he replied, "there will most likely be rain, lasting through the night." He then snuffed out the candle he'd placed on their bedside table, and gently told his wife to go to sleep.

Honor slept fitfully that night beside her husband. When morning arrived with the crowing of the old rooster, it seemed as though she'd hardly slept at all. Her face was pale and drawn, with deep, darkened circles surrounding her eyes. Despite Stukeley's protests, however, Honor insisted upon rising, dressing herself, and tending to some of the household chores.

Throughout the morning Honor again appeared preoccupied, although she tended to her duties as best as she was able to. She refused to eat anything more than a small amount of broth during the morning meal, and would scarcely speak when spoken to. It was also apparent that she was having considerable difficulty in breathing. Every so often she would begin to cough, and whenever she did so, she would clutch at her side as if in pain. Finally, Stukeley could no longer tolerate watching her carry on in this manner. As soon as they were alone together in the dining room, he announced to his wife that he was about to go into the village, and fetch the doctor for her again. When she protested, Stukeley insisted that she tell him what was wrong.

She no longer had any way of avoiding it; Honor had to confide to her husband what was taking place. With tears filling her eyes, she explained to him that their daughter Sarah had been coming to her in the night while he slept beside her. "She wants me to come with her," said Honor. "And soon, I know that I'll be joining out sweet Sarah in another life."

Stukeley's face blanched white, as he slowly lowered himself into a chair. "This cannot be possible," he said in a hoarse voice. "Surely this was a dream you had, and nothing more."

Honor slowly shook her head, and replied, "No, it was not a dream! It was our Sarah. And she bids me to join her."

Stukeley protested, "But, you cannot leave us. Our children still need you so, and I need you. What would this life be worth living without you?"

"I'm sorry," Honor wept. "But I'm so tired, and I don't think that I can resist her any longer."

Now more desperate than ever, Stukeley knew what course of action he must take. He confided to Honor the grisly remedy that their neighbor Jeremiah had suggested. Although Honor was initially horrified, she eventually relented.

Wearily, Honor told her husband, "If it will bring peace to Sarah's wandering spirit, and save our daughter Hannah, then I pray that it be the Lord's will."

Stukeley wasted little time in once again conferring with his most trusted friends and fellow Grange members. Because the Almanac predicted that the ground would soon be too frozen to dig, they decided not to delay any longer. They therefore set the date of the exhumations for later that very week.

On the night before the grim event was to take place, Stukeley lie awake in bed beside his feverishly slumbering wife. While lying there, he kept a keen eye at the bedroom window, lest the spectral form of Sarah should suddenly materialize within the darkened bedroom. He was resolved not to let the mother of his children be taken from him. After all the many years they'd been together, the prospect of life without her now seemed unbearable. So many questions now weighed heavily upon his soul, for which he had no answers. If only his dear old Grandpa Pardon, a wise and devout man of the cloth, were still alive to advise him! But no, the burden of responsibility was now his and his alone.

Stukeley himself had spent some hours searching the Scriptures, but could find nothing specific relating to his situation. Still, he could not accept that it was his daughter Sarah returning from the grave to do such harm to those she had loved in life. After all, if Satan possessed power to transform himself into an angel of light, then certainly he could assume the image of Sarah. Perhaps this was even God's way of testing their faith, as the Parson had suggested.

In the near distance, an owl hooted, nearly causing Stukeley to jump from his bed. He then settled back down, momentarily embarrassed by his own foolishness. He ran a hand across his forehead and wearily closed his eyes, knowing that morning would arrive all too soon.

Shortly after sunrise the following morning, Stukeley rose and began tending to various farm chores as usual, while waiting for his neighbors to arrive. He'd spent some hours in prayer before daybreak, asking for courage and fortitude for the task ahead.

It was not until shortly after the morning meal, however, before young Clarke announced, "Pa, we got company."

Rising from his seat, Stukeley glanced out of one of the front windows and saw three of his neighbors – old Jeremiah among them – approaching on foot along the winding pathway. Two of the men held shovels over their shoulders. Resolved in his purpose, Stukeley strode over to the coat pegs on the wall, and reached for his long, snuff-colored overcoat. Before proceeding out of his front door, he paused to glance at his wife Honor, who was still seated by herself near the hearth. A thick wool shawl was wrapped about her shoulders for warmth, and her head was bowed. Whether she was in silent prayer, or merely napping, Stukeley could not tell. He then turned and left the house, to join the others who were outside waiting for him.

Several other men eventually arrived at the small Tillinghast family plot to assist their friend and neighbor. Numbered among them were Mr. Wilcox, Mr. Reynolds, Mr. Whitford, Mr. Moony, Mr. Gardner, and two young farm hands that worked for the Tillinghast family during the warmer seasonal months. Following several minutes of chatter, during which old Jeremiah and the others reassured Snuffy that they were taking the right course of action, the digging commenced.

Although none of the three graves had yet been adorned with stone markers, the earth mounding them was still relatively soft, and fairly easy to remove. The first of the graves to be unearthed belonged to Stukeley's son Andris, who'd been the most recent burial. Together, several of the men used ropes to haul the crude pine box up from the grave. They then set it upon the ground beside the freshly opened grave, and used their spades to scrape some of the remaining earth from off of the top. Mr. Wilcox, Mr. Gardner, and Stukeley proceeded to remove the nails from the lid with the tools they'd brought along. The men then tied cloth bandanas over their mouths and noses, before removing the lid.

As the lid of the crude pine coffin was lifted off and placed aside, the men gathered round to examine the remains contained within. Even with the cloth bandanas covering the lower parts of their faces, their nostrils were instantly assaulted with the strong stench of decay. It was soon evident to all that the body of young Andris was well on its way to returning to the earth, despite the fact that he'd been buried only several weeks. The clothing that remained intact on his putrefying young body was damp and soiled from a small amount of water seepage lining the bottom of the coffin. Nonetheless, Stukeley motioned old Jeremiah to step forward for a closer examination. Jeremiah obliged, going over to the pine coffin and leaning upon his walking stick for support, while inspecting what remained of young Andris. He then glanced up at Stukeley and the others, and slowly shook his head no before stepping back. Stukeley himself tenderly replaced the lid back on top of the coffin, pausing to whisper, "Forgive me, my poor son." They then secured the lid once again with the nails they had loosened.

Before moving onto the next grave, the men pulled down their bandanas and took a brief reprieve, fortifying themselves by passing around a jug of hard cider that had been supplied by Stukeley. One of the men placed a hand upon Stukeley's shoulder, and asked him, "How are you fairing, Snuffy?"

Stukeley replied that he was holding up, and thanked his neighbor for his kind support. Stukeley then addressed the rest of the gathering, telling them, "Again, I wish to thank you all for being here today, my friends, to assist me with this most unpleasant task."

"Think nothing of it, Snuffy Stuke," said the man who stood closest to him. "I speak for all, when I say how often you have helped so many of us in this community."

All of the men who were present agreed. One of them added, "Speaking for myself, I and my family would not be where we are, if you and your wife had not aided us with your charities, when we'd struggled in starting our own farm."

An unspoken dread floated among them, that a similar blight might someday strike their own families, if they did not deal with this situation here and now. Taking a deep breath, Stukeley said, "Well... let's get on with it, then." They moved over to the next unmarked grave, and began to dig.

When Ruth's pine coffin was raised out of the open grave and the lid pried open, it quickly became evident from the stench wafting up that her body was also in a proper state of natural decay. Her bodily frame appeared skeletal beneath the dampened shroud that covered her body, and while her hair remained full, the skin on her face had become taught and shriveled. Jeremiah again stepped forward to more closely examine the body, before declaring to the others that she did not appear to be "the one."

The jug was once again passed around, and conversation shared, before they began exhuming the third and final grave, which of course was Sarah's. Of all the three graves of his recently deceased children, this was of course the one over which Stukeley felt the most trepidation. Each afflicted member of his family had reportedly seen Sarah, and now even Honor claimed to have been attacked in the night by her deceased daughter. More than anything, Stukeley was now hoping that Sarah's body, the longest to have lain within the earth, would be reduced to decay just as both Ruth and Andris' bodies had been.

Sarah's coffin was finally unearthed, lifted up out of the grave and set upon the ground. This pine coffin, in particular, had been well crafted. After all, Sarah had been the first to succumb to the mysterious illness, and Stukeley did not anticipate having to construct two more coffins in such a close amount of time, especially during the mist of harvest season. As the men began the process of extracting the nails from the lid, Stukeley reminded himself that Sarah had been given a proper Christian burial, and that he himself had secured her coffin shut. Surely, he reasoned, this was sufficient precaution to prevent her from escaping her grave at night, even in spirit form.

When the final nail was loosened from the coffin lid, Stukeley and the others once again placed their cloth bandanas back over their mouths and noses, and proceeded to remove the lid. Nothing, however, could have prepared them for the sight they beheld. Together, the men gasped and drew back in shocked disbelief. Instead of decaying, Sarah truly appeared as if she were alive!

It was the condition of Sarah's face, which was the most shocking. Her once lovely blue eyes were now wide open and staring, their color having turned to a reflective, cloudy gray. Although she wore a tightly bound cloth chinstrap to prevent her jaw from gaping, her lips were now parted, with the corners turned slightly upwards into a ghastly smile. Her tongue also slightly protruded between the still gleaming white upper and lower teeth. Sarah's complexion appeared quite ruddy, and her lengthy golden tresses were in a manner that suggested her hair had grown. The flesh of her hands, which were resting upon her chest, also looked fresh and ruddy, and her fingernails appeared to have noticeably lengthened. All in all, the body of Sarah Tillinghast, which should have been even more advanced in decay than the others, appeared extremely lifelike.

"Good God! She looks as if she were alive," said Mr. Wilcox, echoing the others' thoughts.

Stukeley Tillinghast's face blanched white. He reeled and staggered, nearly losing his balance, before Mr. Wilcox and Mr. Reynolds rushed over to help steady him. Old Jeremiah once again dutifully stepped forward to more closely examine Sarah's body, leaning over on his walking stick until he was nearly face to face with Sarah.

One of the men instinctively said, "Careful, old man," as if he feared that Sarah's life-like corpse might suddenly lunge up and attack him.

After a cursory examination, Jeremiah glanced up. With an intense expression on his wizened features, he informed Stukeley and the others, "We've found the one."

Stukeley's heart sank within him as he realized that he no longer deny the truth. Sarah's body had been taken over by an unholy spirit, and was being used to prey upon the lives of his family members. Jeremiah had been right all along, even though Stukeley had secretly hoped that his words had been nothing more than rantings of a senile old man.

Jeremiah now hobbled over to Stukeley, gently placed a gnarled hand on his arm, and told him, "You know what you have to do now, Snuffy."

Stukeley lowered his gaze and nodded. One of the men approached him, and hesitantly offered, "Snuffy, if... if you feel that you're unable to do this... one of us will do it for you."

Gathering his resolve, Stukeley replied, "No, my friend. I thank you, but this task is now mine, and mine alone." His friend nodded and stepped away, appearing greatly relieved.

While Stukeley prepared himself, Jeremiah and the others became emboldened enough to surround Sarah's coffin, and began remarking to each other on just how unnatural her state of preservation appeared to be. Jeremiah even began poking at her hands with his oak walking stick, while another gently prodded her with his spade, as if to see if she might suddenly begin to move on her own. They were all amazed at how pliable her limbs were, instead of the stiffness that they expected.

The other men then obligingly moved aside as Stukeley stepped forward, brandishing a large, freshly sharpened hunting knife that had once belonged to his father. He knelt down beside the pine coffin, reached down with his knife, and began cutting open Sarah's white burial shroud. Her breasts, still surprisingly ample and full, were exposed to the late afternoon sunlight.

With Stukeley's permission, one of the men made a small gash on Sarah's left shoulder, upon which a small amount of dark blood trickled out. There could no longer be any doubt.

Stooping forward, with his hunting knife poised in both hands over the middle of Sarah's chest, Stukeley closed his eyes for a moment, and whispered to himself, "God forgive me. This is not Sarah. This is not Sarah."

With strong resolve, to save the life of his dear wife Honor and their daughter Hannah, Stukeley then forcefully plunged the long knife into Sarah's chest. He was certainly familiar with the butchering of livestock, and he wished to get this over with as quickly as possible. As the slaughter continued, the men heard the cracking sound of Sarah's ribs and sternum, and she looked as if a piercing scream might suddenly escape from her parted lips, as her limp body heaved with Stukeley's efforts. Her clouded, staring gray eyes were particularly disconcerting, as her head with its long flaxen tresses, lolled back and forth in a grotesque manner. It actually gave the illusion that the dead eyes were glancing at each of them in turn. Finally, three of the men came forward and knelt down along with Stukeley, to help hold the body in place. The men who knelt beside Stukeley instinctively recoiled, as what sounded like a soft groan, or grunt, escaped from Sarah's lips. Stukeley himself paused for only a second or to, before continuing to carve away.

With another cracking of bone, Sarah's large, yellowish heart was exposed. As Stukeley began severing the arteries with his knife, an issue of thick, dark blood unexpectedly spurted out, spraying onto Stukeley and two of the men beside him. Stukeley merely flinched, while the other two let out exclamations of disgust. A sickening-sweet odor seemed to emanate from the dark blood, as the men used their bandanas to wipe it up. One of the men, a young farmhand who worked for Stukeley, suddenly sprinted away to loudly retch. Stukeley continued slicing, until the heart was completely severed. He then lifted it out and deposited it into a nearby wooden bucket, leaving a dark gaping hole in the center of Sarah's chest.

The other of the two farm hands, standing nearby, attempted to pray aloud. "Our F-Father," he stammered, "wh-which art in Heaven...h-hallowed...b-b-beee...Thy n-n-name. Thy k-k-kingdom c-coooome..."

For the first time since they'd arrived, Stukeley suddenly found himself having to choke back his tears. Upon noticing this, one of the men who stood beside the young farm hand lightly touched his arm to silence him, while quietly thanking the lad for his effort.

In the fading sunlight of this late autumn afternoon, Stukeley and the others quickly kindled a small campfire at the edge of the small cemetery. When the fire was sufficiently ablaze, Sarah's heart was placed in the center of it. Old Jeremiah lit his clay pipe and watched along with the others, as the heart was quickly reduced to a blackened lump of charred flesh. As the jug of cider was passed around one last time, Stukeley refused to drink. Instead, he used the edge of a spade to break up what remained of the heart, before dousing the fire and covering it with earth. He and the other men then set about the task of hastily reburying the bodies of Sarah, Ruth and Andris. Before the small contingent of men left the Tillinghast cemetery, Stukeley once again thanked them all for their assistance. The men all assured their friend "Snuffy Stuke" that he'd done the right thing, while pulling up the collars of their overcoats against the stiff, chill breeze that had picked up. It had been a long and trying afternoon, and the men were anxious to return to the warmth of their own homes and families... with quite a story to tell. Old Jeremiah paused to pat Stukeley on the shoulder and reminded him that this had been the only proper action to take. He then hobbled off with the aid of his walking stick, to join the others.

One of the men was heard to ask, "Did you observe the mocking smile on Sarah's blood-red lips?"

Another commented, "I distinctly heard her scream, when Snuffy plunged the knife into her chest."

"Quite right!" the man beside him agreed, adding, "And did you see the way she looked at us all, just before she expired?"

Wearily, Stukeley gathered up his own tools, along with the now empty cider jug, before making the short journey back home in the gathering darkness.

Scarcely one month following the exhumations which took place in this small Rhode Island farming community, the entire country went into mourning over the loss of General George Washington, its chief Founding Father and first United States President. At age 67, General Washington had rapidly succumbed to a sudden throat infection at his home at Mount Vernon. The General had also been severely weakened by blood loss, after his attending physicians had ordered that he be bled a number of times in the course of his illness. Altogether, about five pints of blood were removed from him. One of General Washington's final requests was "...do not let my body be put into the vault in less than three days after I am dead," to prevent the possibility of premature burial.

As the winter months passed, and a new century dawned, Honor Tillinghast did gradually begin to recover from her illness. Neither parent received anymore reports of nocturnal visits from Sarah. Stukeley began to consider that the gruesome "remedy" which he and his neighbors had carried out just might have taken effect. All those who'd been involved also agreed that the old buzzard must have been right, after all! It truly seemed to Stukeley that his prayers had been answered, and that the omen predicted in his fateful dream had been thwarted.

By the time spring arrived, Honor had made a complete recovery. Once again, the Tillinghast orchards were in full bloom, and promised to yield one of the most bountiful crops in the entire county. Unfortunately, Stukeley and Honor's daughter, Hannah Tillinghast Hoxie, suffered a relapse of her own illness, and died at the age of twenty-eight. She was buried in West Greenwich, in her husband Joseph's family cemetery. The general consensus among Stukeley's neighbors was that Hannah's illness had simply been too far advanced. Honor had been spared, because the "attacks" from her daughter had been stopped in time for her to sufficiently recover.

With the seasonally warmer weather having arrived, Stukeley and his two youngest sons, Clark and James visited the small family burial ground and spent an afternoon placing unadorned stone markers at the head of each of the three graves. Stukeley spoke very little during this task. Once the stones were in place, he bade his sons return to the house, explaining that he'd tend to the cleaning up of the area himself.

"Yes, Pa," said James. He and Clark began making their way back to the main house, to get ready for suppertime. Both of them understood that their Pa wanted to be alone here by himself for a while.

As he stood alone in the warm late afternoon sun, Stukeley's thoughts once again returned to that wretched afternoon five months earlier, when he, his neighbors and two of his farmhands had stood in this exact spot, having unearthed the three pine coffins. The face of Sarah was still vividly fresh in his mind, staring up at him with her glassy eyes, and with her parted lips revealing her white teeth as if in a ghastly smile. It was an image that would undoubtedly continue to haunt his dreams throughout the remainder of his life. He also vividly recalled the cracking of her bones as he'd carved the heart out from his daughter's exposed chest, as well as the gasp that had escaped through her parted lips.

"It was not Sarah," he once again reminded himself, as his tears began to flow. "It was some vile spirit from hell, who'd violated her body for a corrupt purpose." Stukeley then thought of Hannah, who he'd recently helped to bury with his son-in-law, Joseph. Suddenly overcome with grief, Stukeley sank to his knees, and buried his face in his hands. "Forgive me, Sarah," he said between his choking sobs. "May God forgive me for what I have done to you, daughter. I… I only sought to save your dear mother and sister… and to prevent any more of our family from being taken."

It was then that Stukeley became aware that a warm, gentle breeze had picked up around him. Somehow, he felt as if he were no longer alone here among the three graves of his children. An inexplicable feeling of peace washed over him, as what felt like a hand gently touched his right shoulder. Turning to glance up, he saw no one. And yet the touch had been undeniable. It was a familiar, comforting touch, similar to the way Sarah used to come up behind him and touch him when she was a young child, and wanted his attention. Could it have been Sarah's angel, he wondered? Or perhaps even Sarah herself? Now feeling somewhat calmed, Stukeley stood and wiped the tears from his eyes with the back of his hand, before making his way back to the house.

Supper was ready by the time Stukeley arrived to take his seat with his family. As Honor efficiently served them, just as she'd always done prior to her own recent illness, Stukeley observed just how careworn her feature had become over the last several months. And yet, her loving smile was still ever present for each of them. Stukeley led them in prayer before they began to eat, thanking the Almighty that through His divine mercy, the family was here, together. Honor herself seemed to sense the change in his demeanor, suspecting that something may have happened, although she said nothing.

That night, Stukeley lie awake beside his peacefully sleeping wife. Honor herself had spent some time secluded in the bedroom quietly weeping, as she did each night after retiring. Stukeley and the rest of the family always afforded her this time for privately mourning her lost children. And now it was his turn to silently mourn. And yet, he again thought of how his shoulder had distinctly been touched that afternoon, and he prayed that this had been a sign that his actions had been in accordance with God's will… or if they were not, that he'd at least been forgiven.

Sometime later, Stukeley eventually began to drift off to sleep. He was in a state between wakefulness and sleep when a bright light seemed to be manifesting before him. As the light became clearer, he knew that he was once again standing amidst his orchards, which were again in full bloom. A sweet fragrance filled the air, similar to the scent of roses mingled with honeysuckle. Stukeley closed his eyes and breathed deeply of the fragrance. It was then that he heard a familiar female voice calling to him, softly and gently. "Papa… Papa…"

Opening his eyes, Stukeley beheld his daughter Sarah standing there in front of him, her arms outstretched as if in supplication. She appeared lovelier than he'd ever seen her, dressed in a flowing white gown similar to the one she was to have worn on her wedding day. Her flaxen locks were cascading over her shoulders, and her face was radiant in the sunlight, like that of an angel, and her blue eyes sparkled with life.

Stukeley closed his own eyes, as tears began streaming down his face.

"Please don't cry, Papa," whispered Sarah, stepping forward and lightly touching his arm. "I am at peace now. I will always love you and Mama. I bid you good bye now, Papa, until we see each other again." Sarah then reached up and gently kissed him, the touch of her lips warm against his cheek. When Stukeley opened his eyes again, Sarah had stepped back, and was standing smiling at him. However, she was no longer alone. Standing there with her, also attired completely in white, were Ruth, Andris and Hannah. They were all smiling at him now. Stukeley would have reached out to embrace them, but they turned and began walking away, gradually fading from his sight as they did so. Before his children vanished completely, he also noticed a tall, radiant figure among them, who seemed to be leading them.

At the first ray of sunlight, Stukeley awoke to hear the early morning birds chirping in the nearby branches, signaling that daylight would soon follow. The shrill, familiar crow of the rooster alerted the family that livestock needed feeding, along with a multitude of other daily farm chores. Upon rising from bed in the semi-darkened room, Stukeley noticed that Honor was also awake, and that she was looking up at him with a contented smile on her face. For a moment, he considered telling her of his comforting vision of Sarah and their other children, wondering how she would accept this. Stukeley then decided to wait until a later time. For now, no words were necessary as he sat back down upon the bed beside his wife, gently clasped her hands in his, and tenderly kissed her forehead.

Throughout the years, the legend of Stukeley Tillinghast, his prophetic dream and his daughter Sarah has been told and retold throughout the vicinity of southern Rhode Island, often with varying takes on the tale, as well as a variety of embellishments. For many years, the story was handed down locally by oral tradition, with the first known published version appearing in 1888, in "The Belief in Vampires in Rhode Island," authored by Sidney S. Rider.

Stukeley, Honor, and their fourteen children were real people who resided in the Pine Hill section of Exeter, Rhode Island, in the latter part of the 18th and early 19th centuries. Much of the legend is apparently based upon fact. Although the original Tillinghast farmstead is long gone, a small, largely neglected and rather obscure historical cemetery lays behind a stone wall on Forest Hills Drive in Exeter (#14) where Honor, her husband Stukeley, and at least some of their children are buried. Honor's stone, although slanting to the side, is located in front of the cemetery and is among the most prominent. The stone claims the date of her death as December 3, 1831. She lived a long life of 86 years. Her husband's stone, located beside hers, is inscribed simply with the initials "S.T." Slightly further back is the gravestone of Stukeley (or Stutley) Tillinghast, Jr., who died on March 13, 1848 at age 74. In the center of this historical cemetery are a row of semi-evenly spaced, small field stones which are extremely weathered and which bear no inscription. It is commonly believed that these stones mark the graves of Sarah Tillinghast and at least two of her siblings.

There are those who claim that the Tillinghast Cemetery is haunted to this day, presumably as the result of the violations of the three graves which took place in 1799. One paranormal investigator I know claims to have captured some indistinct photographic anomalies while recently visiting this cemetery. Others have reported experiencing the sensation of someone standing directly behind them, only to turn around and discover that no one is there. If you happen to be in the area, and are considering visiting this particular cemetery yourself, please be respectful of the fact that Historical Cemetery #14 borders private property.

**Tillinghast Cemetery, Exeter, RI**

# Chapter 10

## Hidden Haunts of the Blackstone

The Blackstone River is a powerfully flowing fresh water river that begins in Worcester, Massachusetts, and flows southward, over the Slater Mill dam in Pawtucket, Rhode Island, into the Seekonk River in Providence, eventually flowing out into Narragansett Bay. The steadily moving water traverses approximately 45 miles and along this route, the fresh water begins mixing with salt water and becomes brackish.

The Blackstone River derives its present name from the Reverend William Blackstone, a contemporary of Roger Williams who established the first English settlement in Rhode Island in 1635, in what is now known as the Blackstone Valley. In 1793, Samuel Slater opened the Slater Mill in Pawtucket and the dam was constructed to power the mechanical spinning machines in the mill complex. By the mid-to-late 1830's, as the Industrial Revolution was well underway, dams had been constructed on practically every mile of the Blackstone River.

Along with its rich history, the Blackstone River is also known for numerous reports of unexplained ghostly sightings. Its history also contains elements of tragedies that have occurred over the years. It is because of this history and the reports of unexplained phenomena that Carl L. Johnson decided to incorporate the Blackstone River as part of the popular Ghost Tours he conducts at the Slater Mill site.

One such tragedy, which took place on Tuesday, August 18th in 1925, is the wreck of the pleasure steamboat Mackinac. The Mackinac had taken employees of Pawtucket's J. P. Coats Co. to a company outing in Newport. Carrying more than 670 passengers, the Mackinac was making its way out from Newport Harbor, on its way back to the Pawtucket River after a day's outing. About 15 minutes after the Mackinac left Newport Harbor, a boiler aboard the ship somehow exploded. It is believed this was due to a weakened wall. Within seconds, the Mackinac and its passengers were engulfed in a cloud of vapor. Some passengers jumped overboard and were later rescued. Many, however, were not so fortunate. Fifty-five individuals were killed in the disaster, or later died from injuries incurred in the explosion.

A makeshift holding center was set up in the train station at the border of Central Falls and Pawtucket. (That train station is still there to this day.) A crowd of ten thousand people thronged to the train station looking for survivors.

A contemporary newspaper relayed a gruesome account of The Mackinac Disaster:

Captain Charles E. Riggs, commanding officer at the hospital had summoned every available navy physician as well as priests and ministers from the naval vessels in the harbor as soon as the wounded victims began to come in. Inside the hospital two wards were prepared. So swiftly did the sufferers come that many were placed on the floors outside the wards. The majority of those who died at the naval hospital were in such bad shape, the physicians said that they could only try to make their last moments as painless as was medically possible.

"Please kill me, I'm suffering so," a brawny Pawtucket policeman pleaded to nurses. An hour later death relieved him from all pain. The officer, one of three killed, was so scalded that the skin on his hands hung in strips. His features were burned so black that he was barely recognizable.

Amid the moaning and screaming victims walked clergymen of all denominations giving spiritual aid. The more seriously injured were all in a separate room and it was here that the Catholic priests walked from cot to cot giving the last rites to some only seconds before death came.

The night of horror presented scores of pitiful sights. A girl whose life was despaired of cried out continually, asking why she should die.

In the first group of injured landed was a 10-year-old girl. As Patrolman Timothy Sullivan went to her side she held up her scalded arms and pleaded, "Please blow on them, they burn so."

~ *New York Times, New York, NY 20 Aug 1925*

The chief engineer of the tour boat Blackstone Valley Explorer, Ramon and his passengers have glimpsed the spectral images of a man, a woman, and what may perhaps be their little girl, walking together along the banks of the Blackstone River. These figures appear to be attired in clothes from the first quarter of the 20th Century. But when Ramon and others have called out to these forms, asking if they need help, they will consistently fade back into the shadows, and vanish from view.

Instances of phantom boats have also been reported. Vessels that seem strangely out of place and out of time have reportedly been seen gliding noiselessly along with the current of the Blackstone River, usually during the early evening hours. Occasionally dim spectral human figures can even be glimpsed riding within these phantom boats. However, these sightings tend to be very fleeting.

During a Ghost Tour led by Carl Johnson, which took place on an early evening in May of 2009, tour guide Karen Kaplin had an actual sighting of one of these mysterious phantom boats. Standing near the edge of the wall that borders the Blackstone River from Slater Mill, she suddenly called Carl's attention to a boat, gliding precariously close to the drop off of Pawtucket Falls.

"Is there supposed to be a boat out there?" she asked.

By the time Carl glanced over there, the boat was already gone. Because these phantom boats tend to appear mainly in the early evening hours (for reasons unknown), people on the Ghost Tours have also witnessed them.

Should you be fortunate enough to glimpse one of these boats, most likely at twilight, do not hesitate to try to snap a photo, take video footage or at least call somebody else over as a witness. These phantom boats tend to vanish quickly, and actual evidence captured of this phenomenon would be considered invaluable!

The unfortunate tragedy of poor Albert A. Jackson is yet another source for unexplained occurrences along the Blackstone. We do not know why on December 21, 1905 (the Winter Solstice) Mr. Jackson dared the strong current of the river, through the water in front of the Pawtucket Falls. Perhaps he was celebrating the holidays a little early that year, and may well have been inebriated. But upon doing so, his foot and leg became caught in a crevice. Try as he might he was unable to free himself and the current pounded him, continually forcing his head under the freezing water.

It was not until the next morning that the lifeless body of Albert Jackson was discovered bobbing in the Blackstone River. A Pawtucket citizen named Robert Byrne went up to the rocks below the falls in a boat and, getting upon a ledge, crawled up to the rock that held Jackson's body in place. The swirl of the water brought the body partly to the surface allowing Byrne to pass a noose line over the shoulders. Another boat positioned above the falls held the line in place, allowing the use of an oar as a lever to pry the body loose.

Officials determined the left foot had been carried under the rock and the pressure of the water kept it there. A block and tackle had to be lowered from off of the Main Street Bridge to retrieve his body.

But curiously and sadly, Main Street Bridge has been the site of numerous suicides.

Carl Johnson speculates, "If somebody wants to leave this life, there must be an easier way. However, I think some people have become despondent, and the river seems to call to them."

The last instance as of this writing was said to have occurred in 2004. A lady, having been informed by her physician that her husband was terminally ill and about to die, ended her own life by jumping off the Main Street Bridge into the Pawtucket Falls. By a sad twist of fate, her husband later recovered his health.


The Blackstone Valley also happens to be prone to a lot of storms, particularly hurricanes. The geography of the Blackstone Valley is actually a big hill, which begins in Providence, climbs up through Pawtucket, Centrals Falls and Cumberland, topping off at Precious Blood Cemetery in Woonsocket. That is its highest point of elevation.

Now, one storm that came raging through the Blackstone Valley was Hurricane Diane in August of 1955. Hurricane Diane flooded Precious Blood Cemetery so severely that the western embankment was washed away, exposing coffins. Many of those coffins slid down the embankment, went out into the Blackstone River, and were borne away with the current. One of those coffins actually ended up lodged in the raceway at Slater Mill! Some made it all the way out to East Providence and Narragansett Bay, eventually ending up being washed away in the Atlantic Ocean. Some were recovered, but to this day, some bodies were re-interred in Precious Blood Cemetery, and nobody really knows if they are in the right graves. A woman whose father was a police officer on duty then said it really cannot be described how horrific that was, seeing coffins strewn on lawns, many with the lids open.

An urban legend is attached to this true account, almost too amazing to be true. It even made the local newspapers at the time. The story of a married couple residing in Cumberland, Rhode Island tells us of the wife who had become terminally ill, and to make matters worse, discovered that her husband was having an affair with another woman. Understandably hurt and resentful, she told her husband, "You know, if I should die before you, and you marry that woman, I'll come back to haunt you!" Well, as fate would have it, she did pass on prior to her husband, and was interred in Precious Blood Cemetery. Subsequently, the man did indeed marry the other woman. And in that great flood from Hurricane

Diane, the wife's coffin was one of those that washed downhill into the Blackstone River and floated down with the current, finally coming to rest on her former husband's front lawn, with the lid of the coffin wide open. According to eyewitnesses, one of the deceased wife's arms was raised, as if in an accusatory manner.

Aside from these profound events in history, it has also been speculated that the the powerful current of the Blackstone River, combined with its high mineral content within the rushing waters (including silicone, mica, gold, and quartz) may perhaps provide an energy source for some of the paranormal activity occurring within the vicinity of the Blackstone Valley.

In 2008, The Atlantic Paranormal Society investigated part of the Blackstone Valley region when an episode of the hit TV series "Ghost Hunters" was filmed at the Slater Mill historic site. TAPS founders Jason Hawes and Grant Wilson did seemingly find some evidence of a child spirit within the water wheel pit of the Wilkinson Mill, through communication with a K2 Meter. The huge water wheel is of course powered by the flowing currents of the Blackstone River. Their communication with the spirit, who claimed to be a young boy named Eduard, was so consistent that Jason invited the spirit to come home with him to be a playmate for his 8-year-old daughter.

In closing, I would like to mention a few interesting facts concerning about Reverend William Blackstone, after whom the Blackstone River is named. Having relocated from Boston, Reverend Blackstone was the first white settler to make his home along the banks of what was formerly known as the Pawtucket River. He rode a white bull instead of a horse. And, he introduced rose bushes and the Yellow Sweeting variety of apples to Rhode Island, which were not indigenous to the Colonies.

Reverend William Blackstone died May 26, 1675, at the age of 80 years. Ironically, his mortal remains seem to have been "misplaced." When his grave was in the process of being relocated some years ago, his bones were placed in a box and nobody seems to remember who had them last. They were going to be interred with a monument to the Reverend William Blackstone. Today the monument is there in

Cumberland, but his remains are not. They may be stored in a garage or someplace else now long forgotten. If we cannot locate Jimmy Hoffa, then perhaps neither will we find Reverend William Blackstone. But please, local residents, check your attics before throwing anything out. We would appreciate it if the Reverend William Blackstone was returned as soon as possible.

Nether River

By Carl L. Johnson (Composed and recited for Mills and Mysteries: A Ghostly Experience!)

Looking down the Blackstone River,

Causes me to quake and shiver,

When I think it might deliver,

Those sad souls whose lives were claimed.

Ceaselessly I see it flowing,

With the chill wind soft blowing,

And I pause here never knowing,

Of those lost ones left unnamed.

Moonlight on the weather dreaming,

Carried by the water's streaming...

Spirits flown that now are dreaming,

Of this River never tamed!

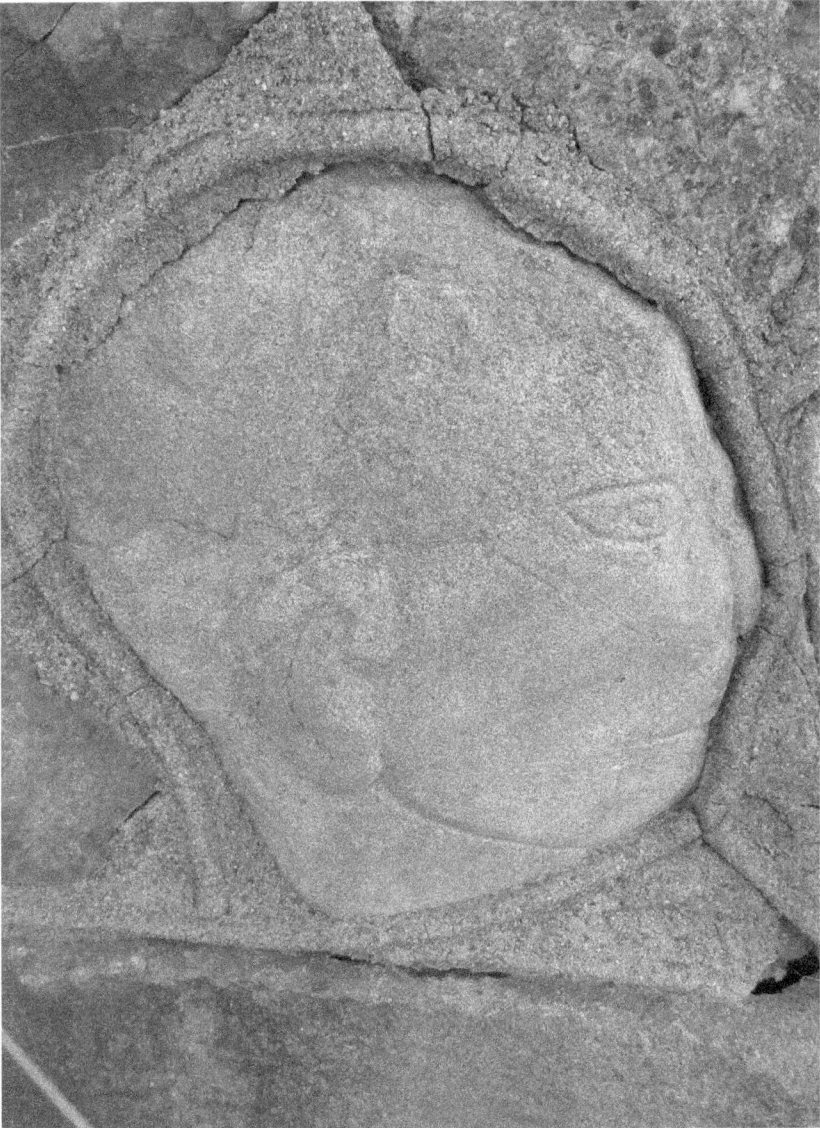

**Mysterious face carved in Blackstone River wall.**

**Carl Johnson leading a tour**

# Chapter 11

## Ashland, MA

New England Anomalies Research was first contacted about the Ashland case by our close friend and colleague, David Manch. David was a senior member of New England Paranormal at the time. He and two of his other team members were involved with an ongoing investigation at a private residence in Ashland, Massachusetts. David certainly had some interesting observations to share with us about this case, and from all indications, they were dealing with some serious issues at this house.

In fact, the activity they'd documented so far seemed to indicate that a malevolent presence might be at work. Their client was a man in his early thirties named Michael Rochford who lived alone in a one-story house nearby to his parents. However, because of recent mysterious disturbances, he no longer felt comfortable staying in the house by himself.

According to David, a number of bizarre accidents had occurred within Michael's house over the last year. It began when Michael had suddenly lost consciousness right after he'd been taking a shower. While this of course could have been an accidental slipping in the shower stall, or some other natural explanation, Michael seemed to feel that this may have been done deliberately to him by an unseen presence. Also, a roommate who'd been staying at the house had undergone a sudden and radical personality change. Even though he and Michael were the best of friends, his roommate had even attacked Michael and, allegedly, had no recollection of the incident afterward. Along with the personality change, Michael claimed that his friend's eyes had suddenly gone black, just before he'd flipped out and attacked him.

Supposedly no one was able to live comfortably in the house for very long, which caused Michael to begin wondering if some sort of unseen hostile presence might be cohabiting with him. Even his parents agreed that the house itself seemed to have an unnatural feel to it whenever they visited. Michael himself eventually tried taking some action by placing a wooden cross upon a chair in one of the spare bedrooms, and hanging rosary beads above it. He'd then left the house for a period of time, and when he'd returned, he found the chair overturned with one of the legs broken, and the wooden cross upon the floor in an upside-down position. The rosary beads were also lying upon the floor even though Michael swore that no one else could have gotten into the house while he'd been gone, with absolutely no signs of a forced entry. It was shortly after this incident that Michael had decided to seek intervention, and he'd contacted New England Paranormal.

David had been accompanied by Bill Norris and Michelle Mowry on the initial investigation, which had taken place that past January of 2011. Almost immediately after being welcomed into the house by Michael and his father Buddy, both David and Bill felt overcome with a heaviness feeling, although Michelle was not affected. A few minutes after the team had entered, they noticed that the lights briefly appeared to dim. Without warning, the client, Michael, suddenly ran from the house and vomited on his front lawn.

Undoubtedly the most peculiar thing that David experienced during their investigation was when he happened to glance over at Michael and his dad Buddy. Buddy's face suddenly seemed to "blur." According to David, it was the strangest thing he'd ever witnessed during a paranormal investigation.

The client had also recently invited a psychic over to investigate his house. This psychic had told him that there were multiple spirits present in the house, and one malevolent female spirit in particular, who was perhaps a former occupant.

David concluded his report to us by saying, "The client was somewhat emotionally taxed, but I am fairly confident an entity was present that was feeding off of that stress, and this could have been the result of a cursed doll (my personal theory on the case)."

Having worked closely with Sandra and myself before, and knowing our experience with extreme cases, David asked if we'd be interested in doing a follow up with Michael, including a religious house clearing. Sandra and I agreed, along with other members of New England Anomalies Research. The next step would be to contact the client that David had referred to us, take care of the necessary paperwork, and then set up a date for our visit.

As it turned out, Sandra and I had been scheduled to give a paranormal presentation at the local library in Ashland on a Saturday afternoon in March. Since the client's home was located in relatively the same vicinity, we decided to kill two birds with one stone, and arranged to swing by to perform the house clearing right after our library presentation.

It was a full house at the library that afternoon, with people coming from the local community who were interested in hearing our talk on the paranormal. Our presentation of course also included video of actual paranormal phenomena, and listening to examples of EVP from many places we'd investigated over the years. Sandra and I were pleased to have N.E.A.R. members Lisa Dowaliby, Nathan Mayer and Richard Palasiewicz in attendance that afternoon, especially since they would be assisting us with our client following the presentation.

Our lecture on the paranormal was very much a success, and we remained for nearly an additional hour taking personal questions from audience members, as well as a book signing. When we were finally ready to leave, it turned out that we still had enough time to stop for a bite to eat before arriving at our client's house.

Out in the parking lot, Richard Palasiewicz graciously offered to drive. As we were about to hop into Richard's SUV, Sandra asked, "Anyone have any suggestions as to where we might stop for sustenance?"

Richard replied, "There's actually a pizza joint right in the center of Ashland. We can stop there on our way to the client's house."

Everyone agreed that pizza sounded great, and we all climbed into the van, with myself riding shotgun. Along the way, Richard casually mentioned to us, "You know, guys, I just hope having pizza doesn't give me indigestion. Sometimes it just doesn't agree with me. Pizza and I tend to fight each other."

Lisa teasingly told him, "Oh, no, Richard! We're not gonna have to deal with that tonight, are we?"

Nathan suggested, "We can always stop somewhere else for fast food if you'd rather, Richard."

"Nah, really guys, I'll be fine," Richard assured us.

After dining heartily at the local pizza restaurant in preparation of the long night ahead of us, we all set off for our client's home, which was about twenty minutes away.

With Richard once again behind the wheel, we went over our basic protocol for the evening. Because the house we were going to had already been investigated by David and his team, we were not planning on conducting a full investigation ourselves. Instead, we intended to interview the client and then record data throughout the house, while Sandra and I performed the religious clearing.

Sandra said, "And hopefully, if all goes according to plan, we'll be out of there and on our way home at a reasonable hour."

In the back seat, Nathan asked, "Are there any other details we should be aware of, before we arrive at the client's house?"

Sandra replied, "Just that David mentioned a slight gas leak in the basement. He and his team members checked it out though, and they said it wasn't at a dangerous level."

I added, "Also, David mentioned that at one point while he was at the house, Michael Rochford and his father were seated on the sofa, and he noticed that Michael's father's face was starting to 'blur' in some mysterious way."

"Really?" asked Lisa. "That sounds freaky. Do you suppose it could have been a trick of the light?"

"Well, possibly," I said. "But according to David, he was directly facing both Michael and his dad at the time. And David is extremely objective, so I tend to trust his judgment. But we'll just have to see what we ourselves experience when we get there."

We were only about fifteen minutes away from our client's house while discussing these things, when Richard suddenly let out a groan, and said, "Uh-oh."

Concerned, I asked, "Richard, what is it? Are you alright?"

"Not really," he replied. "I think the pizza I ate has just caught up with me."

Indeed, I noticed that Richard was suddenly looking a little green around the gills, so to speak. In the backseat, Lisa said, "Oh, no, Richard! I guess you really shouldn't have indulged in that pizza after all."

Sandra asked, "Are you going to be okay, Richard? Do you need one of us to take over driving?"

Richard answered, "No... I just have to find a bathroom, really quick. Like, pronto!"

Unfortunately, there were no gas service stations or even fast food places within our immediate sight. But since we were now only several minutes away from our client's house, we were all hoping that Richard would be able to endure the remainder of the short distance. (Richard himself was especially hoping this!)

Relief was almost in sight as Richard turned his van onto the client's street, and kept up a steady speed. Sandra said encouragingly, "We're almost there, Richard."

Lisa added, "See if you can hang on just a few minutes longer."

"Oh, believe me, I'm doin' my best to hang on!" Richard said through his gritted teeth.

Finally, we arrived at the house, and pulled into the driveway. With his left hand already on the door handle as he shut off the engine, Richard announced, "I'm afraid I'm not gonna have much time for introductions, folks."

"That's okay, we'll take care of that," I assured him. "You just do what you have to do."

Without first bothering to unpack our equipment, we quickly disembarked from Richard's van, and hastily made our way to the front entrance door of the client's home. We were welcomed in by Michael Rochford, a young man with short dark hair and a somewhat stocky build, who appeared to be in his late twenties or early thirties. His parents were also there to help with the interview.

Richard quickly introduced himself, and added, "First order of business, do you have a bathroom I could use?"

Michael replied, "Sure, it's right down the hall there, on the left."

"Thanks," said Richard, and instantly dashed down the hallway.

Michael called after him, "Just watch the seat in there, it's a little loose." But Richard was already in the bathroom with the door closed.

I explained, "It's been a long trip, and he ate something that didn't quite agree with him."

"Oh," said Michael, nodding. "I understand."

I then held out my hand and said, "By the way, I'm Keith of New England Anomalies Research. This is my wife Sandra, and our team members Lisa and Nathan. And you've already just met Richard."

"Nice to meet you all," said Michael, as we all shook hands. "And these are my parents, Buddy and Cheryl Rochford."

Michael's parents seemed to be a very pleasant, middle-aged couple. In fact, I immediately thought that Buddy bore somewhat of a resemblance to actor Martin Sheen in his younger years, while Cheryl was a slim, attractive woman. Michael then invited us into the parlor to begin our interview.

After we'd set up our recording devices, I asked our client to state his name. "Michael Rochford, son of Buddy and Cheryl Rochford," he said.

I asked Michael, "Now what's your religion?"

"Roman Catholic," he replied.

"And how old are you?" I asked.

"I'm thirty-one now," he said.

Sandra said, "This is somewhat personal, but I have to ask if anyone involved is currently taking any prescribed medication, or under a doctor's care." The answer was negative.

I asked Michael, "So, how long now have you been experiencing activity in this house?"

"In this house? Pretty close to almost two years," he said. "I would say it started a few months after I moved in. I bought the house three years ago now in July, and I didn't really notice anything for the first couple of months. The first thing that might have happened…I'd just gotten out of the shower, and the next thing I knew I was unconscious in the back of the shower house. My friend was picking me up for work that morning, and he was the one who helped me out. So I don't know if I slipped or was pushed or whatever, but I really didn't think anything of it at the time."

Lisa asked, "What was the next thing you noticed?"

Michael replied, "Well, then I had a roommate move in, and he was living in the room down at the end of the hall, and he literally started acting crazy. He was smashing pictures over people's heads, and you would talk to him, and it was like his eyes weren't even there. He became extremely violent to the point that he was attacking me in the middle of the night while I was sleeping, punching me."

Buddy added, "And then he'd be completely normal again, after he came out of it."

Lisa commented, "Wow, it sounds like things got pretty violent during these episodes."

I asked, "You never noticed any personality changes in him before this?"

"No, never" said Michael. "But it got to the point that I had to kick him out; he was so violent."

"Did he have any sort of sleep disorder that you knew of?" I asked.

"None that I'm aware of," said Michael. "And then right after I kicked him out, things started happening to me a lot."

Sandra asked, "What sort of things were happening to you?"

Michael replied, "I started hearing growls, and hearing my name called a lot."

As if on cue, a low growling sound was suddenly heard quite audibly within the parlor. Lisa glanced up and asked, "Did anyone else just hear that?"

Apologetically, Richard said, "That was just my stomach again. Sorry, guys."

We all broke into laughter again, and Sandra clarified for the recording, "Not an EVP."

Lisa said, "Gees, Richard, do you need to use the bathroom again??"

"Naw, I'm all set for now," Richard said with a casual wave. "No emergency this time."

Continuing with the interview, I asked Michael, "Now, you were saying that you've heard things audibly here?"

"Yeah," said Michael. "I've heard knocking, growls. I've heard my name called. I've heard voices."

I asked, "What do the voices say, other than calling your name?"

Michael said, "Um, it's hard to distinguish. It sounds a lot of times like whispering conversations."

"Any particular time of the day or night?" I asked.

"Yeah, it's usually around three in the morning when things start picking up," Michael replied. "You know, two-thirty, three in the morning. And whenever I sleep on the couch, like clockwork I wake up at three in the morning, and there will usually be something going on. A lot of times, I'll hear footsteps running up the basement stairs really loud, but they always stop just when they get to the top. Also, it sounded like something was always walking around up in the attic. You know, heavy-footed. And sometimes there will be knocks on my outside doors, and no one will be there."

Nathan asked, "How many knocks in a row will there be?"

"I think it's usually three in a row," said Michael. "Yes, I'm pretty sure it's three."

Cheryl asked, "Is that significant?"

I replied, "Well, it can be. We like to try and establish if there's any numerical pattern to the activity."

"Oh, I see," said Cheryl.

Sandra asked Michael's parents "Have either of you experienced anything in this house?"

Both Buddy and Cheryl claimed that although they hadn't experienced any actual activity in the house, they both felt uncomfortable there. Buddy claimed that he disliked being in the house alone for any length of time, and Cheryl absolutely refused to enter the house alone.

Lisa asked, "How about other family members?"

Michael said, "My younger brother who's going to be a senior in high school experienced something. We hadn't told him anything about what was going on here, because we didn't want to upset him. Well, one day he was mowing the lawn. And when he went by the spare bedroom, he claims he saw a dark figure with red eyes looking out the window at him."

Buddy added, "Then right after seeing that, he was attacked by bees right outside the house."

"Yeah," said Michael. "Right after seeing it, he got stung by about twenty bees. Ironically, he'd never been stung in his life before then."

Sandra asked Michael, "What was the next thing you experienced?"

Michael replied, "Well, at first there were a lot of weird noises and stuff, but nothing really malicious. Then one morning last September, I'd just woken up, and I suddenly couldn't even move my right leg. The EMT's had to come and take me to the hospital. And I wound up being in the hospital for three months."

Lisa asked, "Three months? What was wrong?"

Michael replied, "They said I had some rare blood infection. And I basically had to learn to re-walk and everything. And when we got back and we came in the house, the feeling was just awful. So I remember, we put a chair in the far end room with a crucifix on it, and rosary beads hung over it. My dad and I came back two days later, and we found the chair was pushed all the way out of the room."

Buddy said, "We couldn't explain it, because nobody else had a key to this house."

"What did you do then?" I asked.

Michael said, "Well, my dad put the chair back in the far bedroom the way it was before, with the cross set on it and rosary beads hanging over it. And when we came back a day later, this time we found the chair all smashed in the hallway, with the crucifix upside-down leaning against the wall. And the rosary beads were on the floor in the bedroom."

Nathan asked, "So what happened then?"

Michael said, "Well, after that was when we had a couple of investigations done. David came with his group, and they got a couple of EVP's that were direct responses to questions. One said, 'Get out of here!'

The other one said, 'Come,' when he asked 'Should we go in the other room?'"

Sandra said, "David mentioned to us that you also recently had a psychic visit this house, is that correct?"

Michael replied, "Yes, that's correct. She said that there are multiple spirits here, probably from an Algonquin Indian burial ground on the property. But she also said that there's a dominant spirit of a woman here, that comes and goes through a 'portal' that's in the bedroom at the end of the hallway. I'll show you that later. The psychic said that she may be the spirit of a woman who lived here before. The woman's son actually stopped by here once, but he refused to enter the house when I invited him in."

Lisa commented, "Hmmm... that's certainly interesting. Did he mention ever having experienced anything in this house?"

"No, he didn't mention anything to me about that. He seemed in a hurry to leave," said Michael.

Sandra said, "As I recall, David also mentioned that there was some history of an antique doll?"

Buddy Rochford instantly said, "Oh, yes, the doll. Tell them about the doll, Mike."

Michael said, "Yeah, well, my parents live right down the street, and my uncle also used to live there years ago, until he became a priest. And as a priest, he went to Spain and brought back an antique little doll for my younger sister, when she was about, what, one or two at the time, Dad?"

Buddy said, "Yeah, I think she was two."

"At first, my younger sister became very attached to the antique doll," said Michael. "And she'd sleep with it every night. But after a while, she started waking up with scratches on her face. Not only that, but she said the doll was talking to her at night. So after that she became really scared of it."

Richard commented, "I don't blame her."

Buddy added, "She would put the doll face down every night. And every morning it would be sitting upright."

I asked, "Did she have a name for this doll?"

Michael said, "My sister called it 'Gaga.' That was the name she made up for it."

"Where is that doll now?" I asked.

Buddy replied, "We got rid of it. We threw it into an incinerator."

Sandra and I shared a quick glance with each other.

Nathan asked, "And did the activity stop, after you got rid of the doll?"

"Yeah, it seemed to," said Michael. "As I said, my uncle was a priest, so he came to bless the house. But some time afterward, he ended up killing himself, by jumping off a bridge. It all tied in together."

"He jumped off a bridge??" asked Richard in shocked surprise.

Buddy said, "Yes, he did. And no one really knew why he did it."

Michael added, "Yes, and that was about two years ago now."

"Do you know which bridge that was?" I asked.

"I don't," said Michael. "I know it was in Rhode Island. Maybe either the Newport Bridge or the Jamestown Bridge."

Lisa asked, "Were you in touch with him at all at the time?"

Michael replied, "No, he pretty much stayed away from us after the house blessing. I think he'd originally gone to Costa Rica to learn Spanish. And then after that he went straight to Spain, and stayed abroad for a few years. And it was soon after he finally came back, that he ended his life."

As our interview with the family was concluding, Sandra asked Michael, "What would you like to see accomplished from our visit here tonight?"

Michael said, "I want this place to be livable again. As it is, I'm paying for a house that I'm not even living in." Michael was adamant that he wanted the negative activity in his house to stop.


Immediately after the interview, Michael, Buddy and Cheryl gave us a tour of the entire house, which did not take long. As David had previously told us, the atmosphere of the house did seem quite gloomy, mainly due to the low lighting. In the far bedroom at the end of the hallway, Michael showed us the broken chair that had allegedly been damaged by an unseen presence, and the wooden cross that had reportedly been found in an upside-down position.

I told Michael, "We'll be sure to pay special attention to this room while we're conducting the blessing."

"Thanks, I'd sure appreciate that," he said. "I have a very uneasy feeling about this room in particular."

Sandra and I began our spiritual clearing of the house in the basement. Both Nathan and Richard were documenting the process on video, while Lisa was recording on audio. Michael also accompanied us, while his parents remained upstairs. Recalling that David had mentioned that there had been a slight gas leak in the basement, I asked Michael about this. He informed us that it was only a slight problem, and that he'd soon have it taken care of.

Sandra and I recited an "Our Father" and conducted a thorough blessing of the basement, which included praying out loud for any lost or wandering spirits to be conveyed to their proper abode, on the authority of Jesus Christ. Before leaving the basement, I also anointed the windows and the doorways with blessed oil, while Sandra liberally sprayed holy water about the basement.

Back upstairs, we made our way as a group down the hallway, stopping in each room with Sandra and I reciting chosen Scripture passages, as well as anointing the doors and windows with blessed oil and water.

We then entered the far bedroom. Because this was the room in which the psychic had reportedly sensed the existence of a portal, I made certain to pay special attention to the wording I used when praying, and to the anointing of this room.

At the time, I thought it may have been my imagination, but it seemed to me that Michael appeared to be somewhat uncomfortable in the room with us while we were blessing it. However he remained silent, and did not voice any objections to what we were doing.

We concluded by blessing the attic, the kitchen area and the parlor, again anointing all access ways. I also said a prayer of protection for each of the family members as well as our team members, and anointed their foreheads with blessed oil. Sandra in turn said a prayer of protection for me, and anointed my forehead.

When the clearing was done, all three members of the Rochford family told us that the atmosphere within the house did feel considerably lighter. We spent some time explaining to them that much of maintaining the positive atmosphere within the house was now up to them... especially Michael, who would be the one moving back in.

Both Sandra and Lisa stressed to Michael just how important it was to create a positive environment for himself while living there. Lisa especially advised him about not allowing himself to be victimized, and of taking control over his situation. Sandra and I also advised Michael on the importance of positive relationships, and of trying not to become isolated. I encouraged Michael, Buddy and Cheryl to remain in contact with us, and to let us know how things were going.

Michael and his parents expressed that they were extremely grateful for us having come to the house to help them, and assured us that they'd stay in touch. Buddy placed a hand on his son's shoulder, and asked, "Well, Mike, do you think you'll be giving this place another try?"

"That's my plan," said Michael. "Hopefully things will be a lot better now. It feels so much lighter in here already."

As the family was again thanking us and wishing us a safe trip back home, Buddy humorously added, "And Richard, make sure you stay away from that pizza from now on."

"Oh, don't worry, I've learned my lesson about not mixing pizza and investigations in the same night!" said Richard.

We all shared a laugh, and left that evening on a positive note.


While we were on our way home, Lisa mentioned to me, "By the way Keith, did you catch the look on Michael's face when you were blessing that bedroom where the broken chair was?"

"I kind of caught his expression out of the corner of my eye, and I sensed some hostility, but I didn't really get a good look at him," I said. "Why do you ask?"

Lisa said, "Well, I was looking right at him, and from the look in his eyes, he seemed like he was about to flip out and start becoming violent. I didn't know if he was about to attack you, or what!"

"Well, thankfully he didn't," I said. "But one thing that David mentioned he experienced, but that we didn't, was Buddy Rochford's face suddenly blurring. It didn't seem to happen to anyone else, either."

Sandra said, "I'd imagine that was probably a one-time occurrence. Too bad David didn't catch it on video when it happened."

I said, "But, I've actually witnessed this phenomenon occur myself."

"You have?" asked Nathan.

"Yes, years ago, back when I was a teenager," I said.

Lisa asked, "Wasn't it freaky what they were saying about that doll, that the uncle who was a priest brought over from Spain?"

Richard said, "Yeah, and then he wound up committing suicide by jumping off of one of the big bridges!"

Sandra said, "The doll probably had some sort of attachment to it when he bought it. And by the way, it's considered dangerous to burn a cursed object."

"It is?" asked Richard.

I explained, "Yes, because it could possibly cause retaliation. So when they mentioned that they'd thrown the doll into an incinerator, we were wondering if that may have added to some of their problems."

The subject of our conversation then returned to some good natured ribbing of Richard and his digestive problems of earlier that evening. Lisa told him, "Your favorite food was obviously fighting you tonight, Richard!"

"Yeah, it was," he agreed. "Now I wish that we'd just stopped at a local coffee shop, or some other place."

Nathan said, "Next time Richard, you'll just have to let me suggest where we should stop. I'll be sure to choose some place a lot safer for you."

With a laugh, Richard said, "Alright, alright, next time I'll just have to listen to Nathan!"

Throughout the next couple of weeks, as time allowed, we meticulously went through our video footage and audio recordings from Ashland. However, we did not find anything in the way of paranormal evidence, not even so much as a minor EVP. Whatever spirit force had allegedly been tossing furniture about the house and wreaking other havoc had apparently not been active on the night that we were there.

Hopefully the clearing that Sandra and I performed would be effective, and the advice which our team members had given Michael would have a positive effect on him.

On a comedic note, within the week following our trip to Ashland, Lisa somehow managed to find a photo of an outdoor parade where someone wore a large slice of pizza costume... and directly beside them someone was costumed as a toilet! The two characters were obviously dancing together in the parade.

Lisa posted this picture on Facebook for all of us to see, knowing how much Richard and the rest of us would all appreciate the significance. Sandra and I sure had a hearty laugh over it, and I asked Sandra, "How the heck did Lisa manage to find this??"

Sandra replied, "Leave it to Lisa, and she'll find a way."


Since we did not hear from Michael Rochford for the next couple of months, we assumed that this was a good sign. We of course hoped that the house clearing we'd conducted was having a positive, lasting effect, and that Michael was following through on our advice.

Several weeks later, however, we heard from David that Michael was complaining that some paranormal activity was once again starting to pick up in his house. By summertime, Michael also contacted us again, and informed us that because of the increased activity he'd once again found it necessary to move out of his house. He was also asking if we could get back up to Ashland sometime soon, and perform another house clearing.

David also informed us that in the interim since we'd been there, Michael had invited yet another paranormal research team to investigate his house. Fortunately, it was a team with which we were very well acquainted: the New England Center for the Advancement of Paranormal Science (N.E.C.A.P.S.), run by our mutual friend Michael J. Baker.

Although N.E.C.A.P.S. was an excellent paranormal research team, they tended to take a strictly scientific approach to their investigations, and Michael Rochford obviously felt that he also needed spiritual intervention. Sandra and I therefore agreed to arrange for a return visit to Ashland, Massachusetts.

Because of our caseloads, combined with work and family obligations, the soonest we could arrange for a return trip would be mid-to-late August. Finally, we were able to schedule a return visit to the Ashland house for Saturday, August 20th. Unfortunately, neither Lisa nor Richard would be available to join us this time. But we did have N.E.A.R. members Kim Frye, Nathan Mayer, Valerie Moskowitz, David Grist, plus Jeanine and Daniel Calkin joining us this time, and we could certainly rely upon all of them to be competent investigators.

When we arrived at Michael Rochford's house, his parents Buddy and Cheryl were again there with him waiting to greet us, just like the last time. They welcomed us in, and we introduced Kim, Valerie, Dan and Jeanine to them. They of course remembered Nathan and Sandra and I from our previous visit.

Nathan said, "So, Michael, I understand that the activity here has picked up again."

"Yes, it has," said Michael. "In fact, I haven't been living here for months."

Taking in our surroundings, it was immediately apparent that the interior of the house was just as dimly lit as it was during our previous visit, creating an overall gloomy atmosphere. Somehow, the feeling of unwholesomeness within the house seemed even more pervasive than before.

After the Rochford's had given us a tour of the house for the benefit of our members who had never been there before, we all congregated in the parlor to interview Michael and his parents. I began by asking,

"Michael, could you give us an overall review of what's taken place here since our last visit here?"

Michael replied, "Well, as you know, several months ago this place was made unlivable for me, because of everything that was going on here. I had this place investigated by New England Paranormal, and they also experienced some things here. Then you guys came, and everything was great for a while. I moved back in, and things were fine for three or four weeks. Then it was on a Thursday night, I was here just watching TV, and I thought I heard footsteps and a couple of voices, but I didn't think too much of it. Then on that Saturday, I was here with my friend, and we both saw a shadow dart down the hallway. And then we heard loud bangs coming from my bedroom. So we both went in there to check it out. Then while we were both in there, my friend was standing about three or four feet away from me, looking at me. And all of a sudden he saw me just get picked up and pulled back about ten feet, and slammed up against the wall! So we got outta here, and I haven't been back since, except for when Michael Baker and his team came."

Sandra asked, "So you haven't been here since April, correct?"

"Yeah, it's been since April," said Michael. "But it was the night before Easter that I actually got attacked."

I asked, "Now, your friend who witnessed the activity with you, has he been back here since?"

Michael said, "Not since he came to the investigation with Michael Baker. He won't come back, not after that night. He said he was bedridden for about seven days."

"Really?" I asked. "What happened to him?"

Michael replied, "He said it was a sudden back spasm, something that never happened before. He couldn't even move. So after that, he didn't dare come back to this house." Michael lowered his head and added, "In fact, I could write a list of friends who won't even come to my house now. They've all heard or seen something."

David Grist said, "I understand that you had a psychic here, and that she said there's a portal in that bedroom down the hall."

"Yes, that's correct," said Michael.

I asked, "Now, again, what spirits did she mention?"

Michael said, "She actually mentioned a multitude of spirits, especially with all of this being Native American land, which it is. She also mentioned the woman who was the mother of the son I bought the house from. But when I met the woman's son, he wouldn't come in. He wanted to leave all his furniture here."

With a light hearted laugh, Kim asked, "And that didn't tip you off at all?"

"No, not at the time," Michael replied humorously.

David asked, "Now what have you actually seen here? You've seen shadow figures?"

"Yeah," said Michael. "I've seen a large black mass going up and down the hall several times. I've seen a chair that was moved straight across the room in there. My original roommate, I tried to talk to him. His eyes... it was like they weren't even his eyes at all. I tried to reason with him, but it was like he wasn't even there. He'd have sudden outbursts, he was picking up pictures, and smashing them over my other friends' heads. He was totally violent and out of control for no reason. And once he moved out of the house, he was back to normal."

Kim asked, "Have you also experienced feeling violent?"

Michael replied, "No, but I've dealt with heavy bouts of depression since he moved out. So it's nothing I've noticed, but other people might."

Kim asked, "Do you have any history of depression, or anything of that sort prior to getting into this house?"

"No," said Michael. "Not until I moved here, no,"

"Did you start having experiences as soon as you moved into this house?" asked Kim.

Michael said, "Not initially, I thought the house felt great when we bought it. Now a couple of times I've come in and got physically sick within five minutes. I had to go right back out and throw up. I felt nauseous and started sweating. A panic thing, or whatever."

Sandra asked, "Well, if we did an intervention like the one that we did when we were here in March, would you attempt to move back in again?

Or would you want to wait until N.E.C.A.P.S. finishes their research, and gives you some feedback. What would your plan be?"

"I'd try to move back in again, and see how it went," said Michael. "The house had a good feeling for at least three weeks, after your last visit here."

I said, "And you mentioned that the activity began starting up again right before Easter?"

"Yes, it was the Thursday before Easter," said Michael. "I was on the couch watching TV, and I thought I heard my name, but I didn't think anything of it. And I thought I heard a whispered conversation down the hall. I went to bed and didn't think anything of it. And then that Saturday night was the night I was here with my friend, and we saw the shadow way down the hall, heard the voices coming from my room, and I just got pissed and started yelling at it. It then grabbed me from behind and dragged me up against the wall."

I asked, "Do you ever talk to this entity, or these entities? Do you ever address them yourself?"

"The night I got thrown I did," said Michael. "I started swearing, and telling it to show itself. Next thing you know, I got tossed. I put the chair with the cross and the holy water on it. Both times I did that, it reacted."

"So that was Easter Holy Week," I said. "And that would have been Maundy Thursday that happened, correct? The day before Good Friday."

"It was Thursday that I heard something," said Michael. "And it was Saturday night that I was thrown against the wall. Come to think of it, that happened past midnight, so it was actually Easter Sunday, around one in the morning, when I got thrown."

Sandra said, "Michael, last time you mentioned that your uncle was a priest, and that he brought a doll over from Spain for your younger sister."

"Yeah, my uncle who committed suicide, by jumping off of a bridge," said Michael.

Jeanine asked. "Does anyone have any idea why he chose to end his life?"

Michael's dad Buddy shrugged and said, "We don't really know. I assume he was going through some sort of serious depression, but he didn't leave any suicide note or anything."

I then asked, "Michael, you haven't done any kind of divination, have you? Like Ouija boards, or anything like that?"

"No, I certainly wouldn't risk doing that," he said.

Dan said, "I recall something about you hearing loud footsteps, around the time that New England Paranormal was here."

"Oh yeah, the footsteps," said Michael. "We were in the spare bedroom with David, and four or five of us all heard the footsteps coming up the stairs. We were in the spare room at the end. It was right after the EVP said, 'Come to our room.' And within a couple of minutes we got very loud footsteps going up and down the hallway. The floor was just vibrating with the footsteps."

Sandra asked, "When N.E.C.A.P.S. was here, I assume they also conducted an EVP session, correct?"

"Yes, they did," said Michael.

Jeanine asked, "And what were the results of that EVP session?"

Michael replied, "Well, when Mike was here, we were all doing an EVP session in the room. And he had a couple of girls with headphones on listening with the microphone in there. And he started asking it religious questions. He asked if it had a problem with religious artifacts. And both girls at the same time heard it say, 'Hell, yes!' They both said it was crystal clear. Unfortunately, they didn't catch it on their recordings. But they swore they both heard it."

Sandra said, "Well, even an EVP session could possibly be construed as provocation."

Michael said, "Oh, they did try provoking it, to try getting a reaction from it."

Nathan asked, "And did that get a reaction?"

"Yeah, it sure did," said Michael. "At one point I felt a really hot hand grab my left arm. For about a week-and-a-half later I had a red hand print on my left arm. I remember I jumped up, thinking my friend grabbed me. But he was about five feet away on the other side of the bed, when we were doing the EVP session. I've still got the picture of a red hand print on my left arm, and I sent it to Mike, too. It felt really hot when it grabbed me."

It was now about ten PM, and we decided to commence with the house clearing. Our procedure went pretty much as it had the last time,

with Sandra and I conducting the actual clearing and our team members documenting the entire procedure. We began with the basement, and worked our way though each of the upstairs rooms including the attic, leaving the parlor for last. Again, I paid special attention to the bedroom at the end of the hallway, where the psychic had said there was a portal though which spirits were gaining access to the house.

When then requested that the entire family gather together in the parlor with us, where Sandra recited the Prayer to St. Michael:

"Saint Michael the Archangel, defend us in battle. May God rebuke him, we humbly pray, and do Thou, O Prince of the Heavenly Host – by the Divine Power of God – cast into hell Satan and all the evil spirits, who roam throughout the world seeking the ruin of souls. Amen."

Everyone in the room repeated "Amen" in unison.

Sandra concluded by reading Psalm 23 out loud, after which I anointed Michael's forehead with blessed oil. The deliverance prayer had fortunately not resulted any violent reaction on Michael's part.

When I asked Michael how he felt, he breathed a sigh of relief, and said that he felt as if a weight had been lifted from off of him. We of course also reminded Michael and his parents that they were welcome to contact us, and to keep us informed about how there were doing. "We'll be sure to keep in touch," Buddy assured us. Again, they expressed their gratitude for our intervention on their behalf.

Before we left, I told Michael, "Remember, your parents also have a God-given spiritual authority of protection over you as well. No matter how old you are Michael, your parents are still your parents."

The second blessing we conducted seemed to have a more lasting effect on Michael's house, since he was able to move back into it and live comfortably. The deliverance session also seemed to have personally helped Michael a great deal. He now had a better understanding of how to protect himself against psychic attack, and he also had the positive emotional support of his family.

**NEAR members filming on location**

# Chapter 12

## Haunted Tavern On Main

Located in the town of Chepachet, Rhode Island, the Tavern on Main certainly boasts a long and dramatic history. The name Chepachet itself is a Native American word meaning "Devil's Bag." Previously known as The Stagecoach Tavern, it was originally built in the mid-1700's, to accommodate travelers along the main stagecoach line leading from Providence into Massachusetts and Connecticut. Those travelers stopping off at the tavern could dine and find overnight lodging if they so desired, while stagecoach drivers could exchange their horses for fresh ones if need be.

In 1842, the tavern became the setting for a dramatic moment in Rhode Island history. Thomas Wilson Dorr, a Chepachet resident and prominent lawyer, was elected Governor of Rhode Island by the People's Party. The main issue of Governor Dorr's cause was to procure voting rights for non-property owners in the state of Rhode Island. When incumbent Governor Samuel King refused to relinquish his position, Governor Dorr called a convention of the general assembly, held in the tavern, on the Fourth of July, 1842. Governor King promptly responded with a general call to arms to put down what has historically known as the famous "Dorr's Rebellion." Governor Dorr's troops were stationed nearby, atop Acote's Hill (now a large cemetery bearing the same name). The night before the arrival of King's troops, Dorr and his troops, realizing they'd be hopelessly outnumbered, decided to withdraw to their "headquarters" at the tavern. They subsequently barricaded themselves inside. When King's troops did arrive, they began firing through the front door of the tavern. Horace Bordeen was struck in the thigh from a shot fired through the keyhole. Otherwise, there were no casualties aside from a cow, inadvertently shot and killed during the melee. Dorr's troops were eventually forced into surrendering.

The proprietor of the tavern at this time was Jedediah Sprague, who was forced to admit Governor King's troops into his establishment. Because supporters of Dorr's cause were continuing to stage minor demonstrations throughout Chepachet, King's troops decided to remain as uninvited guests of the tavern, taking full advantage of Sprague's "hospitality" throughout the summer months of 1842. A document dated from 1844 states that during their occupation, King's troops consumed 2,440 dinners, smoked 11,500 cigars, drank 34 flasks of liquor, 37 gallons of brandy, 29 gallons of West India rum, 24 bottles of cider, and 12 bottles of champagne. Unfortunately, Jedediah Sprague never received any monetary compensation for his wares.

During the latter part of the 19th century and continuing into the 21st century, the tavern (since renamed as Tavern on Main) has undergone many changes and seen various owners. It has served as a rather drab apartment building, a pub, a billiard parlor, and more recently as a restaurant with an adjoining bar. During renovations in 1998, the owners uncovered what turned out to be a surprise package of sorts, about a foot below the foundation. Wrapped in an oilcloth was a surprisingly well preserved sawed-off shotgun, upon which were inscribed the initials "FJW." Historical research revealed that this weapon would have belonged to Frederick J. Williams, employed as an armed guard by the Providence to Worcester stagecoach line in the early 1800's. Mr. Williams was a regular visitor to The Stagecoach Tavern, since this was one of his scheduled stops along the way.

With such a long and active history, it is not surprising that the tavern is also reputedly haunted… although the exact identity of whom or what may be haunting this establishment remains a matter of speculation. Patrons and wait staff alike have reportedly been lightly tapped either on the shoulder or the back of the neck by an unseen presence. Small items such as table settings have been known to suddenly turn up missing, only to reappear in unusual places. Upon one wall of the dining room hangs the framed, black and white photograph of an attractive yet forlorn looking woman attired in late 19th Century clothing. It is the spirit of this woman, said to be waiting for the return of her long lost lover, which is believed to haunt this particular section of the dining room. Also seen on occasion, the apparition of an older gentleman attired in what appears to be a military uniform, dating from sometime in the 1800's. However, he has yet to be identified.

Even more disconcerting is the occasional appearance of a mysterious "ghost child," the spirit of a young boy, perhaps five or six years old, wearing what appears to be long blue night shirt. Although the identity of this young boy is unknown, he has been briefly seen darting about in various locations in the tavern. This illusive spirit is usually glimpsed when the building is nearly deserted.

Growing up in the neighboring town of North Scituate, located to the west of Chepachet, I'd often heard rumors of the tavern being haunted. Recently Sandra and I, along with our team from New England Anomalies Research, decided to contact the present owners of Tavern on Main, and entertain the opportunity of a paranormal investigation. We were pleased to learn that they were extremely receptive to the idea. Since the set date of our investigation coincided with the Halloween season, a local TV news station would be covering our investigation as well. Besides Sandra and me, our team members participating in this investigation included my brother Carl, Chris Finch, and Russ Brisette. The five of us arrived at Tavern on Main shortly after the dining room had closed to the public for the evening, with the news crew arriving minutes later. The present owners welcomed us into the dining area, informing us that we'd have this area to ourselves for our investigation. A long-time resident of Chepachet and former employee at Tavern on Main, Eva also attended the gathering that evening.

After we'd discussed some of the décor of the dining room, during which I highly complimented the owners on the impressive display of antiques and collectibles adorning the walls and low overhead ceiling beams, we all sat down to chat with Eva and the owners. We talked a bit about the actual history of the building itself. They informed us that it was originally built as a two and a half story dwelling back in the early 1700's.

We then moved on to the subject of the ghosts that may, in fact, be haunting Tavern on Main. Eva immediately perked up, indicating that this was one of her favorite subjects, considering her familiarity of the tavern and its history.

"Oh, there's definitely at least three different spirits in here," she said without hesitation. "They've been seen and felt by a lot of people in this building over the years. One is the ghost of an older man, who wears an old fashioned military uniform, who's been seen in this room a few times. But nobody seems to know who he is."

When I asked Eva if she'd personally experienced anything unusual at the tavern, she replied that she'd been lightly pushed from behind by an unseen hand, although it felt like it was in a manner more playful than threatening. Further, many times she'd placed down various items such as table settings, only to have them wind up missing seconds later. Sometimes these items would never be found again.

Eva added, "There's also the ghost of a little boy who's sometimes been seen in different places in the building. He's reportedly been spotted a few times over there by the ladies room, although he's been seen in other places too. Those who see him always describe him as wearing a blue shirt."

Eva also relayed an incident that happened several years prior when a bartender named Ron, as he was closing the bar section for the night, had just piled all of the stools on top of the bar, per his usual routine. Ron then momentarily stepped out of the room to unlock one of the outer doors so the overnight cleaning crew could enter. When he returned only a matter of seconds later, each of the stools had been removed from off the bar and set back upright on the floor.

Eva explained, "There was no way humanly possible that anyone could have set the stools back down so quickly."

"No sound of any commotion when this happened?" I asked.

"No, no sound at all," said Eva.

We also discussed the case of an old upright piano once in a corner of the dining room that seemed to have a mind of its own. For some reason, only certain people at certain times would be able to play it. Otherwise it would remain unplayable. On at least one occasion, it even spontaneously began playing by itself, until one of the bartenders lifted the cover to the keys. The music then suddenly ceased. Although the old piano was eventually sold, it was apparently somewhat reluctant to go. At least twice when the previous owner would demonstrate it over the phone for prospective buyers, the keys would play just fine. However, when the prospective buyer would arrive, the keys refused to cooperate and would not play at all.

Eva also informed us, "We've had a couple of psychics here in the past, too."

When I inquired if the psychics divulged any significant information, Eva explained that they were able to identify two of the spirits haunting the Tavern on Main by name. The woman in the framed photograph on the wall was supposedly named either Ellen or Mary Elizabeth. When speaking of her, the staff now always refers to her as Mary Elizabeth. According to at least one of the psychics, Mary Elizabeth was once a guest at the tavern who used to sit at the particular booth over where her picture now hangs, waiting for her lover to return to her as he'd promised. Tragically, he never did return, and Mary Elizabeth eventually died, heartbroken and alone. Her lonely spirit still continues to keep vigil in that same corner booth, year after year, in the hopes that her lover will someday return to join her.

The little boy who is sometimes seen wearing a blue shirt is supposedly named William, although the reason his restless spirit haunts the tavern remains unknown. At least two other spirits, whose exact identities are also unknown, are said to haunt the dark recesses of Tavern on Main. One is the older man in uniform who has been seen in the dining area, nursing an injured left arm, presumably a war injury. The other is an unidentified older woman who simply sits in one of the chairs and observes people.

As a group, we then focused our attention on the framed photo of the woman, who is referred to as either "Ellen" or "Mary Elizabeth." While the news cameraman filmed a close-up of this photo, Eva explained that Mary Elizabeth is never malicious, but is simply mischievous at times.

"She'll just pull little pranks, like taking candy out of the candy dish when no one is looking," explained Eva.

Sandra commented, "She does have a very wistful expression in the picture, as if she actually could be waiting for her long lost lover to return."

NEAR member Chris asked, "But there's no actual verification of who this woman in the picture actually was?"

"I really don't know," replied Eva. "But I love that picture. I opened the frame up just recently, because she's my favorite, but there's no name or anything on the back of the photo."

Nearby on the same wall hung a framed photograph of a gentleman with a waxed mustache, looking as though it may have come from the same era as the woman's picture. Indicating this framed photograph, I asked Eva if anyone had any idea of the gentleman's identity.

"We're not sure who he is either," said Eva. "He could be a ghost, for all we know."

"He probably is by now," Carl suggested with dry humor.

Eva said, "Or maybe he could even be the soldier who we see, the older man. We don't know." Referring back to the portrait of the woman, Eva suggested to us, "If you talk to her, she might react to you."

"We'll keep that in mind," I assured her.

After the TV news crew had separately interviewed each member of our paranormal research team, we turned the dining room lights down low and began our investigation. Sandra soon began picking up some significantly high level readings while doing a sweep with the electromagnetic field detector she held. Also significant was that she happened to be in front of the corner booth, which is the very section of the room where most of the paranormal activity is said to occur. We quickly checked for nearby outlets or electrical sockets, to see if we could rule out any possibly electrical source which might be causing her EMF to spike. When we'd eliminated interference by fixtures, outlets, etc., I began snapping photos in the immediate area. In two of these photos, which I took within seconds of each other, an illumination of light appears to be emanating at the bottom from an unidentified source.

We next conducted an EVP session in the area of the corner booth, where the framed photograph of "Mary Elizabeth" adorns the wall. Although we captured no definite voices on audio tape during the session, about an hour into our investigation, Russ' camera suddenly began to totally malfunction. Being the "open-minded skeptic" in the group, he was particularly puzzled.

"I don't understand it," he said. "I've used this camera so many times with no problems, and I just put in fresh batteries. But I was only able to take two pictures, and then it completely stopped working, tonight of all nights."

The following morning, Russ was surprised to find that his camera was again in perfect working order.

Before the evening was over, local author and paranormal investigator Thomas D'Agostino and his wife Arlene Nicholson joined us, themselves having had multiple experiences at the tavern. In fact, Tom and Arlene actually had their wedding ceremony performed in the upstairs dining room, known as the Dorr Ballroom.

Tavern owner David Lumnah has set up a series of "haunted evenings" at Tavern on Main, during which Tom and Arlene give a lecture and present evidence of the paranormal. Their presentation includes a video showing what may be an illuminated figure moving from right to left in the dining room. In the video, a moving figure momentarily obscures the light on the wall as it passes by. This footage was taken by a local student, and Tom has been unable to find any rational explanation for the moving figure that appears on the video.

At the conclusion of each presentation, Tom and Arlene then lead patrons on a paranormal exploration through the tavern, utilizing cassette recorders, dowsing rods and heat sensitive equipment. Tom informed us that on one occasion while he and his wife Arlene were conducting an EVP session at the "haunted booth" in the dining room, the lights flickered on and off several times, seemingly in response to their questions.

At one point during the session, Tom asked, "Is there anyone here who would like to speak with us?" When he played back the audio tape, a voice could be heard asking, "Why?" Later, while Arlene was sitting in the bar area chatting with a friend, her drinking glass that was resting on the bar suddenly shattered, sending splinters of glass flying everywhere. Fortunately no one was seriously injured. However, when a crystal expert later analyzed the glass, he could find no natural explanation as to why it would have suddenly exploded the way it did.

Tom also mentioned to us about the young woman who was fatally shot in the tavern, on a chilly December night in 1973. It is believed by some long time patrons that her restless spirit is responsible for at least some of the ghostly phenomena happening at the tavern.

Although we were unable to determine exactly who is haunting Tavern on Main, or why our investigation did prove to be an interesting experience. Tom D'Agostino has since captured an EVP of a child's voice in the downstairs section, repeating a question he had just asked. When Tom asks, "Is it time to go to bed?" a voice on his recording can be heard saying, "time to go to bed." in a sing song, child-like way. Tom has also caught a woman's voice telling him to go to the bar, on two separate occasions.

We do feel some element is present that occasionally interferes with electrical appliances and equipment, and has the capability of relocating small objects. Also, the TV newscast of our investigation that aired on Halloween night did much to boost local interest in the tavern and its history. Based on recent accounts, the tavern's unseen inhabitants remain quite active as well.

Andrew Lake, founder of Greenville Paranormal Research, has also had his own experiences at Tavern on Main. On the evening of October 30th, 2007, Andrew was upstairs in the Dorr Ballroom when, to his shocked surprise, an antique washboard hit him on his left shoulder and the side of his head! He'd been seated with his back to it, about a foot and a half away from the shelf it was resting upon, when the washboard hit him and then flew across the table. He never found any satisfactory explanation as to how this could have possibly happened.

A few years later, on October 28, 2008, Andrew was once again in the Dorr Ballroom with a small group of guests. During an EVP session, Andrew had asked if the small boy was there and if he could reveal his presence. Andrew also began asking questions about Thomas Dorr. Before he could get very far with those questions, everyone suddenly heard the sound of small shod feet running from the arched ceiling, down the wall and then in a tight circle on the dining room floor. A gentleman in their group assumed it was the owner's wife and the bus boy making these sounds at the other end of the dining room. However, they both came out of the wait staff station, making it quite clear that they also had just heard the footsteps.

**Forlorn Lady portrait, Tavern On Main**

# Chapter 13

### A Visit From the Reaper

(The following is a true account, although the names of certain individuals involved have been altered to protect their identities.)

In the month of April in 2004, TAPS had recently been contacted by a family residing in the Berkshires, in western Massachusetts. From what the family had told us, they were experiencing some disturbing paranormal activity in their home, and they were anxious to know whether we might be able to help them resolve their situation. Because the family claimed to be experiencing some potentially dangerous spirit activity, and older children were involved, we decided to make this case a priority. Brian Harnois, Sandra and I formed the investigative team, with of course. Sandra and I prepared to perform a religious cleansing if the clients so requested.

Joining us on this investigation would be a new team member, Joe Greene. Joe was a very pleasant, intelligent young man in his early twenties, of slim build and average height, with his wavy brown hair tinted slightly reddish. Joe had recently completed his training in TAPS as a field investigator and had been welcomed in by our co-founders Jason Hawes and Grant Wilson, and the rest of the team. Having proven himself to be an enthusiastic and responsible individual, Joe had also expressed an interest in furthering his training. Respectfully, he had approached Jason and Grant, as well as Sandra and myself, and asked if he might receive additional training in some of the heavier aspects of paranormal investigation, specifically extreme encounters with inhuman spirit entities. Not that Joe was eager to rush headlong into a potential demonic situation. On the contrary, he wanted to gain some experience as cautiously as possible, in order to be more prepared should he ever have to deal with such a situation.

The four of us set off from Warwick, Rhode Island late on a mild April Saturday afternoon, with Brian driving. During the lengthy drive to the Berkshires, Sandra, Brian and I discussed with Joe what he might expect on a case such as this, and exactly how we were going to proceed. While we cautioned Joe to be prepared for the unexpected, we also advised him that we would be proceeding under controlled conditions, and that most of the time even these types of investigations went without major incidents. Although Joe admitted that he was feeling just a little apprehensive, he was very much looking forward to this being a learning experience and he was also hoping to assist in helping out the client and her family.

Joe told us, "Earlier today I was talking about this with my friend Greg, explaining to him about what I'd be doing tonight. And he told me there's no way that he'd dare to go into a situation like this."

Sandra said, "That's right, you've mentioned Greg before. Isn't he supposed to be coming with you to a TAPS meeting sometime soon?"

"Oh yeah, maybe even next week," said Joe. "I don't think he wants to become an investigator, but he respects what we do, and he'd really like to meet everyone. And he said he's really looking forward to hearing about some of your interesting adventures."

I added, "Who knows, Joe? Maybe you'll have a story to tell him after tonight."


It was still fairly light outside when the four of us arrived at the client's residence. Jackie DuPont, a slim, pleasant dark-haired woman in her forties greeted us and welcomed us inside her two-story home.

"You're the people from TAPS!" she said with a bright smile. "Thank you so much for coming all this way. Please, come on in and make yourselves comfortable."

Accompanying Jackie that evening were her sister Megan and Jackie's 15-year-old son Dustin, and 13-year-old daughter Crystal. Jackie explained that her husband was out working the night shift, and that her two other teenage daughters, Teresa and Jennifer were out visiting with friends.

As soon as the introductions had been made and we were all seated comfortably in the parlor, Brian and I switched on our audio recorders and Sandra commenced with the interview. Beginning with the standard line of questions, Sandra asked Jackie if she knew how old the house was.

Jackie informed us that their house was built in 1935, and that she and her family had moved in exactly six years ago on April 30th. Sandra asked if they had any pets, to which Jackie replied that they presently had a tabby cat, and a small black terrier named Rocky. She added that they used to also have a beautiful Rottweiler, but had died just over a year ago.

Sandra asked if they practiced any specific religious faith or beliefs. Jackie answered that although they did not regularly attend church, she was of the Catholic faith, and still regularly said her prayers.

Sandra asked, "Do your pets ever seem to react to things that family members may not see or hear?"

Jackie replied, "The dog and the cat we have now don't seem to react to anything. But the Rottweiler was never afraid of anything, at least not until after we moved in here. Then suddenly he started acting afraid and jumping at things no one else could see and then he'd go yelping and running as if something was chasing him, and he'd hide behind me."

Megan added, "And one day I was here house sitting for Jackie, and a box of matches suddenly slid off of the coffee table and onto the floor by itself. And at the same exact time Chrystal's alarm clock radio suddenly went off. So I pulled the plug on the alarm radio and went running upstairs, pulling the Rottweiler by the collar!"

While continuing to jot notes on her interview form, Sandra asked, "Have any members of the family experienced any unusual odors in the house?"

Jackie replied, "Sometimes there will be what I can only describe as a wicked graveyard smell within the house, but it comes and goes." All the other family members concurred with this, including Megan.

I asked Jackie, "Have you considered the possibility that perhaps a small animal may have died somewhere within the house? I mean, we have dealt with this before, and found a logical explanation for an odor of decay."

Jackie replied, "No, I don't think it's that. My husband has checked this house from top to bottom, but he didn't find anything. And we even called in an exterminator once, and he said the house was clean."

Sandra said, "Now this next question is something I have to ask as part of the interview, but it will be kept completely confidential. Are any members of the family currently taking medications, or under a doctor's care?" None of them acknowledged taking any medications or under a doctor's care.

Sandra asked Jackie, "Are you familiar with the history of this house, such as former occupants?"

Jackie replied, "All I really know is that a man named Earl lived here before we moved in. In fact, we have a neighbor who knew Earl, who told us he died of cancer."

Sandra asked the family, "To your knowledge, has anyone in this house ever used a Ouija board or other divination device?"

Jackie replied, "My daughter Crystal and I played with a Ouija board once. But the indicator kept spinning around, and that really freaked us out! After that we figured once was enough, so we put it away and never played with it again."

"Where is the Ouija board now?" I asked.

Jackie said, "Believe it or not, I actually had it right in my bedroom closet, because I was gonna give it to you guys and ask you to get rid of it for me. But when I went to get it earlier today, it was gone, even though I was sure of exactly where I left it."

Crystal added, "We looked all over the house, but we just couldn't find it."

Brian glanced at Sandra and me, and commented, "Missing Ouija board, huh? Doesn't that sound typical!"

Sandra, Brian and I had recently assisted with a case for New England Paranormal where the client's Ouija board was also suddenly and mysteriously missing.

Sandra then asked Jackie and her family what other kinds of activity they had been experiencing.

Jackie said, "Well, it actually started with the kids. Dustin was upstairs in his bedroom, and...well, you tell them, Dustin."

Dustin explained, "Well, I used to have a computer in my room. One night I was sleeping, and I suddenly woke up, and the keys to my computer were pressing by themselves. So I came running downstairs and told my sister Teresa what was happening, so she came in and saw it too."

"Anything else?" I asked.

Dustin said, "Sometimes up in my bedroom, things will suddenly go flying off the shelf, like my model cars and stuff. And then more recently, my radio shut off by itself. You have to shut it off either by hand or by the remote, and the remote's nowhere to be found."

Crystal said, "Dustin, tell them about the plastic bag."

"Oh, yeah," said Dustin. "One night I was down here on the couch, when all of a sudden a plastic shopping bag came flying by along the floor. It did it like three times, and each time I jumped up and turned the light on, until finally my sister asked me, 'Dus, what's going on?' So I told her what was happening."

Jackie added, "But my bedroom seems to be the center of activity, whether I'm alone in there or not. It's in there that I've actually been seeing things."

"Seeing things?" I asked. "What sort of things are you seeing?"

Jackie explained, "Four years ago we had this kind of shiny, reflective silver paper on the walls inside my bedroom. And one night I was in bed, when I saw a tall, thin reflection on the silver wallpaper. We had a friend staying over, a real tall kid, so naturally I thought it was him standing in front of the hall light. So I turned around, but no one was standing there. And then my daughters also started seeing what they described as a tall thin figure in my bedroom. Now, at first we thought it might be Earl we were seeing... you know, the guy who used to live here... because we figured he must have been very thin while he was sick."

With a laugh, Megan added, "And then we all got nervous because we used to sing that song 'Good Bye Earl' all the time, when it was playing on the radio. So we figured maybe we caught Earl's attention."

The song 'Good Bye Earl' by the Dixie Chicks was considered to be controversial because it was a song about the murder of an abusive husband. Some radio stations at the time even refused to play it.

I asked, "Do you find the presence of Earl disturbing?"

Jackie said, "No, not really. Because if it was Earl, I don't think he's bad. In fact, good things seem to happen when Earl's around."

Sandra asked, "What kind of good things happen when Earl's around?"

Jackie said, "Well, there was one time when I woke up in the middle of the night, and I clearly felt someone sitting on my husband's side of the bed, even though my husband was at work. And all of a sudden I could smell Popsicles. So I turned on the bedroom light, but no one was on the bed. And then I got up and went out into the kitchen, and found that a box of Popsicles had been left out, and they were just about to start melting onto the rug. So I think maybe Earl was alerting me to that."

"Interesting," said Sandra. "Have there been any other interventions from Earl?"

Jackie said, "Yes, another time, my daughter Teresa was insisting that she was going to go out, despite warnings of severe thunderstorms for that evening. And she had just switched off her bedroom light when suddenly it switched itself right back on again. So Teresa accepted that as a sign from Earl, that he was warning her not to go out, and she stayed home."

I then said, "Jackie, you mentioned that your bedroom is often the center of activity. What negative things have you experienced in there?"

Jackie replied, "Well, one night I suddenly woke up around three AM gasping for breath. I had the sensation that I couldn't breathe, like a weight was pressing down on top of me. I felt cold and my hair stood up. Then I looked around, and I saw that there was this dark figure standing in the room with me. It was so tall, that at first I thought it may have been floating, but it wasn't. And all I could think of was the Reaper, because that's what it looked like."

"The Reaper?" asked Brian. "As in the Grim Reaper?"

"Yes, exactly like the Grim Reaper," said Jackie. "It was so tall that it had to duck down to avoid hitting the ceiling. It was wearing what looked like a black robe with a hood. And even though the room was completely dark, I was still somehow able to see it."

I asked, "Were any facial features discernible?"

"Oh, yes," said Jackie. "From what I could see, it had deep-set, coal black eyes. And all I could think of was the character in that Stephen King movie, 'Storm of the Century.' And it had a wide evil grin like a skull. I'll never forget the way it looked right down at me and smiled!"

Joe asked, "Has anyone else seen this figure? The reason I ask is because I'm just trying to rule out the possibility of sleep paralysis."

I added, "Sleep paralysis can sometimes also be accompanied by hypnopompic hallucinations, say, when the body is not yet fully awake."

Jackie replied, "Oh, but this was no hallucination, because both my son Dustin and my two eldest daughters have seen it in my bedroom, too."

Turning to Dustin, Joe asked, "Really? You've seen this same exact figure in your mother's bedroom?"

"Oh, yes," said Dustin. "In fact, that's why I was staying in my mom's bedroom overnight, to see if I'd see it too. Then I woke up sometime around three in the morning, and I felt like I was unable to catch my breath. And my mom and I both looked over, and sure enough, we both saw this tall dark figure standing there looking down at us and smiling. It was so tall it was up to the ceiling."

Sandra asked, "And your daughter Teresa also saw the same exact thing?"

Jackie replied, "Yes. She was staying in my room with me while my husband was working nights. I have to admit I was afraid to sleep in my bedroom alone. And she saw the same black, gigantic figure that I did. We both witnessed it at the same time!"

Sandra said, "It's too bad your daughter Teresa isn't here tonight, so we could get her take on this too."

Sandra asked, "Chrystal, have you ever seen the 'Reaper'?

"No, and I don't ever want to," Chrystal replied without hesitation.

I asked Jackie, "Has your husband ever seen this figure?"

Jackie said, "Nope, he's never seen it, but he's heard it in our bedroom. One time John and I went away to Florida for a couple of days to check out a house down there, and the same night after we came back we were both suddenly woken up in the middle of the night by what sounded like a loud 'clap' right over our faces. It was so loud that it woke both John and me up out of a sound sleep. So I think maybe that was the Reaper's way of letting us know he resented us being gone for a couple of days, and for us thinking of moving to Florida."

Directing the next question to Jackie's sister, Sandra asked, "Megan, have you ever seen this tall spectral figure while you've been over here?"

"No, I've never seen it," Megan replied. With a laugh she added, "And if I did, believe me, I'd be outta here!"

Sandra then asked if anyone had anything to add about their personal experiences in the house. Jackie, Dustin and Chrystal all claimed to have heard footfalls on the ceiling upstairs in Dustin's room, coming from the attic directly above.

Jackie explained, "But it's not really an attic; it's more like a crawl space, even though what we heard sounded like a full party going on."

Dustin and Chrystal both verified that they'd had friends staying overnight who had also heard that same dancing and partying going on above Dustin's bedroom ceiling.

Dustin said, "It wasn't mice, because it was really loud stomping, and you could hear what sounded like women's voices laughing and singing along with it."

During the last minutes of our interview, it was revealed that Jackie's eldest daughter Teresa had actually dabbled in occult practices more than was originally explained. In fact, she was known to have worn a pentacle, and may even have used the now missing Ouija board upstairs in her bedroom.

Sandra asked, "Before we conclude, is there anything anyone else would like to add?"

With a nervous laugh, Jackie said, "Well, the Reaper will probably appear or do something tonight, because he always does when we talk about him."

Brian Harnois' reaction to this was, "Bring it on!"

I could sense that Jackie's statement had caused Joe to feel rather uneasy, although he was doing his best to conceal it. For my own part, I doubted that an actual manifestation of the 'Reaper' would occur with us ready with our recording devices, although I was certainly prepared for anything unexpected.

Sandra of course remained practical, and politely asked Jackie, "Now, what would you like to see accomplished by our visit here tonight? I understand that you've mentioned you'd like a blessing conducted here in your house, is that correct?"

Jackie replied, "Oh, yes, definitely, I would like a house blessing. I want this thing that looks like the Reaper gone! I don't think that it's a regular ghost, and I'm really concerned that it will eventually harm one of us."

Brian said, "Don't worry, Keith will do a thorough blessing throughout this entire house."

I explained, "Of course, we can make no guarantees of spirit removal. But the blessing will hopefully lessen the activity."

"Thank you," said Jackie. "We certainly appreciate anything you can do."

While getting out a supply of blessed oil and water from my bag, and placing a small blessed crucifix around my neck, I asked, "So, you mentioned that there is a small attic space just above Dustin's bedroom? Is it at all accessible?"

Jackie replied, "Yes, it is, but as I mentioned it's not really an attic, it's more of a crawl space. Would you need to get up there?"

"Just enough to reach in and spray some blessed water," I said. "I wouldn't need to get all the way in."

Jackie said, "We use a step ladder when we want to get up there."

"Good, that should be fine," I said.

Shortly before we commenced with the house blessing, Megan announced that she had to get back home. Immediately after Megan left, I told Jackie that with her permission, we would begin the blessing in the basement and work our way up, blessing each room along the way until the entire house was spiritually cleansed.

Jackie told me, "I understand. Thank you, Father."

"Oh, I'm not a priest," I said. "I'm a demonologist."

While the three members of the DuPont family remained together in the first floor parlor, Brian, Joe, Sandra and I made our way downstairs into the cellar. The blessing went smoothly and without incident. I began by leading the others in praying an 'Our Father' and calling upon angelic protection for us and the family upstairs. At my request, Sandra also recited a Scripture passage from Ephesians, Chapter 6. Sandra assisted me in anointing all access ways in the cellar, such as doors and windows, with blessed oil and water, while Brian and Joe took audio recordings and EMF readings. When the blessing of the cellar was completed, we made our way upstairs to begin blessing of the first floor rooms.

When we arrived back upstairs, Jackie anxiously asked us, "Did you guys experience anything down there in the cellar?"

Brian replied, "No, nothing at all. It seems pretty dead down there, if you'll excuse the pun."

I explained. "It's not uncommon for us to experience very little activity during a blessing, because the entities tend to lay low. Most of the time, they certainly avoid announcing their presence."

Jackie said, "Well, I'll be surprised if you don't get some activity up here. When you're in my bedroom, the Reaper will probably appear to you, so be careful. It considers that his territory." Dustin and Crystal both nodded in agreement.

I thanked Jackie for the warning, and assured her and her children that we would proceed with the utmost precaution.

When we did get to Jackie's bedroom, Joe performed a sweep through the room with his Gauss meter. When he came to Jackie's nightstand, the meter suddenly began spiking.

"I've got a reading of 9.0 over here," he informed us. The baseline had been set at 1.0. When Joe moved closer to the digital alarm clock, Joe said, "It's obvious that this digital alarm clock is causing the indicator to spike."

Brian said. "Good call, Joe. We'll have to let Jackie know about that after we're done in here."

We then proceeded with the actual blessing of Jackie's bedroom. I said aloud, "We are under the protection of the Holy Spirit, and surrounded by the Armor of God, according to St. Paul's letter to the Ephesians."

I then asked Sandra to recite aloud a passage from Deuteronomy, Chapter 2: "Hear, O Israel: Thou art to pass over Jordan this day, to go in to possess nations greater and mightier than thyself, cities great and fenced up to heaven, a people great and tall, the children of the Anakims, whom thou knowest, and of whom thou hast heard say, 'Who can stand before the children of Anak!'"

Continuing with a prayer of my own, I said, "And under the authority of Jesus Christ, we ask that anything of an unholy spiritual nature be cast out from this room, and replaced by a mighty and holy angel of God, to protect all who enter here, and all who sleep here. We also ask that any lost or wandering spirits that may linger here, be sent to their proper abode."

Sandra and Brian then assisted me with anointing the bedroom windows and closet door, while Joe continued documenting the procedure. Sandra also sprayed a liberal amount on holy water onto the bedspread and on the bedposts. Glancing at Joe, I noticed that he appeared to be calm and focused, despite Jackie's warning that the Reaper would likely appear to us within the bedroom.

When we emerged from Jackie's bedroom, she and her son and daughter seemed a bit surprised that no manifestation had occurred. I explained to them that we had performed a very thorough blessing in the master bedroom, and that we had also prayed for angelic protection.

Sandra added, "One thing I noticed, Jackie, is that your digital alarm clock on the bureau is very close to where your pillow is. Now, I'm not suggesting that you have epilepsy or anything like that. But sometimes an electrical device such as a digital alarm clock may trigger a form of temporal lobe epilepsy, which actually could cause feelings of dread, and even hallucinations. Now, the only reason I mention this is because we picked up very high EMF readings in your bedroom, especially near the digital alarm clock. So, just as a suggestion, you might think of moving it a little further away from you."

"Thank you Sandra, I'll certainly try that, and see if it makes a difference," said Jackie.

The blessing of the remainder of the first floor area went completely without incident. The family had overheard much of our procedure, and I did get the impression that they were somewhat relieved to see and hear us on the job, moving through their house in an attempt to dispel whatever negative energy may be present.

We were then ready to bless the second floor. Dustin offered to accompany us upstairs to pull down the ladder leading to the attic. As they had mentioned, the attic itself was actually nothing more than a crawl space. However, I certainly found sufficient room to climb up and spray holy water in all four corners, while praying, "In the name of the Father, the Son, and the Holy Spirit, may this area be blessed and sanctified. Amen."

It was not until we were performing the blessing of Theresa's bedroom... the last room in the upstairs area we had left to bless... that we began to encounter some trouble. Just after Sandra recited Scripture from Hebrews, Chapter 9, and I was about to pronounce the blessing, the atmosphere within the bedroom suddenly began to become noticeably thickened.

Dustin mention, "I don't know if anyone else is feeling this, but did the air in here just become heavier?"

Brian said, "Yeah, now that you mention it, the atmosphere in here does suddenly feel a lot heavier. Anyone else noticing this?"

Sandra agreed, "It does feel a little more oppressive in here than it did a moment ago."

Now more than ever I was wishing that Theresa was here tonight, to share some details. It would have been helpful if she could tell us if she'd attempted spirit conjuration... and if so, specifically what spirits. I then looked over at Joe, who seemed to be breathing a little heavy.

"How are you holding up, Joe?" I asked. "Are you doing okay?"

Joe nodded and said, "Yes, I'll be okay. Thank you for asking."

I then asked Sandra to read Psalm 91 as a prayer of protection, which she did clearly and confidently. When she had finished reading this Scripture, we all noticed that the feeling of heaviness in the bedroom had lessened considerably.

After this, I said, "In the name of Jesus Christ, and on the authority of His shed blood, if any unholy entities have been summoned to this house and to this room through the law of invitation, then we render this contract as null and void, by the power of the Holy Spirit. We pray that any lost or wandering spirits be conveyed to their proper abode by mighty and holy angels, and that an angel of peace be sent to guard all who enter and leave this room, and anyone who may sleep here. May this room be bound and sealed against any spirits of perdition that may have previously held dominion here. And we bless and sanctify this room in the name of the Father, and of the Son, and of the Holy Spirit. Amen."

Sandra sprayed a liberal amount of holy water about the room, especially onto Theresa's bed, while I anointed the doorways and windows with blessed oil. I also anointed the bedroom mirror as a precaution, in case Theresa or anyone else had performed any form of 'mirror magic' in the bedroom.

The blessing of the entire second floor was now successfully completed, and the surrounding atmosphere no longer seemed quite as oppressive. Whether the thickness had been caused by a preternatural force, or whether it had merely been a lack of ventilation upstairs, it had suddenly and noticeably lifted.

The five of us returned back downstairs to the first floor parlor to where Jackie and Chrystal were anxiously waiting for us. I informed them that things were now taken care of, and that the activity she'd been experiencing should be kept at bay now. Dustin added, "They completely blessed the upstairs, Mom, including the attic and Theresa's bedroom, and it does feel a lot better up there now."

"Thank goodness," said Jackie with a sigh of relief.

In conclusion to the house blessing, Sandra read Psalm 23 with all of us gathered together in the parlor. I then offered to anoint Jackie, Dustin and Chrystal with blessed oil. All three of them said they would like that very much.

I anointed Jackie first, making the sign of the cross on her forehead with blessed oil and saying, "In the name of the Father, and of the Son and of the Holy Spirit, may you be protected from unholy and negative forces. And may you be guarded by holy angels of God. Amen."

"Amen," said Jackie. "Thank you, Father."

Once again, I politely and with a touch of humor explained, "I'm not an ordained priest."

"Oh, I'm sorry, I keep on calling you that," Jackie apologized with a laugh.

Smiling, I said, "It's understandable, given the circumstances."

I next anointed Dustin's forehead and Chrystal's forehead, and recited prayers of protection for them, doing the same for Sandra, Brian and Joe. Sandra in turn anointed my forehead and said a prayer of protection for me.

Before leaving, we advised Jackie, Dustin and Chrystal that as long as they and the rest of the family maintained a positive, faithful attitude within the house, the blessing we had just performed should remain effective. I explained that I had also done a binding, which should prove very effective in keeping the spirits from returning to harass them.

Sandra said, "And as you heard when we were doing the blessing, we also invoked angels to watch over you and protect you. Also, I cannot emphasize enough how important it is not to invite these negative spirits back in by performing any sort of divination. Now I know you don't use Tarot cards or Ouija boards, but you mentioned that at least one of your daughters had done so in the past."

Jackie told us, "Yes, but Theresa doesn't have anything at all to do with the occult anymore. And like you said, I really wish she was here to talk with you people tonight."

I said, "Ideally, I wish both she and Jennifer had been here tonight, so we could have interviewed them both and I could have anointed them also. But I want to remind you, that as a parent, you have much more of a God-given authority over your children than I do."

Joe stepped forward and added sincerely, "Remember, Jackie, just like Keith and Sandra were saying, this is your house. Try not to give in to fear, or allow whatever may be here to push you around."

Sounding somewhat more resolute, Jackie said, "You know, you're absolutely right. This is my house and I'm tired of living in fear."

Brian said, "That's what we like to hear. And just remember, if you need us for anything, we're only a phone call away."

"I'll keep that in mind, and I'll let my husband know that too," said Jackie. "And again, thank you all so much for coming out tonight, and for all you've done to help us."

After we had packed up our equipment and were on our way out the door, Brian added with a chuckle, "And let us know if that Ouija board finally shows up."

Jackie replied, "Oh, I certainly will, if it somehow manages to turn up. But we looked everywhere for it, so I have no idea where it could be."

It was now a brilliant moonlit night as we began making the drive back from the Berkshires, discussing the DuPont case along the way. Sandra, Brian and I complimented Joe on what a fine job he had done that evening.

With a nervous laugh, Joe said, "There was a moment there where I really started feeling overwhelmed, and I wondered if I was going to get through it."

Brian said, "Oh, you mean in the upstairs bedroom, when the air started getting really think and oppressive. Yeah, I was feeling that, too."

"But you did fine, Joe," I said. "The important thing is that you held it together, and remained very professional."

"Largely thanks to you guys being so supportive," said Joe.

Sandra reminded him, "And before we left, you also helped advise Jackie to stop obsessing over the 'Grim Reaper' and giving into her fears."

"Yeah, good job, man," said Brian.

"Thanks so much," said Joe. "At least I can say I made it through my first possibly inhuman spirit case."

Brian said, "You know, I still wonder about the two daughters that weren't there tonight. Especially Theresa, who Jackie said was dabbling in the occult. I'm just wondering if there's any possibility that she may have intentionally hidden that Ouija board somewhere... maybe at her friend's house."

Sandra said, "Well, let's hope that's not the case, and that the blessing we performed is allowed to take effect."

Joe asked, "How effective are the blessings that you perform in these cases?"

Brian replied, "Believe me, dude, the blessing that Keith and Sandra perform are extremely powerful."

Sandra added, "Of course, Joe, a lot is up to the client as well. So hopefully, like we were discussing earlier, Jackie's daughter will refrain from 'dabbling' in the occult."

"Yeah, I see what you mean," Joe agreed. He then asked me, "Keith, in your opinion, what type of spirit do you think was in that house?"

I replied, "In my personal opinion, it was an inhuman entity, and they'd given it further access by opening doors playing with a Ouija board. I don't think the spirit of the former owner Earl was ever there, although he himself may even have had an attachment. Of course, we'll never know that for sure."

Both Sandra and Brian concurred with me.


Later that evening when we pulled into the lot in Warwick where Joe Greene's car was parked, Joe told us, "Hey, again, thanks so much for allowing me to come along with you guys tonight. I really appreciate it."

"Yeah, you did a great job tonight, dude," said Brian, tapping knuckles with him.

Sandra said, "Thank you so much for joining us tonight, and for helping out. It was a pleasure working with you tonight, Joe."

"Aw... thanks, guys," said Joe, smiling and adjusting his glasses.

I said, "Thank you Joe, and I hope we get to meet your friend Greg at the next TAPS meeting."

"Oh yeah, Greg's really looking forward to meeting all of you," said Joe. "And I'm sure he'll be interested to know about what I experienced tonight. Naturally I'll keep the family name and location confidential."

During that week following the investigation, I listened to the audio recording of the investigation of the Berkshires case, and came up with one barely discernible EVP. It was recorded near the end of the client interview, when we were discussing the house blessing, and it seemed to be a voice simply saying "Why?"

Things seemed to have settled down at the DuPont residence, as they did not report any new sightings of the 'Reaper' within the following week. The blessing we performed apparently had a positive effect, and Jackie was hopefully following our advice about taking control of her house.

At our next meeting of TAPS, held at our usual local coffee shop, Sandra, Brian and I were naturally looking forward to sharing the details about the DuPont case with our fellow team members. Our friend and fellow TAPS member Donna LaCroix was especially excited to know all about what we'd experienced, telling us, "I'm so anxious to actually get to go on an investigation myself! You guys have all the adventures."

Sandra said, "You're certainly welcome to come with us sometime, Donna. We'd love to have you join us on an investigation."

Grant Wilson had just taken a seat and joined us. Overhearing our conversation, he mentioned to Donna, "We haven't really had that many cases lately. Things have really been slow."

Sandra said, "Actually, Keith and Brian and I have been very busy lately. We've been going out on cases practically every weekend for the past several months."

Grant was obviously pleased to hear that we'd been so diligent.

One thing we noticed was that Joe Greene had not yet arrived at the meeting, although he was usually one of the first ones to arrive. Sandra, Brian and I certainly wanted him to be present for our review of the DuPont case, so he could add his own perspective of what the four of us had experienced there.

However, it was not long before Brian Bell shared some rather disturbing news with all of us at the meeting that evening. He informed us that Joe Greene had just contacted him, to let him now that he would not be at the meeting because his best friend Greg had tragically committed suicide a couple of days ago.

We were naturally all shocked and saddened to hear of this. I asked Brian, "Did Joe say why his friend Greg committed suicide? Or how?"

"No." said Brian. "Joe didn't give me any other details than what I've just shared. All I know is that his friend Greg took his own life, and that Joe is of course devastated by this sudden loss. Joe also said he's not sure when he'll be back, but that he needs to take some time away from the group for now."

Jason Hawes said, "That's certainly understandable. He should of course take all the time he needs."

Donna commented to Sandra, "His friend Greg must have been so young, probably in his early twenties, like Joe,"

Sandra said, "He probably was. In fact, I think Joe once mentioned that they went to school together."

Brian Harnois added, "And Joe was just talking about his friend Greg when he was with us the other night. I wonder if the poor guy will be back by next week?"

"I don't know," I said. "But I'd certainly like to express my condolences to Joe, when he comes back."

Brian, Sandra and Donna and the rest of the members all said the same.


Joe Greene never did return to TAPS. After the sudden death of his friend Joe apparently decided to separate himself from the paranormal investigation field altogether. We of course respected his decision as well as his privacy, and wished him the best of luck.

As for the Dupont family, they reported no further sightings of 'the Grim Reaper' or other activity, so a follow up visit with them was not required. The last we heard, they were continuing to live peacefully in their home in the Berkshires.

# Chapter 14

## Stone's Public House

Located in Ashland, Massachusetts, Stone's Public House is well-known for its great food and drink...and its notorious haunting activity. Built in 1832 by John Stone, it was opened as a local hotel to accommodate passengers of the new railroad that was to be built along John's own property. In fact, the original name of his establishment was The Railroad House. From contemporary accounts, John Stone himself was quite a formidable character. He was a farmer, a captain in the militia and a prominent local businessman. The Railroad House officially opened on September 20, 1834, to an enthusiastic crowd of approximately 300 people, although this may be a modest estimate.

Although John Stone operated the Railroad House for less than two years, he continued to live on the property, while leasing the building to a series of other innkeepers. John Stone died in 1858, and ten years later the business was bought by W.A. Scott.

Throughout the next several decades, the building fell into a state of neglect, until it was bought and saved from demolition in 1976 by Leonard "Cappy" Fournier. Mr. Fournier had ambitious plans for the building. He immediately set about restoring the establishment to its former glory, and reopened the place as the John Stone Tavern. It was later renamed Stone's Public House, and the establishment continues to function as a highly successful inn of Irish-American heritage flair, with excellent food and drink as well as popular entertainment. Cappy Fournier is also the first to give public credence to the otherworldly activity that takes place within the building.

Among Fournier's staff, bartenders have reported water taps repeatedly being turned on by themselves, causing endless frustration. Patrons also frequently report being touched and groped by invisible fingers, although to my knowledge no one has run out screaming as of yet.

Cappy Founier has also welcomed a number of psychics and paranormal investigators to investigate his establishment. One item that has been of particular interest to both psychics and investigators alike is a young girl's bloodstained dress discovered within the fourth floor attic. This dress is believed to date back to 1862, and to have belonged to a 10-year-old girl named Mary J. Smith, who was tragically killed by a passing train just outside of the hotel. Some contemporary eyewitness accounts from both staff and patrons alike describe a mysterious little girl being spotted in different places in the building. She will usually be seen briefly peeking around corners or scurrying through the hallways, before vanishing from sight.

In 1984, Ralph Bibbo, the founder of ECHO (Education Concerning a Higher Order), conducted his own investigation at the inn. Ralph claimed that during the course of his investigation, he communicated with several of the spirits haunting the inn, including a former maid named Sadie. He also claimed that a spirit presence informed him that a New York boarder named Michael was accidentally killed by John Stone in the year 1845, after a card game gone horribly wrong. John Stone allegedly accused Michael of cheating him out of $3,000. After the murder, several persons who witnessed the crime helped carry Michael's body downstairs and secretly buried him in the basement. Such was the loyalty of secrecy between John Stone and his band of close associates!

In the late summer of 2004, members of the Atlantic Paranormal Society, including my brother Carl and I, conducted an investigation at Stone's Public House. The investigation was filmed for an episode of the first season of the TV series Ghost Hunters. During the course of our investigation, Steve Gonsalves was able to debunk a reported "floating light" anomaly, which turned out to be merely reflections through the windows caused by passing headlights in the first floor dining room.

In the fourth floor attic, Steve showed us the little girl's bloodstained dress that supposedly belonged to Mary J. Smith. TAPS investigator Brian Harnois wound up "borrowing" this dress, and took it home with him overnight to appease a little ghost girl who was supposedly haunting his apartment. According to Brian, the trick temporarily worked, and he promptly returned the dress. In that same attic, we also came across an antiquated local newspaper, which by an uncanny coincidence, was dated exactly one hundred years ago to the day of our investigation that night!

Brian Bell and I also found a "death portrait" of a young child. A member of the staff explained to us that the portrait used to be publicly displayed in the downstairs area. However, the customers found the otherworldly stare of the child in the portrait a little too disturbing, so it was relocated to the attic. The thought crossed my mind that some sort of spirit attachment may be associated with this death portrait. Brian Bell agreed with my assessment, and I performed a cautionary blessing over the child's death portrait.

I prayed, "In the name of God, we ask if there are any children here, that they would not remain earthbound, but that their angels convey them to Heaven."

On a lighter note, another scene filmed, but did not make it onto the episode, was what came to be known as the humorous "dancing demonologist" scene, in which my brother Carl partnered with fellow TAPS member Donna Lacroix while the local band was still playing shortly after our arrival!

While we were there, we also learned of a darker side to the hotel's history. During the latter part of the 19th century, the hotel fell into disrepair and became known as a place of ill repute. Apparently drunkenness, prostitution and violence became the norm for this establishment, and rumors of murders that were covered up circulated, including the infamous card game gone wrong involving John Stone himself.

Although we did not experience a great deal of paranormal activity that evening, we did come away with an appreciation for the history of Stone's Public House, and our investigation made for an interesting episode of Ghost Hunters.

Of all those who have investigated the alleged paranormal activity at Stone's Public House over the years, perhaps no one has invested more time and energy into this project than independent researcher David Francis. A resident of Upton, MA, David's interest in Stone's Public House first began as a teenager when his dad took him there and explained to him about some of the haunting aspects of the building. However, it was not until some years later, as an experienced paranormal researcher, that David began seriously investigating Stone's Public House, often teaming up with other investigators.

In April of 2008, David Francis met with David Retalic of Haunted Happenings for a full walkthrough of Stone's Public House. They were both truly amazed as they ventured through the old hotel and saw all the areas of the building that were closed off to the general public. Upon carefully ascending the rickety staircase, they found the third floor area to be in a dilapidated state of disrepair. Inside each of the third floor rooms, the blue-green copper stems of the former gaslight system were still plainly visible. This was the same basic condition that we ourselves found the third floor to be, when filming for Ghost Hunters.

That same evening, David Francis sat at his desk listening to the recording he had made on his Olympus voice recorder of his walk through of Stone's Public House. While reviewing his data, he discovered what seemed to be an example of an EVP. It was a voice that he at first assumed was saying "You're all drunk." However, upon conferring with Cliff Wilson of the Ashland Historic Society, they came to the conclusion that the voice on the recording was actually saying, "Huge room... jeez."

In August of that year, David Francis assisted in organizing a complete investigation at Stone's Public House, which comprised of several local paranormal researchers. Among these researchers was David Retalic, as well as my brother Carl Johnson and Laura Casey from New England Anomalies Research. They were also joined by members of the Paranormal Investigation and Research Organization (PIRO) from the University of New Haven, Connecticut, and independent researchers Amy Connelly, and David's brother, Mike Francis. With this number of investigators, every section of the establishment would be covered.

The team decided that their base of operations would be set up in the storage area of the second floor. Although no one reported experiencing any activity during the first few hours of the investigation, things eventually began to pick up. At one point, David Francis was taking a turn monitoring the closed circuit cameras, when he felt a firm tap upon his right shoulder. Assuming it was his brother who'd been standing nearby, David asked, "What is it, Mike?" When Mike did not respond right away, David turned around, and saw that his brother was standing on the other side of the room, not paying attention to him. David also noticed that investigator Amy Connelly was also in the room but was standing too far away to have just touched him. Since neither Amy nor Michael could have possibly tapped David on the shoulder at that moment, he mentioned it to them, and noted the incident as unexplained.

At almost that same moment down in the basement, David Retalic experienced something a bit more disturbing. He was alone in a small area between two of the larger rooms when suddenly a sizable rock came flying seemingly from out of nowhere and struck him on his forehead just underneath the brim of his hat. The force of the blow caused David to stumble backwards, nearly losing his balance. Understandably somewhat shaken, he quickly returned back upstairs to the second floor and alerted the others as to what had just happened. In fact, as David and Michael Francis and Amy Connelly examined him, they could see a visible gash on his forehead where the rock had struck him, and a lump was even forming along his scalp line. Unfortunately the incident was not captured on camera. But for David Retalic, he needed no further convincing that Stone's Public House was genuinely haunted. In fact, he decided that he did not need to return to investigate the place after what he'd personally experienced that night.

Carl and Laura had concentrated most of their investigation that evening in Room 23, which is a guest room located on the third floor. They managed to capture an EVP of what sounded like the voice of a little girl, either cooing, giggling or possibly even crying. Carl and Laura had to wonder if this voice had any connection to 10-year-old Mary J. Smith, who is believed to have owned the tattered, blood-stained dress now preserved in the attic.

Another investigation at Stone's Public House was organized by David Francis the following summer. In preparation for this investigation, David decided to conduct a preliminary walkthrough of the building accompanied by Michelle Mowry and friend Christina Ottman. At one point during their walk through, while David was recording audio, he and Christina happened to be discussing a mutual friend named Mike. When David later reviewed his audio recording, he discovered that an unidentified female voice on the recording had responded by asking, "Well, how is Michael?"

Three weeks later the summer investigation was held. Joining David on this venture were friends Beth and Lance Towne, Christina Ottman, Nathan Mayer of New England Anomalies Research, Michelle Mowry of

New England Paranormal and Cliff Wilson, president of the Ashland Historical Society. This night they decided to begin by concentrating their investigation on the third floor. They split up into two teams, each setting up in the two separate guest rooms at opposite end of the floor.

David was in the far room located nearest to the railroad tracks. While in this room he placed a small, liquid-filled ball-style compass onto an old patio chair cushion, to monitor for any possible magnetic fluctuations. David then began their EVP session by asking, "Are there any relatives of John Stone present in this room?"

Suddenly Beth Towne exclaimed, "David, the compass just moved on its own!"

Thinking she meant that the compass was spinning inside its case, David quickly switched on his headlamp and glanced over at the cushion where the compass had been placed. However, the compass was no longer there. It was discovered resting beside the center chimney in the room, about a foot and a half from where it was placed. David replaced the compass on the cushion and tried in every conceivable way he knew to get the compass to jump off from the cushion, but his efforts proved ineffective. He even tried pounding on the cushion, jumping up and down, and kicking it with his foot, but he simply could not get the compass to roll out onto the floor. It also seemed logical that the compass falling off the cushion and onto the floor should have produced some sound, but he and Beth had heard nothing. Neither could Dave find a trace of any such sound on his audio recording.

Although no other extraneous activity was experienced at Stone's Public House that night, the audio recordings the investigators had made yielded at least several rather clear examples of EVP. One in particular could be considered a Class A recording. It was recorded in the same third floor room where the compass had mysteriously moved, by the other group of investigators after they had switched rooms with David's group.

In the recording, Michelle Mowry addressed the spirit of Mary J. Smith. Michelle mentioned to Mary that people have heard her giggling throughout the building, and that her voice may have recently been recorded by two other investigators. This is immediately followed on the recording by a little girl's voice distinctly responding "Yes."

Also during this EVP session, Michelle asked Mary Smith if she could please move the compass again, and mentioned to Mary that she had a little girl at home. At this point in the audio file a car is heard passing outside, and as it trails off the same girl's voice shouts, "GO AWAY!"

Note: I have also experienced this when recording for spirit voices, where the spirit will seemingly "ride the acoustical wave" by using sound vibrations that are already in the air – either the sound of a vehicle trailing away, or somebody in the room having just spoken - to communicate.

A loud bang can also be heard on the recording, although it was not heard by any of the other investigators who were present at the time. Dave considers this EVP session to have yielded important results, because of the intelligent responses to the line of questioning.

Throughout subsequent investigations at Stone's Public House, David Francis and others have found that EVP seems the most frequent form of possible paranormal evidence. These recorded disembodied voices also sometimes correlate with actual historical data. For example, one evening while Cliff Wilson and David were recording for evidence within the bar area, Cliff recorded a voice saying, "Tiddy ran – he missed it." This comment on Cliff's recording could possibly be referring to a police officer named George Tidsbury. Officer Tidsbury was a friend of the W. A. Scott family who ran the hotel from 1868 until 1904. According to Cliff, George Tidsbury had unsuccessfully run for public office at least a few times and this phrase could be an echo from a long ago conversation that may have taken place in the barroom.

Over the past several years, multiple other voices speaking names and various other brief messages have also been recorded within the building. During one of his subsequent visits to the inn, while conducting background noise level recordings for future comparisons, David Francis captured a masculine voice on audio, clearly saying the name "Lawrence." This could possibly be referring Lawrence Scott, the son of owner W.A. Scott, who died at the age of 35 in the building on December 20, 1885. His cause of death was from cirrhosis of the liver.

Sounds like the moans of an adult female have also been recorded throughout the building. Historical research has uncovered an article from the Ashand Advertiser dating back to the late 1880s, mentioning that George Scott, the eldest son of W.A. Scott, had violently attacked a chambermaid on one of the hotel staircases. This attack led to George being committed to an asylum in Worcester, MA, where he died in 1897.


Quite obviously, many of the disembodied messages captured on audio recording with Stone's Public House seem to tie in with factual historical data. And although much of the evidence collected at this location is in the form of EVP, sightings of a ghostly little girl and other manifestations continue to be reported fairly regularly. David Francis and other investigators welcome any information that may provide additional insight into their ongoing research of the paranormal phenomena at Stone's Public House. David can be contacted at: http://independentparanormalresearchmassachusetts.weebly.com/

**Stone's Public House**

# Chapter 15

### "Uncle Frankie"

(The names of the clients in this story have been altered to protect their actual identities.)

In early December of 2004, our friend and fellow investigator, Brian Bell, who was of course also a former member of TAPS, contacted Sandra and me. He needed our assistance on a case he was independently investigating in Riverside, RI. A family was supposedly being haunted by a recently deceased relative. In fact, the wife and mother of the family actually happened to be an old friend of Brian's from some time ago.

As Brian explained it to us, "I haven't seen my friend Anne for a few years. But just recently, she happened to be watching a past episode of Ghost Hunters, and she recognized me on it. She and her family have been experiencing a haunting for the past couple of months, ever since her brother-in-law passed away. In fact, the haunting mainly seems to be centered on her fourteen-year-old daughter."

Sandra and I readily agreed to assist Brian with his investigation. We were especially relieved to know that the case was local, and would therefore not necessitate us having to travel out of state. Joining us on the investigation would be my brother Carl, as well as two people who were new team members of Brian's.

The following Saturday evening, December 11th, Carl, Sandra and I met up with Brian and his team at a local coffee shop in Riverside. Mary, a slim young woman in her early twenties was very interested in becoming involved in paranormal exploration. John Hawkins, who was in his late twenties or early thirties allegedly possessed a certain amount of psychic ability. John would be assisting in the investigation primarily as a sensitive.

We arrived at the clients' home less than fifteen minutes later. Present inside the house with Anne were her husband Sal, their fourteen-year-old daughter Amy, their sixteen-year-old son Justin, and their friends Phil and Shannon. The parlor was decorated for the holiday season, with a brightly-lit Christmas tree set up near Sal's easy chair. As we sat in the comfortably warm parlor, we switched our tape recorders on and began our interview with the family. According to Anne and Sal, most of the phenomena seemed to center on their fourteen-year-old daughter Amy. Ever since Sal's brother Frank had died suddenly of a heart attack two months earlier, strange phenomena such as cold spots, rapping noises and the unexplained movement of small household items had been occurring within the house, usually when Amy was present in the room. Because Sal's late brother had always been particularly close to his niece, and very protective of her, they had come to the conclusion that the ghost of Frank might still be lingering in the house and watching over her, sort of as a guardian spirit.

Sal explained, "Christmas was always my brother's favorite time of year, and it was his job to decorate the tree for us every year. He was really good at it, and decorated the tree in his own special way."

Anne added, "That's why we think he's suddenly become active, because we've just put up the Christmas tree and the other decorations."

We were informed that the rapping in the house usually picked up during the early evening hours. However, the spirit activity was not confined just to their house. Apparently "Uncle Frankie" was also following his niece to school. According to Anne, the rapping sounds would often start up while Amy was seated at her desk.

Brian Bell interjected, "Do you mean to say, that while Amy is sitting there at school, her Uncle Frank actually starts making rapping noises around her?"

"Yes," said Anne, "and she's very upset about it, too. Not that Amy minds Uncle Frankie being near her and watching over her, but she always winds up getting in trouble with her teachers; they consider her a behavior problem. And she's also being hassled by some of the other students in her class as well. They make fun of her and call her names, like 'Ghost Girl.' And some of them feel uncomfortable around Amy, and refuse to socialize with her. Isn't that right, Amy?"

Amy, who had remained silent up until this time, answered, "Yeah, I don't have too many friends now, because they're all scared to be around me. And it's been happening more and more lately."

Carl asked her, "How often would you say it happens in the course of a school week, Amy?"

"It's been happening more and more lately, usually every day," she said.

Sandra asked, "And how does this make you feel, Amy?"

"Pretty bad," said Amy. "I feel like I'm getting into a lot of trouble, for something that's not even my fault, and that I have no control over."

"Have you tried asking Uncle Frankie to stop?" I asked.

"Yeah, I've tried asking him, but it still keeps happening," Amy replied.

I asked the family, "Do you have any particular religious beliefs?"

"Yes, we're Catholic," said Anne.

"To your knowledge, has a blessing ever been performed in this house?" I asked.

"No. At least not since we've been living here," said Anne.

"Have you consulted with the clergy about your situation?" I asked.

"No, we haven't," Anne replied.

At the conclusion of our interview, Carl asked Anne and Sal, "So, what would you like to see as a result of our investigation?"

Anne answered, "We'd like to find out if this is really the ghost of my brother-in-law Frank." Sandra asked, "And if possible, would you like to see this activity stop?"

Anne said, "Well, yes, especially considering how it's been affecting Amy at school. Lately she's becoming more and more depressed and miserable."

Brian asked Sal, "And how do you feel about it, Sal? Would you like to see the activity stop?"

Sal replied, "Yes, I suppose I'd like to see my brother's spirit at rest. If it is Frank, I'm sure he still feels very connected to us, his family. But I think he should move on."

"I totally agree," I said.

Sandra said, "I'd also like to add that my husband Keith and I would also be willing to perform a religious blessing in the house after our investigation, if that's something you'd be interested in having done."

Anne thought for a couple of seconds, and replied, "Yes, that might be something we'd be interested in having done."

"We could do it tonight immediately following the investigation, depending on what we find," said Sandra. "Or we could come back and do it at a later date. It's just something you may wish to consider."

"Thanks, we appreciate that," said Anne.

I asked the family, "Would you happen to have a picture of Frank available?"

"Yes, right over here," Sal replied. He reached over in his easy chair, and picked up a newspaper clipping from the small table next to him. "This is my brother's obituary, with his picture on it."

Sal handed the obituary to us, which we all passed around. In the small black and white photo, Frank appeared to be a heavy-set man in the prime of life, bearing a strong resemblance to his brother Sal.

"He looks a lot like you," Brian commented.

Anne agreed, "Yeah, they looked a lot alike. And you can tell from the picture that Frank was a fun loving guy."

"Is this a recent picture of Frank?" I asked.

"Yes," said Sal. "In fact, that was taken just last year, only a few months before he died."

Seated over on the sofa, Anne and Sal's friend Phil said, "Now at least you can see who you'll be talking to, in case Frank chooses to communicate with us tonight."

Brian said, "So, you've been here before when Frank communicates with the family."

"Yes, several times," said Phil. "We've sat right here in the parlor and had conversations with him."

Phil's wife Shannon explained, "We'll ask questions, and if Frank's in the mood to talk, he'll answer by knocking on the floor."

"Interesting," said Brian. "So, when Frank answers, is it like he's tapping out a code?"

Anne answered, "No, not really like a code, because he only taps once, whenever he answers."

"Well, then if it's alright with you, maybe we can try contacting Frank after we've investigated the rest of the house," Brian suggested. "Do you think that maybe he would communicate with us later on?"

"That's entirely possible," said Anne. "As long as we have Amy here in the room with us, he may even talk with strangers."


We then began our investigation. After splitting up into two teams, we spent time in each room of the two-story house, taking various readings and recordings. However, it was not until Sandra, Brian and I reached the basement that we began experiencing any possible activity.

At one point Brian asked, "Is it me, or does it suddenly seem a little colder down here?"

Sandra said, "Now that you mention it, the air does seem to be a little chillier than it did just a moment ago."

Brian checked his digital thermometer, which registered only a slight fluctuation. "It was sixty-seven degrees in here; now it's sixty-five."

Turning to Justin, Anne's teenage son who joined us on the investigation, Brian asked, "Has anyone experienced anything unusual down here, that you're aware of?"

"Yes," Justin answered. "In fact, I recently had some of my friends over, and while we were down here in the basement, it started getting real cold. And then the overhead light suddenly became dim for a minute or so. That was when some of us started freaking out because we were convinced something was down here with us."

Brian checked his digital thermometer once again. "Well, it's only gone down a few degrees in here. Nothing real significant."

We then checked for possible drafts, and actually found them coming in from all of the upper basement windows.

"I guess that accounts for the minor drop in temperature," said Brian. "You can even feel how the wind's picked up outside."

Sandra then asked me if we should begin an EVP session, to which I agreed. I asked Justin, "Do you understand what Electronic Voice Phenomena is?"

"Yeah, I think so," he replied. "It's when you try to record voices from spirits using a tape recorder."

"Exactly," I said. "And you're welcome to join us for our session if you'd like, especially since you live here, and have experienced what's going on. It's completely up to you."

With a shrug, Justin said, "Yeah, sure, why not?"

While audio recording we asked a series of simply phrased questions, such as "Who are You," "How long have you been here," "Did you once live in this house," "Is your name Frank" and "Do you have any messages for us?" Justin quickly caught onto the technique, and began asking rudimentary questions along with us.

After approximately ten minutes of asking questions, we decided to pause and review our session for any possible evidence. Our recordings revealed no immediate trace of EVP. We then radioed the other team members who were upstairs on the second floor, to ask if they'd been experiencing any activity.

Carl responded over the hand-held radio, "No, it's been pretty quiet up here so far. We haven't really been experiencing anything." Brian told Carl it had also been pretty quiet in the basement, and that we'd meet him and the others downstairs in about ten minutes.

Before we ourselves went back upstairs, Brian suggested to Justin, "Listen, Justin, would you mind asking your sister to come down here for a few minutes? Since most of the activity has reportedly centered on her, we might get some reaction with her down here with us."

"Sure, I'll go up and ask her," said Justin.

A few minutes later, Amy had joined us in the basement. "So, what would you like me to do?" she asked us.

Brian said, "We'd like you to try and contact your Uncle Frank. Maybe try asking him a few questions, to see if he'll respond."

"Okay, I'll give it a try," she said. "Uncle Frankie… are you here?"

We waited in silence for about ten seconds, before Amy repeated, "Uncle Frankie, are you here? It's me, Amy."

We waited another few seconds, when Amy said, "There, I think he just answered."

Justin said, "Yeah, I heard it too. He just knocked on the floor."

"I'm afraid I didn't hear anything," said Sandra.

"Neither did I," said Brian. "Please try asking him again, Amy."

Amy asked again, but neither Brian nor Sandra or I heard anything. Amy and Justin told us that Frank was answering very quietly, but was probably having trouble being heard by us because the floor was concrete. Brian asked, "Well, where are the knocking sounds coming from?"

"Right about here," said Amy, indicating a spot on the floor directly in front of her.

Brian knelt down and placed his hand on the spot Amy had indicated. "Go ahead, ask again," he said.

"Uncle Frankie, can you please give us a sign that you're here?" asked Amy.

Brian waited for a second or two, then looked up at us with a surprised expression. "I just felt it, very lightly, right where my hand is," he told us.

Amy addressed the spirit of Frank again as Brian confirmed that he could again feel the vibration.

"It's like a quick, very light thump," he said, inviting both Sandra and I to try to feel it ourselves. Sandra and I both attempted to feel the thump in response to Amy's questions, but the results were inconclusive. Although we did feel a slight thumping vibration, we could not be certain it was actual paranormal activity.


After we'd returned upstairs, John Hawkins and Carl briefly ventured outside with Amy. They stood outside of the house on the sidewalk, as Amy again attempted to establish contact with her deceased uncle.

"Uncle Frankie, are you out here with us?" she asked. Bending down and touching the cold sidewalk surface, both Carl and John could feel a definite tap in response to her question.

She asked, "Frankie, could you please tap for us again?" And once again, they could feel a definite tap. In fact, when they listened carefully, they could even hear a very slight tapping sound along with the vibrations.

Once back inside, John and Carl verified to the rest of us that they had indeed experienced a tapping out on the sidewalk, in response to Amy's questions. Therefore, we all agreed to sit with the family in the parlor, and make a group attempt at contacting "Uncle Frankie." Amy once again agreed to act as the catalyst.

As she did down in the basement, Amy began by asking, "Uncle Frankie, are you there?"

This time, as everyone remained quiet, we could all hear a soft, single tapping sound emanating from the parlor floor. Amy's mother Anne excitedly asked everyone, "Did you all hear that?"

We all acknowledged that we did, although the tapping sound was so soft it was barely perceptible. Brian instructed, "Anne, ask if this is really Uncle Frankie we're communicating with."

Anne asked, "Uncle Frankie, is this really you we're communicating with?"

In response, there came another barely audible tap from the floor, which caused everyone to glance at each other in amazement. Amy commented to her husband Tony, "It looks like your brother Frank is awake, and he's willing to talk with us. Maybe he's used to everyone being here now."

"Yep, I guess he is," said Tony, nodding in agreement.

Brian then asked Anne, "Do you think that Frank might respond to me, if I asked him a question?"

"Sure, give it a try," Anne encouraged him.

Brian asked, "Frank, do you know who we are?"

His question was answered with another quiet tap from the floor. "Hey, he's responding to me!" Brian said excitedly. He then had another question. Indicating his young friend Mary, Brian asked, "Frank, do you like the pretty girl being here?"

This time Brian's question was answered with a somewhat more definitive tap, causing him and everyone else in the room to laugh, and Mary to blush self-consciously.

Now that Brian knew he could get answers from Uncle Frankie without Amy's assistance, he enthusiastically began asking question after question, each time receiving a soft tap in response. Sandra and Carl and I of course wondered to ourselves if someone might be downstairs, tapping these from underneath the floor. However, everyone was present and accounted for in the parlor, including Anne and Sal's friends Phil and Shannon. A quick check back down in the basement reaffirmed to us that no one was down there.

Anne also informed us that Frankie was able to perform a few little "parlor tricks," so to speak, such as accurately guessing people's ages. Since Brian was anxious to test this out, Anne's daughter Amy demonstrated for us by asking, "Uncle Frankie, can you tell me how old I am?"

We all listened carefully, as fourteen evenly spaced raps sounded on the parlor floor. Excitedly, her mother Anne said, "See? Fourteen, that's exactly right."

"That's impressive," said Brian. "Now I'd like to ask him Mary's age, since Frank would have no way of knowing that."

"Sure, go for it," said Anne.

Brian glanced down at the parlor floor and asked, "Frank, do you see Mary, the pretty girl who's seated over there? Can you tell us what her age is?"

We all listen attentively as twenty knocks were evenly tapped out. "Wow!" said Mary. "Yes, that's my exact age."

"Now I'm impressed," said Brian. Turning to Sal, he said, "Your brother really seems to be right on."

Frank, or whoever was communicating with us, was also accurate in guessing Brian's age, as well as his friend John Hawkins'. He was off by two numbers when tapping out my age and Carl's age, but again accurate with Sandra. The entire scene seemed reminiscent of a typical Victorian Era spirit communication session.

I then suggested to Brian and the others that since "Uncle Frankie" was obviously now in the parlor with us, they might try posing for a "family portrait," so to speak, with Frank right among them. Brian liked my suggestion, and asked everyone to gather around the sofa for a family Christmas picture. He himself would also pose with the family. Brian also requested that Amy ask Frank to appear over his head in the photo. Obligingly, Amy said, "Uncle Frankie, it's time for our family Christmas photo, and we'd like for you to be in it with us."

Her dad specified, "Ask him to appear over Brian's head."

"Oh, yeah," she said. "Could you appear over Brian's head?"

After the family was seated together around the sofa, along with their friends Phil and Shannon, Brian positioned himself with them and said, "Alright, Frank, I'm your new buddy. So if you're able to appear right above my head, now's the time to do it for your Christmas picture. Can you do that Frank? Can you try to appear above my head for your Christmas picture?"

Sandra and I snapped a few pictures, but, unfortunately, no ghostly manifestation appeared in any of the photos. With Phil's permission, I also asked if Frank could be so kind as to appear over Phil's head while I snapped another picture. But once again, Frank failed to make an appearance for the camera. Brian jokingly suggested, "Maybe Frank's camera shy."

"Was he camera shy in life?" I asked Sal.

Sal replied, "No, I don't recall him being camera shy at all while he was alive."

Brian jokingly said, "Let me guess, Frank... everyone get the hell out of my house, right?"

Everyone laughed when an immediate thump sounded from beneath their feet.

Brian was also eager to resume the question and answer session with Frank. He began asking Frank what he thought of the way his sister-in-law decorated the Christmas tree this year, without his assistance.

Through a series of taps, it was determined that although it may not have been up to Frank's own personal standards, the tree decoration this year was acceptable.

Anne said, "I was saying to Frank the other day that I didn't do as good a job decorating the tree as he would have done."

Brian asked, "You can live with it, right Frank? No pun intended." Another tap sounded in response.

"He seems to be revving up a little bit," said Carl. "I think he likes the mode of conversation. Not as interrogating, more conversational."

"Yes. Less serious," said Brian.

Referring to the angel on top of the Christmas tree, which was slightly lopsided, Anne asked, "Frankie, should Sal fix that angel?"

With a single tap, everyone agreed meant yes. I then said, "Ask Frank if he likes angels."

Brian asked, "Frank, do you like angels?"

This time Frank gave no response. I said to Amy, "Ask him, does he see angels now?"

"Me?" she asked.

"Yes, please," I said.

Amy asked, "Frankie, do you see angels?"

But again there was only silence. Finally Brian said, "The heck with angels. You just want to see more pretty girls, huh, Frank?"

"My kinda' guy!" said Brian when everyone heard an immediate knock, seemingly of approval

"Some things just live on," Carl said.

I once again commented on the picture of Frank in his obituary, saying, "He sure looked as though he had a sense of humor."

"Oh yeah, he did," said Sal.

Carl said, "You need a sense of humor when guys like us come around."

The time was now shortly after 9:00 PM, and we decided to wrap up the investigation for the evening. To conclude his communication with Frank, Brian promised, "Next time we come to visit, I'll bring a CD with your favorite Christmas songs on it, and we'll also bring the pretty girl back. She's going to spend the whole night flirting with you. How does that sound, Frank?"

The whole group laughed with the definite thump in response.

Before leaving, we explained to the family that we would review our data for evidence, and contact them perhaps midweek with our findings, if any. We also offered to return for another visit, perhaps before Christmas if they needed us.

Carl said, "Personally, I have no doubt something here. It could be the impression of Frankie's personality. Everything we've experienced here tonight seems to verify that."

Brian agreed. "It obviously seems to be the case, that it's Frankie, just sticking with you guys. It seems to me that he's not here because he doesn't know what he's doing, or where to go, or he's sad, or miserable or lonely. He might be a little frightened about certain things, and might feel the need to be protective, especially towards Amy. But, on the same note, I think in general he just likes being with you guys."

"This is a human's personality," said Carl.

"Really," Brian agreed. "Even though he may be a spirit now, he's still your Frankie." He then asked, "Isn't that right, Frank?"

We all waited for a response, but there was only silence. Sal asked, "Frank, you miss your pork chops?"

A couple of seconds passed before the next thump. Carl said, "I noticed a respectful pause before that one."

"Oh, yes, Frank loved his pork chops," said Anne.

"Good stuff," said Carl.

Brian said, "I guess Frank just needs to warm up to so many strangers, coming in here with cameras and recorders."

"In some cases, spirits can be very perceptive," said Carl. "Time isn't in the same frame as it is for us. But still, he sees all of us, and he's not going to know everything about us right away, so he's going to have to get used to this barrage of people."

"We'll be coming back to visit him, and say hi to him," said Brian.

Amy said, "I don't know how anyone else in my family feels, but I feel there's nothing wrong with talking to him."

"And obviously Frank's not confined just to this house," said Carl. "So that way he can be watching over you, being part of your lives"

"In fact," said Brian, "I'm under the impression that you guys want him to stay with you."

"If it's Frank, then I'd want him to," said Sal.

Brian said, "But it depends, like he said, on whether it's actually Frank," said Brian. "Is this Frank I'm talking to? Frank, are you still with us? Frank?"

Once again, there was no response. Amy asked, "Frank, are you still there?"

"He's not answering," said Brian.

Sal told us, "He's probably gone to bed."

"Do you think he'll be active at all again tonight?" I asked.

Sal said, "No, he wasn't last night. In fact, last night he went to bed earlier; he hardly did anything."

Anne said, "He started around four-thirty, and ended like at eight-thirty."

"And it's nine-thirty now," said Carl.

I asked the family, "By the way, was Frank of the Christian faith?"

Anne replied, "Yes, he was Catholic like the rest of us. Why do you ask?"

"Just curious," I replied.

"Like we said, we'll be in touch as soon as we've finished reviewing our recordings. In the meantime, if the activity picks up or if anything changes, be sure to let us know, and we'll schedule another visit." Brian reminded the family as we left the home.

Before leaving Brian also made certain to say, "Good night, Frank. We'll see you again."

Back outside, as the chill wind whipped about us, Brian asked Sandra, Carl and I, "Well, overall, what did you guys think?"

Carl replied, "Interesting, to say the least, especially for an initial visit."

Sandra said, "I'm still somewhat skeptical, as to where those knockings may have been coming from…"

"To me, it was reminiscent of a session with the Fox sisters," I said.

Mary asked, "The Fox sisters?"

Carl explained, "The Fox sisters were mediums from New York in the mid-1800's. Their sessions with alleged spirit communication became the foundation for the Spiritualist movement."

Turning to John, Brian asked, "John, were you picking up on anything tonight?"

"Not really a whole lot," said John. "It was just too confusing during that question and answer session, with so many people at once."

"Yeah, I understand," said Brian.

Throughout the next few days, Sandra remained skeptical about the noises in the home the family had so readily attributed to "Uncle Frankie." Although everyone we'd met that night in the house was present and accounted for, this in itself did not rule out the possibility of "parlor tricks." Then again, the tapping sounds Carl and John had experienced on the sidewalk outside of the house contributed to the evidence of a spiritual presence. While Sandra and I both agreed that obviously some sort of intelligence was behind the rapping sounds, we also considered the possibility that the fourteen-year-old daughter Amy could be somehow causing the phenomena herself, even perhaps on a psychic level. After all, she was admittedly a lonely teenager who was now receiving negative attention in school, because of the rapping sounds surrounding her.

A third possibility we of course considered, was that this might in fact be an inhuman spirit entity, masquerading as the deceased uncle as a ploy to gain the family's trust. And if this was the case, it was certainly doing a good job of deceiving the family thus far. Since "Frankie" became curiously unresponsive when questioned about seeing real angels, this theory was even more probable.. For some inexplicable reason he, or it, had also avoided answering when Brian asked if it was really Frank that he was talking to.

Although we carefully reviewed our audio recordings from Saturday night, we found no trace of EVP. As for the thumps that had been going on in the parlor during the alleged spirit communication, they were so soft that they were barely audible on the recording. Not only that, but a nearby smoke detector had been intermittently beeping in the background due to a low battery, which interfered with the parlor recording.

As it turned out, we did not have to wait long for an invitation back to the house in Riverside. By mid-week Anne not only contacted Brian, but she also called Carl as well, who'd left his phone number with the family. According to Anne, the activity in their home had suddenly and dramatically increased. Objects were now supposedly flying around in the house, almost as if they were intentionally being thrown at family members. An unfamiliar woman's shoe had also been found on the basement floor, although no one in the family claimed to have put it there. But it was fourteen-year-old Amy who was mainly being targeted. A treasured vanity set upstairs in her bedroom had reportedly been smashed to pieces by an unseen force. But most serious of all, Amy now seemed to be at times manifesting another personality and occasionally speaking in a voice other than her own. Anne wanted to know if we could please make a return visit sometime during the upcoming weekend, to help out her and her family.

Brian telephoned Sandra and me, and told us, "I'm not sure exactly what's going on over there, but when I talked with Anne, she sounded truly terrified. If they're on the level, then this could be an emergency situation."

We therefore arranged our follow-up investigation for that Saturday night, exactly one week from our first visit. Brian also requested that Sandra and I be prepared to perform a blessing, in case the family wanted it. We of course agreed to do so.

Sandra, Carl and I could not help but wonder whether our initial investigation had somehow triggered this sudden increase in the activity. Could the simple fact that we'd been there have ticked something off? The closest I'd come to performing any sort of religious provocation was when I'd inquired if Amy's Uncle Frankie saw angels where he was.

At any rate, we were certainly anxious to return to Anne's house and find out exactly what was going on there. From what she'd told us, she and her family were potentially in real danger.


We arrived back at the Riverside residence early in the evening on December 18th, 2004. Present were Carl, Sandra, Brian Bell, John Hawkins and myself. Brian's friend Mary, who'd been with us on the previous investigation, was unable to join us this time. When Anne and Sal welcomed us inside, they expressed to us how grateful they were to see us again, and informed us that a lot had been happening since our last visit one week ago.

Sandra asked "Are you looking for us to do something about this? Or are you still undecided?"

Sal replied, "Actually we're going to be moving."

"You're moving?" asked Sandra, somewhat taken aback.

"When?" I asked.

"In a week," said Anne. "But we're only moving a street away. We just can't take what's going on in this house anymore, and what's been happening to our family."

At Brian's suggestion, we all decided to sit in the parlor with the family, and do a follow-up interview with them. Family friends Phil and Shannon were again present this evening. As we spoke with the family, everyone was in relatively good humor and very anxious to go into detail about the activity that had taken place since our last visit.

"What type of shoe was it?" Brian asked when the family brought up the shoe found in the basement.

Sal said, "It's a woman's dress shoe, and it looks like it comes from the 'sixties or 'seventies. But nobody seems to know where it came from."

"We'll show it to you when you go downstairs," said Anne. "I don't know what the significance of it could be, unless maybe it belonged to someone who lived here years before."

Carl asked, "Does anyone have any theories as to why the activity suddenly seems to be getting more hostile?"

Sal said, "It seems that when Frank stops for a day or so, something finally happens big time. It's like he's building up for something. In fact, just last night, Anne was downstairs here and it started throwing stuff down the staircase, like her chapstick, soda bottles, and even an alarm clock."

"But last night was really bad, when the alarm clock was thrown" said Anne. "If I hadn't reached my head around that staircase, I would've gotten nailed, or whatever. It's gathering energy form somewhere."

"Was everyone else in the house accounted for at this time?" asked Brian.

Anne said, "Yes, the whole family was together downstairs."

We were also told that fourteen-year-old Amy had been seeing "circles" or orbs while upstairs in her bedroom. She has has been recently found walking around at night as if in a trance.

Brian asked. "Could you explain to us about the disturbance that took place in Amy's room the other night?"

Sal replied, "Last night at about 2: 00 AM, we suddenly heard some sort of commotion going on upstairs in Amy's bedroom. So Anne, Justin and I came rushing into her room to see what wrong. Well, we found that everything in her bedroom was thrown all over the place. The vanity was lying right across the floor. And Amy herself was there in her bed with a book over her face."

"What book?" I asked.

Anne said, "It was one of the prayer books that used to belong to Frankie that had been downstairs on top of the piano."

"So we tried to wake her up, to see if she was alright," said Sal. "But no matter how hard we tried, she just wouldn't wake up. Finally Justin pulled her off the bed and onto the floor, and then she finally came to."

I asked, "Amy, you don't remember any of that?"

"No, and that was the last time I've slept up in my bed," said Amy.

Sal said, "And then when she came down here and went to sleep on the couch, all she did was laugh."

"She laughed?" asked Brian.

Sal said, "She was laughing so loud, and making so much noise, I was afraid that someone in the neighborhood might call the cops on us. And she just kept laughing, and said, 'Don't make me laugh, Frankie, you'll make me pee my pants!' And we all started laughing too, 'cause it was so funny."

"Amy was also having a conversation with Frankie, in her sleep," said Anne.

"Yeah, that's right," said Sal. "She was talking with Frankie about the country club, and about the funeral, if anybody paid for it. But she doesn't remember any of that"

Anne said, "But the night before that, Amy kept saying, 'He's coming, he's coming. Who 'he' is, I don't know. But I sat there and listened for a while, and it was like she was having a real conversation with someone. She was saying, 'Yes, they're here. They're here all the time. They're taking care of him.' To me, that indicates that it could be her Uncle Frankie, because she's having a conversation about her father being all right."

Sandra then asked Anne and Sal, "Does she have any history of sleepwalking?"

"No, not at all," said Anne. "She's never been known to sleepwalk, ever."

Sandra said, "Well, just as a suggestion, you probably should bring this to her doctor's attention, if you haven't already. He or she may suggest a sleep clinic."

Both Anne and Sal agreed that this might be a good idea.

I asked, "Now, I understand that you're moving in a week or so?"

"Yes, the first of the year," said Anne. "But as I said, only a street away."

Brian asked, "Do you think the fact that you're moving has anything to do with the activity suddenly picking up?"

"Yes, I think that it could be a contributing factor," said Anne.

Sal said, "My brother Frank is probably upset over the move. But whether he'll come with us, or stay here in this house, I don't know. I guess we'll just have to wait and see."


After the interview with the family was concluded, Brian decided it was time to begin our second investigation of the house. Sandra and I first set the camcorder up downstairs on a tripod, recording in infrared. Brian, Carl, John, Sandra, and I then began investigating in and around the kitchen, since the family had also reported experiencing sudden cold spots in that area just prior to the disturbances. Just as the last week, the smoke alarm was still beeping intermittently. Brian commented, "Looks like you still haven't changed that battery."

Anne said, "Yeah, it's annoying, I know. But since we'll be moving in a week anyway, I haven't bothered changing it."

Although we initially begin getting some rather high EMF readings in the kitchen area, Brian cautioned us, "Some of these appliances could still be storing an electrical charge. Sometimes the capacitors, like in the TV over there, could still be giving off enough output to render our readings inaccurate for the next twenty-five to thirty minutes or so."

Pointing out the toaster oven and the microwave, Sandra said, "There certainly are a lot of appliances around here. Maybe we'd better come back to this area later on."

The teenage son, Justin, then led us downstairs. While Sandra was setting up our video camera in the basement, Justin indicated a shoe that was placed on a wooden table, and said, "Oh, by the way, this is the shoe that we found on the middle of the floor." He handed it to us to inspect.

It appeared to be a young girl's small, black leather shoe, of a style dating back at least a few decades. Brian asked Justin, "And you say that you and your family simply found this shoe down here?"

Justin replied, "That's right, no one in the family put it there. We have no idea where it came from."

Carl said, "Maybe it once belonged to someone who lived in this house years ago, like your mom suggested."

"Yeah, that's what we were thinking," Justin agreed.

Brian said, "Well, if whoever that belonged to is still here in spirit form, then hopefully she'll make her presence known to us."

"Or he," I said. When everyone turned to look at me, I shrugged and added, "Hey, well, you never know."

After Sandra had finished setting the video camera in place, we returned to the first floor with Amy and Justin, and found the family members gathered in the parlor and dining room.

I asked Amy and Justin, "Nobody's upstairs on the second floor now, right?"

"No, the upstairs should be empty," Amy replied.

Brian approached Anne and Sal, who were chatting with their friends Phil and Shannon in the parlor. "Excuse me, would you mind if we began investigating the upstairs area?" he asked them.

"No, not at all, please do," said Anne. "Just watch out for all the clutter that's up there, especially in Amy's room."

Sal said, "Yeah, it's really a mess up there, what with Amy's smashed vanity and all. We've left it exactly the way we found it. It's a total mess up there."

"We'll do our best to be careful," Brian assured them.

We found the temperature in the upstairs area to be notably cooler than the rest of the house, since the family had not bothered to heat the upstairs for the past day and a half. Brian explained to us, "This is John's first time out actively pursuing this. But I figured we'd see if he can detect anything up here since this is where the family says most of the activity has been taking place."

Sandra asked, "So, you want to give it a try, John?"

"Sure," said John with a shrug. "Like Brian said, I'm pretty new at paranormal investigating. But I do have some psychic awareness, and I can usually tell if there's a presence nearby. In fact, I used to work as an overnight security guard at a large warehouse facility in Central Falls, which was built in the 1840's. And that was when I really started picking up on the presence of spirits all over the place. It got to the point where I had to ask them to back off from me, and keep a distance."

Brian said, "Well, let's got through these rooms up here, and see what we can come up with."

Carl asked me, "Are you recording this, Keith?"

"Yes, I have my tape recorder on," I said.

"We're also doing infrared downstairs in the basement," Sandra added.

John said, "There's nothing down in the basement, except for the lady's shoe they found. But I've never felt anything at all down there. It's all concentrated up here."

Carl suggested, "Well, how about if we start asking some rudimentary questions up here? That way, John can let us know if he picks up on anything. In the meantime, we'll be recording for any possible EVP."

"That sounds like a good idea," Brian agreed.

As we began making our way down the darkened hallway, with our flashlights guiding us, Carl asked, "Does anyone want to respond? Does anyone have a message for us? Frankie, or whoever? Whatever presence wants to make itself known, speak to us. We'll listen."

Sandra asked, "Can you make your presence known to us?"

After a wait of about fifteen seconds, we rewound the audiotape and listened. However, we found no trace of EVP. Turning to John, I asked, "John, are you picking up anything in here?"

John said, "I sense that it's moving about, probably avoiding us. But I feel that it's concentrated in the room up ahead, just to the left."

"That's Amy's bedroom," said Brian. "Let's go see what's up in there."

Upon entering Amy's bedroom and switching on the dim overhead light, we indeed found everything to be in a state of disarray, with the vanity set smashed into pieces as if someone had taken a sledgehammer to it. Shards of broken plastic and glass littered the floor. The bed was still unmade with the covers bunched in a heap.

Brian said to us, "C'mere, and take a look at this. It's totally destroyed this vanity."

"Holy mackerel" said John, as he took a closer look at the wrecked vanity.

As Sandra and I also stepped in for a closer inspection, I said, "So, this is where the devastation occurred. It looks like someone really took quite a temper tantrum in here."

"You got that right," said John. "Because I can feel it."

"You can feel it now?" I asked.

"Uh-huh," said John. "If I took off my jacket right now and rolled up my sleeves, you'd see goosebumps all the way up my arm."

Brian commented, "Whoever did this must be really twisted, or have real serious emotional problems."

Sandra suggested, "Or maybe it's simply a cry for attention, even if it's negative attention."

"That's of course also a possibility," said Brian. "But if this does involve some sort of entity separate from the family, we've somehow got to try and get it to reveal itself."

Turning to John, I said, "Try asking it a question."

John seemed to be feeling somewhat overwhelmed by the energy in the room. "Can you back off just a little bit?" he asked. "I can feel ya. Can you maybe go in the other room? I'm not gonna touch anything in here." After a moment John breathed a sigh of relief and said, "Thank you."

Carl asked him, "Were you just feeling threatened by the presence, John."

"It was just kind of enveloping me for a moment there, so I had to ask it to leave." said John. "But it's totally calm in here now. Nothing like it was before."

Carl said, "I agree, the heaviness in here does seem to have suddenly lightened a little."

Brian asked John, "What exactly is it that you feel, when you're sensing a spirit presence?"

"It's a sensation of cold," John explained. "But not the kind of cold like you feel if you go outside. Just picture a cold that's coming from inside you."

Brian said, "Tell it to come back, and we'll see if we can pick up any evidence."

After taking a deep breath to ground himself, John said, "Come back in. We're waiting for a sign that you're here. Some kind of response, anything." After of moment of hesitation, John said, "Atta' boy."

Sandra and I again both began asking questions for possible EVP. Sandra asked, "Will you remain here if the family leaves? Are you bound to this house?"

"Or will you go with the family when they move?" I asked.

We then took a moment to listen to our recordings, but again no response. Carl suddenly waved our attention over to John Hawkins, who seemed as if he was in some sort of trance.

"Hawkins?" Brian asked him. When he did not respond, Brian again asked, "Hawkins? You alright over there, John?"

John shook his head and seemed to snap out of it. "Whoa," he said. "I just felt it, wicked intense. But then it dissipates. It's coming in and out of the room in spurts, but it won't seem to hold steady."

Brian checked his digital thermometer, and noticed that the room temperature had just dropped three degrees. We also observed some minor fluctuations on the Gauss Master, although nothing significant was registering. Glancing around, Brian asked the spirit, "Why don't you come back here and stay with us; try communicating with us?"

John said, "I sense that it's moving in and out of the room, and that it's avoiding a direct confrontation with us."

"What exactly are you feeling now?" I asked him.

"Vibrations," he replied. "But, like I said, it won't stay in one place long enough for us to communicate."

Turning to Brian, I asked "What's your assessment at this point?"

With a sigh of frustration, Brian told us, "I hate to say it, but John's been feeling it move around, so I just assume that it's very reluctant to communicate at all with us. Maybe it's Frankie, maybe not. But whoever did that to the vanity is obviously extremely hostile."

Carl then addressed the entity by asking, "If this is Frankie, could you please communicate by tapping for us, like you did last week?" But there was no response.

Brian then began losing patience with whatever entity might be playing cat and mouse with us. Referring to the wrecked vanity, he said, "I demand that the foul and weak creature that did this reveal itself!"

John said, "I could feel him for just a moment there, but now he's backing off again."

"This is getting us nowhere," Brian said in frustration. "Carl, would you mind going back downstairs for a moment, and asking if there's any possible way that Amy would be willing to assist us up here?"

"Will do," said Carl. He quickly left to try and convince Amy to join us.

It was now getting late, and the rest of us were also anxious to either establish some sort of communication with the entity, or to wrap up our investigation and go home. While we were waiting for Carl to return, hopefully with Amy accompanying him, Brian asked me, "Keith, you want to try provoking it? You're a lot milder than I am."

"That he is," Sandra agreed.

"Well, alright, I'll give it an attempt," I said. After going over and standing beside the destroyed vanity, I asked, "Are you responsible for this devastation?" After a wait of several seconds, I asked, "Would you like it if this place was exorcised?"

"I just felt that chill sensation again," said John. "Something just came in here."

"Keep going, Keith," Brian encouraged me.

I asked, "In the name of Jesus Christ, are you a human spirit?" Following a short pause, I asked, "In the name of Jesus Christ, are you an inhuman spirit?"

John said, "It's staying in here with us. We're definitely getting some reaction now."

Before I could ask many more questions, however, Carl returned upstairs with Amy.

"Oh, hi," I greeted her. "I'm glad you agreed to join us up here. Do you feel uncomfortable being in this room?"

"Yeah, when I'm alone," she said. "But not with all of us here. Not with you guys standing right here, no."

"Good," said Sandra.

Amy walked over to what remained of her vanity and told us, "I've left this exactly the way that I found it."

Brian said, "Yeah, it's quite a mess. Amy, we've been unable to establish any definite contact with Frankie, or any other presence that may be here. John's been picking up the impression that a presence has been going in and out of this room. So, we were wondering if you could possibly help us to communicate with your uncle, the way you did for us last week. Would you mind doing that for us, Amy?"

"No, I wouldn't mind," Amy said with a shrug. She then casually sat down on her bed with her hands folded. We were all glad that she was so willing to cooperate with us.

Brian asked her, "Okay, Amy could you try asking your Uncle Frankie if he's here?"

"Uncle Frankie, are you here?" she asked.

We waited, but there was no response. Brian said, "Try asking him if he could tap for us, like he did before."

Amy asked, "Frankie, can you tap for us?"

But again no response. Sandra asked her, "Has the tapping still been going on while you're in school, Amy?"

"Oh, yeah, more than ever," she said. "In fact, the other students are giving me so many problems about it, my mother's thinking of taking me out of the school altogether."

Brian then suggested, "Listen, Amy, maybe you can provoke your uncle into responding by telling him you're in trouble. After all, he was always very protective of you, right?"

"Yeah, he was," said Amy.

"Try telling him that men are up here in your bedroom, and that you're afraid," said Brian.

Flatly and without emotion, Amy said, "Frankie, there's men here inside my bedroom, and I'm afraid." She waited a few seconds before adding, "Can you please come and help me?"

With Brian prompting her, Amy continued asking for her Uncle Frankie's assistance, but no response was forthcoming. At one point Brian glanced over at John and asked, "Hawkins? Anything?"

"No," said John, shaking his head. "I'm not picking up on anything in here right now."

Carl asked Amy, "Why do you think your Uncle Frankie would be avoiding you, even when you asked for help?"

"I have no idea," she said. "Like we were explaining, the activity's been picking up a lot since last week, so I don't know why my uncle's not answering me now."

I then asked her, "Amy, would you like what's been happening to you to stop?"

"Yeah, especially with all that's been going on at school," she said.

"You're still Catholic, right?" I asked.

Without hesitation she replied, "I'm a Christian."

"Good," I said. "Do you attend church service?"

"No," said Amy.

"You do read the Bible, right?" I asked.

"No, not really," said Amy.

"I just want you to understand, you don't have to be harmed by this, or made to feel uncomfortable," I explained to her. "If you choose, you can have protection."

"Whoa," said John, taking a step back. "Something in the room just went right by me."

Brian again pressed Amy to try communicating with the spirit presence, but "Uncle Frankie," or whatever it was, seemed unwilling to cooperate. Carl commented, "Strange that Frankie has the ability to totally destroy a solid object like this vanity, but is no longer able or willing to even tap for us."

Amy said, "Yeah, I dunno what's going on with him tonight. Maybe he's still mad."

Sandra asked, "Why do you think he'd be mad in the first place?"

Amy shrugged, and said, "Maybe because we're gonna be moving, I guess."

As it soon became obvious that no further spirit communication would be forthcoming, Brian decided it was time for us to return downstairs and confer with the family.


Back downstairs in the kitchen area, we privately spoke with Anne, while Amy was in another room. We shared our findings with her, as well as John Hawkins' impressions while we were in the upstairs area. Brian said, "Obviously, Uncle Frankie wasn't coming through to us tonight, and neither was he coming through to Amy. We're also all in agreement, that it probably wasn't Frankie who caused all that damage up there."

"Well, what do you think did cause that damage, then?" asked Anne.

As tactfully as possible, we explained that in our opinion, the damages had either been caused by an unknown entity, or perhaps even by Amy herself. Anne seemed to be receptive to what we were saying, and informed us that she'd had a discussion with Amy's high school guidance counselor about scheduling a psychological evaluation for Amy. Even if the disturbances in the house were genuinely paranormal in origin, Anne agreed that her daughter would require extensive therapy.

Carl explained the possibility that Amy was causing things to happen both at home and at school on a subconscious level. "It's believed that some cases of so-called 'poltergeist' activity are actually the result of sporadic psychic energy, put out by a young adolescent going through emotional turmoil," said Carl. "Quite often this occurs with a female adolescent, and your daughter seems to fit the criteria."

Anne asked, "And if Amy is subconsciously causing this activity, what can be done about it? Especially if she's not even aware she's doing it, and has no control over it?"

"Sometimes these situations just seem to end by themselves, when the conflict of the individual is resolved," Carl explained. "But, there's no definite way of predicting this in advance."

John said, "And whatever was upstairs was very elusive, although I was getting the impression that it's mainly confined to the upstairs area."

Anne wanted to know, "But what if it is an entity that's separate from my brother-in-law? Will it be able to follow us when we move?"

I told Anne, "No absolutes, especially since we haven't definitely established exactly what we're dealing with as yet."

Sandra said, "But, like we explained to you last week, Keith and I would be willing to perform a blessing throughout the house, if you and your family would like."

Anne thought this over for a moment, before deciding that she'd prefer to wait until she moved, to see if the activity would pick up again. "Believe me," she said, "if anything starts up again once we've moved, I'll be in touch with Brian immediately, and I hope you can all come back. But for now, I'm hoping that a fresh start will help to change things for the better. This is the house where Frank lived with us, and where all the activity first started, so I'm hoping that everything will be put to rest."

Anne also assured us that she and Sal would be making appointment with specialists, for their daughter's medical and psychological evaluations. Sandra smiled and said, "I'm so glad to hear that, Anne. And you know that our prayers will be with you and your family."

A thorough review of our video and audio footage revealed no anomalous evidence. The Christmas season came and went, and the New Year of 2005 commenced. Although our caseload with New England Anomalies Research was pretty full, we were still curious as to how the family in Riverside was doing. Then, during the first week of January, Brian Bell called and informed us that he'd just heard word from Anne. Apparently the activity had gradually begun to start up in the new home and Amy was again having conversations with Uncle Frankie in her sleep. They were still waiting to get an appointment for Amy to see a prominent neurologist, and were scheduled to have another meeting with Amy's high school guidance counselor.

"Well, at least they're taking steps to get Amy the help she needs," Sandra told Brian over the phone. She also asked, "What about them having their house blessed, like we suggested?"

Brian said, "Anne didn't mention anything about that. But next time I speak with her, I'll remind her about it. In fact, I might need you guys to assist me again with that, if you're available."

We assured Brian that we'd plan our schedules around it, since this case seemed to be a priority. Brian called us again several days later, to say that Anne reported the activity in her new home was still worsening. Brian had offered to return with his crew and with NEAR, to which Anne replied she'd most likely have us back when they'd finished unpacking boxes, and were a little more settled in. She promised to keep in touch, and to contact us immediately if her situation started becoming even more serious. Anne also wanted to finally begin taking Amy to see some specialists.

And then, for some reason, Anne ceased contacting Brian altogether. After not hearing back from her during the next two weeks, Brian tried calling her to check on how things were going, but received no answer. He left another message on the family's phone three weeks later, saying that he was concerned and wished to know how they were doing, but his message was never returned.

And so, Brian simply relinquished the case. During a phone conversation with Brian, I said, "I thought Anne was an old friend of yours."

"Yeah, I thought so, too," he said. "But, I'm sure she has her own personal reasons for not getting back to me, so I have to respect that."


This was certainly not the first time we'd been assisting clients, who had desperately requested our help and who then, for reasons of their own, suddenly decided to cease further communication without explanation. Perhaps they sometimes suddenly wished to remove themselves entirely from every aspect of an unpleasant situation. Sometimes they've sought help from professional counselors and medical professionals, as we of course recommend them to do from the outset if they haven't already… and these professionals may have advised them to refuse any form of intervention, which steps out of the realm of conventional therapy. Again, this was of course their personal choice, and completely understandable.

And of course, the unfortunate instances occur where a rival paranormal group somehow learns about a potentially interesting or "hot" case. They will then sometimes move in and try to discredit the original paranormal group in an attempt to take over the case, assuring the clients that they can do a better job. Fortunately, in my experience these instances of "case jumping" are relatively rare.

Concerning the case in Riverside, RI with which we assisted Brian Bell, we can only hope that the clients benefited in some way from our two investigations, and that their troubled adolescent daughter eventually did receive the help she needed.


As a footnote, our findings from this particular case remain inconclusive. Whether the tapping communications and other activity we experienced were the result of poltergeist activity brought about as the result of teenage angst, or some sort of perpetrated hoax, or by an unknown entity altogether, we were never given the opportunity to fully investigate. One thing we all agreed upon, however, was that we were most likely not dealing with the disembodied spirit presence of Uncle Frankie.

# Chapter 16

### The 'Apex Ape'

The following account took place in the year 1975, and there are still eyewitnesses who will attest to its authenticity. It involved at least several sightings of what was described as some sort of unknown simian primate wandering around the area of the Apex Shopping Center in Warwick, Rhode Island. Among these eyewitnesses was a resident of Smithfield, RI who we'll refer to as "Glen." This is his story.

A rash of reported sightings from local people in the city of Warwick flooded the local police, described as an ape-like creature. However, unlike the standard "Bigfoot" sightings, this creature was described as somewhat smaller in stature, perhaps no more than five foot tall or under. It had supposedly been spotted lurking about in the nearby wooded area of the popular Apex Shopping Center and would sometimes even venture into the deserted parking lot in the evening hours, possibly foraging for scraps of food left over from the shoppers.

Word of this elusive creature eventually spread to other local communities throughout Rhode Island, including the town of Smithfield. In fact, a meeting was held among a tight-knit circle of young Smithfield residents who had heard the story and were intent on either proving or disproving the existence of this creature for themselves. Most of them were in their early-to-mid-twenties at the time. They decided that they would personally investigate this so-called hominid creature, allegedly frightening some of the good citizens of Warwick, as well as other shopping patrons of Apex after dark.

At least three members of this small group of friends decided to venture out together one evening to the Apex Shopping Center in Warwick, and remained in the parking lot until most of the customers had left. And yes, they claimed to have actually encountered the creature! In fact, they returned to Smithfield with reports of having not only heard an unearthly screech emanating from the nearby area of the shopping center but they also claimed to have caught a brief, shadowy glimpse of what appeared to be a stout ape-like creature, lurking on the outskirts of the parking lot. When they had shone the headlights of their car in that direction, they caught a brief yet unmistakable view of two glowing, reddish-yellow eyes reflecting in the headlights. Whatever it was, the creature had let out an unearthly sounding screech, and then swiftly dashed into the nearby woods and out of sight, with an unnatural speed.

The three friends had fled the parking lot, admittedly quite unnerved by what they'd just witnessed. According to their descriptions, the impression they'd had was that this was no known species of primate, at least none that they were familiar with. Further, their brief encounter with this mysterious creature had left them with a peculiarly disturbed feeling. Although they'd been safely within the confines of their car with the doors securely locked, actually hearing and seeing it had literally made their skin crawl, and caused them to be overcome with an instinctual primal terror of the creature. Unfortunately, none of the three witnesses had thought to bring along a camera.

"I sure wouldn't have wanted to be waiting around to take pictures of this thing, whatever it was. After we'd seen and heard it, all I wanted to do was get the hell outta there!" one of the female witnesses adamantly said.

When explaining their experience to family members and close friends, including Glen, they could not wholly account for the sense of dread they'd experienced. They could only describe this feeling as though they had witnessed something otherworldly, something which they shouldn't have seen. While the three witnesses all agreed that the creature was definitely ape-like in appearance, they also all agreed that there was something almost disturbingly "human" about this solitary creature.

Their friend Glen, however, took a rather cocky attitude to their story and scoffed at their claims of the creature they'd encountered having engendered such a feeling of terror.

He told them, "In fact, I'll go down to the Apex parking lot by myself tonight, and either prove or disprove the existence of this creature by myself!"

Although Glen's friends warned him not to go alone, he simply laughed at their concern, and told them that they were letting their imaginations run away with them. Whatever this thing was that they had seen, Glen knew that it had to have a natural explanation, and he assured them that he'd be fine. In fact, he'd even bring a flash Polaroid camera with him, to try and get a snapshot of this creature if possible. And so, that very night after 10:00 PM, against the advice of his close friends, Glen set out alone in his car, to stake out the area of the Apex parking lot in Warwick. He made certain to bring along plenty of soda pop and chips to snack on, for what he anticipated would be a boring vigil of seeing nothing unusual.

Between the hours of 12:00 and 1:00 AM that night, a RI state trooper who was parked along Rt. 295 North witnessed a vehicle pass by him along the highway at a surprisingly high speed. Naturally, the state trooper immediately switched on his flashing lights and set out in hot pursuit. It was not long before he was right behind the driver, clocking him in speeds in excess of 90 mph. Despite the siren and flashing lights, the driver at first refused to pull over. After several minutes into the chase, the driver did eventually slow down, and managed to pull over to the side of the road. When the trooper got out of his police cruiser and somewhat cautiously approached the driver's side of the vehicle, he found the driver to be a young male in his early twenties who appeared to be in a state of emotional shock. Even when the trooper persuaded the driver to roll down his window, he was not immediately able to respond to any of the trooper's questions. In fact, he was hyperventilating.

His breath coming in quick gasps, "Ah-ah-ah-ah-ah-ah," was all he could say. The trooper at first assumed the driver might be experiencing a heart attack or some type of seizure. However, he was eventually able to calm the young male driver down sufficiently to ascertain that he was merely in a state of panic, and that something had badly frightened him. With trembling fingers, the driver produced his license, and gasped that his name was Glen, a resident of Smithfield. The trooper tried to persuade the driver to get out of his car, but Glen was unable to do so without assistance.

When Glen had finally recuperated his senses enough to speak coherently, he apologized to the trooper for not immediately pulling over, explaining that he was simply unable to do so. When the trooper asked Glen what had frightened him so badly, he told the trooper all about the mysterious ape-like creature his friends had reported witnessing in the parking lot of the Apex Shopping Center in Warwick... and how he'd volunteered to stake the parking lot out by himself, since none of his friends would dare to go back there after dark. That evening, he'd ventured alone and had arrived in the parking lot shortly before 11:00 PM. He'd been keeping vigil in the now otherwise deserted lot for perhaps a little over an hour, munching on chips and drinking soda pop – he was not sure exactly how long – when suddenly, he'd heard a high-pitched, unearthly sounding screech emanating from somewhere nearby, which made the hairs on the back of his neck stand up. It was unlike anything he'd ever heard before, even though he'd grown up in a rural area surrounded by woods and was very familiar with most of the sounds of the local wildlife.

And then, he had witnessed a darkened shape emerge from the nearby wooded area into the parking lot. Though slightly hunched and ape-like in appearance, the creature basically walked with an upright posture.

"My God," Chris thought to himself. "It's real… and I'm actually seeing the damned thing!" As Chris continued to watch, spellbound, he noticed that the ape-like creature appeared to be foraging among the scraps in the parking lot. After what seemed like several minutes, but in reality was no more than perhaps twenty seconds, Glen quickly started the car engine and switched on his headlights. This apparently startled the creature, for it suddenly reared up and faced him squarely. The eyes of the creature reflected reddish-yellow in the headlights, and its mouth was open in an apparent snarl, revealing sharp canine incisors. Glen had now reached his limit of endurance.

Without even thinking of trying to get a snapshot of this misanthropic creature, he instantly backed up and then sped out of the Apex parking lot, burning rubber as he did so. As he was pulling out of the parking lot, Glen overheard one final horrific screech from behind his car, causing him to desperately roll up his window and lock his driver's side door without slowing down. He never even bothered glancing into his rear view or side mirrors to ascertain if the creature was pursuing him, deathly afraid of what he might see.

Glen informed the state trooper that he did not even recall speeding along the highway. In fact, the last thing he remembered after leaving the Apex parking lot was slowly coming to his senses and being questioned by the trooper. He had no recollection at all of getting onto Rt. 295, and the only explanation he could give was that in his state of panic, his mind had somehow switched into "automatic." Even though Glen appeared to be totally sincere, the trooper nonetheless subjected the driver to a sobriety test, but found him to be completely sober. He also made a thorough search of the car's interior. All he discovered were the contents of a bag of potato chips scattered over the front seat, as well as a Polaroid camera that appeared to have been hastily tossed aside, and an opened can of Coca Cola which had spilled out over the front seat floor.

Glen's personal encounter with what became known as the "Apex Ape" combined with the state trooper's report and other numerous eyewitness accounts were apparently taken seriously enough at the time to launch an official investigation. The D.E.M. became involved, as well as local and state authorities. The entire area of the Apex Shopping Center and the surrounding wooded area were temporarily closed off and thoroughly explored. The official investigative team thoroughly combed the entire restricted area, and although their extensive search did not turn up the Ape itself, they did find definitive tracks, in the in the form of footprints. After closely examining these footprints, the experts all agreed that they could not possibly have been made by any identifiable species. While these prints were obviously made by some sort of two-footed primate, similar to an adult male chimpanzee or orangutan, the creature seemed to have been "leaping" rather than walking or scurrying. They could tell this by the fact that the individual tracks were made by a bipedal creature, with each set spread about two-and-a-half to three feet apart, indicating a "leaping forward" motion. Not only that, but there were impressions in these tracks resembling claw marks, which had been scratched into the soil every time the creature had leaped. This seemed to indicate that the primate had made a curling motion with its toes, or claws, just prior to jettisoning itself forward with each leap.

It was reported that the search party also overheard a loud screeching in the distance, which was described as the type of screeching a chimpanzee would make, only much deeper and with a great deal more volume to it. During the investigation, experts observed a noticeable absence of the usual signs of other indigenous wildlife (such as birds chirping, squirrels foraging, etc.), which the D.E.M. investigators would normally expect to encounter in such a typical New England wooded area. At the conclusion of this investigation, an official notified Glen and the other eyewitness of their findings.

Unfortunately, if any overt evidence was collected during the investigation, such as recordings of the primal screeching, photographs of the tacks or other specimens, it was never released to the general public. To my personal knowledge no current news reports about the ape-like creature or the subsequent investigation have been recorded. Because the reports of this creature had been causing such a local stir, everything seemed to have been deliberately hushed up. However, almost immediately after the investigation was concluded, the entire wooded area was completely sectioned off with metal fencing by the City of Warwick. Today almost all of the entire area has been cleared and developed, and a Lowes Home Improvement Warehouse presently occupies the space now known as 555 Greenwich Avenue, where the Apex Shopping Center stood for many years.

No further conformed sightings of the mysterious creature known as the Apex Ape were reported after 1975, although several "Bigfoot" sightings have been documented in rural areas throughout Rhode Island. These sightings have occasionally been accompanied by an unearthly screeching. One explanation that has been suggested for the existence of this creature is the "escaped monkey" theory. It is said that during the Hurricane of 1938, hordes of monkeys escaped from nearby Rocky Point Amusement Park, and that these monkeys began breeding in secluded areas throughout the city of Warwick. However, it seems unlikely that a wild monkey population could account for what was witnessed numerous times in the Apex parking lot.

And of course, we still have the eyewitness reports of Glen and a few of his old friends, who still swear by their stories. Glen remains convinced that, although the Apex Ape did somewhat resemble a cross between a large chimpanzee and an orangutan, it was unlike anything that he'd ever encountered before, or since. And in the ensuing years, he's had extensive experience with all forms of wildlife. Glen vividly recalls that the most unnerving aspect of the creature was that its facial features were clearly more human in appearance than simian. Whatever it was, all who have ever encountered this mysterious creature unanimously agree - they will never be able to shake the "otherworldly" impression of it that they were left with.

**The Apex Ape, based on descriptions**

# Chapter 17

## How Sad

It was through our association with friend Robert Tremblay, founder of S.E.R.T. (Spirit Encounters Research Team) that Sandra and I first became acquainted with Michael J. Baker. In 2006, Michael and his production assistant, Anthony Z. Monti had founded an independent film and media production company called New Gravity Media. For their first production, they were interested in putting together a documentary about the paranormal and paranormal investigation. Since Rob and his paranormal research team were currently investigating the Colonial House Inn, located in Yarmouthport, Massachusetts as part of the documentary, New England Anomalies Research founders, Sandra and I were invited to participate. The documentary itself was to be titled "14 Degrees: A Paranormal Documentary," and was scheduled to be released in October of 2007. Besides Sandra and me, the documentary would also feature John Zaffis, Steve Gonsalves, Andrew Graham (our NEAR New Hampshire representative), ISIS Paranormal Investigators, among others.

Sandra and I made the trip to Cape Cod late on a chilly spring afternoon,  arriving at 277 Main Street in Yarmouthport.  Rob welcomed us inside the fabulously historic Colonial House Inn. Andrew Graham and his wife Kathleen arrived soon afterward, and we were certainly glad to have the opportunity for them to join us as part of the investigation team. Rob introduced us to producer/director Michael Baker, as well as his two co-producers, Anthony Monti and Joann Harritos. Michael and his team members were all very affable people, who repeatedly told us just how much they appreciated us driving all this way to participate in their project.

In preparation for our night of investigating and documenting, innkeeper Malcom Perna served us a meal of pasta and fresh New England seafood. We were all delighted to discover that the cuisine at the Colonial House Inn was excellent! Immediately after dinner, Rob sat down with us in the quaint historic dining room and shared some background on the history of the inn.

The original structure of The Colonial House Inn was constructed in the 1730's as a two-story Federal style building, built by the family of Josiah Ryder. It then came into the possession of the Eldridge family and for a century, known as Eldridge House. Sometime in the 1820's, Captain Joseph Eldridge had a house floated over from Nantucket and placed on a foundation at the rear of the building. This house was added to the main building during the 1860's. Captain Eldridge and his wife, Ellen had nine children, although four of them died in infancy. The Captain died in 1856 and left the house to his youngest son, Dr. Azariah Eldridge. Azariah's wife gave birth to one child who died young. Having no heirs, Azariah Eldridge and his wife bequeathed the house to the First Congregational Church in their will.

Over the successive years, the house went through a number of prominent owners, among them U.S. Congressman Thomas Thacher. In 1979, the building was purchased by Malcolm Perna and renovated to include three intimate dining rooms as well as spacious guest rooms, which presently comprise The Colonial House Inn.

Rob informed us that guests reported hearing voices of young children in the hallways and in some of the rooms where no young children were present. In certain rooms, both guests and staff were sometimes frightened by mysterious voices sounding like muffled conversations, or the sound of a woman softly humming or singing to herself. And within two of the upstairs rooms in particular, people had experienced an uneasy feeling of being watched, as if an unseen presence might be in the room with them.

Rob and his S.E.R.T. members had also captured some evidence of paranormal phenomena during a previous investigation at the Inn, including a rather clear example of Electric Voice Phenomena in one of the rooms of a presumably male voice saying "Hello." Rob and his team members also played the recorded sound of footsteps running up and down the stairs in the widow's watch. Although rather inconclusive, we also heard what seemed to be the recorded phantom voices of young children in a stairwell.

Throughout the next several hours of that evening, our two paranormal investigation teams conducted a thorough co-investigation of the sections available to us within the two floors of the building, as well as the basement. All the while Mike, Anthony and Joann were closely documenting our investigation techniques for their project. They were also anxious to capture any possible evidence of the paranormal.

Unfortunately, things were rather quiet that evening, with very little in the way of paranormal activity taking place. However, because one of the S.E.R.T. members had psychically picked up on the impression of a lady dressed in blue down on the lower level, Sandra, Andrew and I decided to go down to that section to attempt an EVP session. While seated around a table, with the New Gravity Media crew documenting the entire session, the three of us began asking a series of pertinent questions, such as:

"Is there anyone present who would like to communicate with us?"

"Are you the lady who was dressed in blue?"

"Can you make a tapping sound on this table?"

"Do you like us being here?"

After about fifteen minutes, we ended our session and reviewed our recordings. Although we found nothing in the way of EVP, on the one section of video footage taken during the session, we detected an anomaly. In fact, while the camera had been focused upon Sandra, a small greenish-blue globule could be seen floating about her face.

While we had no real explanation for this small anomaly, we were able to rule out insects. For one thing, Sandra was completely unaware of it at the time, and it was close enough to her eyes that she certainly would have flinched or reacted in some way. Also, I happened to be sitting close enough to Sandra that I would definitely have noticed even a tiny insect buzzing about her face. Later analysis of the footage also ruled out a dust orb or a camera glitch. We eventually simply labeled this anomaly as inconclusive, rather than paranormal. This footage, which lasts approximately 30 seconds, was included in "14 Degrees."

Shortly after midnight, our two teams decided to wrap up our investigation of the Colonial House Inn. All in all, it had been an enjoyable experience, even if we were unable to capture any overt paranormal activity that evening. The inn itself was an attractively historic building and our meal at the onset of the evening had been satisfyingly delicious!

After Michael Baker and his New Gravity Media team had completed the on site investigation segments for "14 Degrees," they arranged for the personal interviews that would be a significant part of the documentary. Michael rented a local hotel room and scheduled interviews with NEAR members Andrew Graham, Sandra and myself.

Thus it was that on a Saturday afternoon, Sandra and I, along with Andrew and Kathleen Graham, met up again with the New Gravity Media crew at the Comfort Suites, West Warwick, RI. We were on the 4th floor in room number 425.

Before the individual interviews commenced, Kathleen announced that she'd decided to forgo an interview since, although she'd been present at the Colonial House Inn, she'd been an observer rather than an active participant in the investigation.

Kathleen said to us, "As I've told Andrew, he can do the investigating, as long as he doesn't bring anything home with him...that which he recently did."

In his defense, Andrew explained, "Yes, but it was only for about three nights, after we'd done an investigation with Keith and Sandra in Providence. We kept feeling a cat walking around on our bed, but we don't even own a cat. And when we'd turn the light on, nothing would be there. But after three nights, the activity stopped."

Michael, Anthony and Joann of New Gravity all found this account extremely interesting, engaging in a great deal of discussion among us in preparation for the interviews.

When we were finally ready to begin the individual on-camera interviews, with Michael himself acting as the interviewer, he asked us which one of us wanted to go first, and I volunteered. Andrew was next. Each of our segments lasted approximately twenty minutes.

After we'd taken a brief break for refreshments, it was then Sandra's turn to get into the "hot seat" as she referred to it. Now, one thing about Sandra is that while she is very comfortable and at ease while interviewing guests on our paranormal TV talk show "Ghosts R NEAR", she has some reservations when it comes to being in the "hot seat" herself. To make matters even worse, the chair she was now sitting in had no armrests to hold.

In an effort to put Sandra a little more at ease, I teasingly told her, "If necessary, I'll hold your hand."

As it turned out, Sandra's interview went just fine, and she was relieved when it was over. With the interview sessions wrapped up for the day, Michael, Anthony and Joann thanked us all for our participation.

"Great interviews, guys. I can't thank you enough!" Michael told us. "I've already interviewed Steve Gonsalves and John Zaffis, as well as Rob Tremblay, and the ISIS Paranormal Investigators. So after the interview segments are completed, it's a matter of editing them and the investigation segments. So we hope to have '14 Degrees' completed and ready for release by this October."

Andrew said, "Great, we're really looking forward to it."

Sandra and I also invited Michael and his New Gravity Media crew to appear on "Ghosts R NEAR" to talk about the project when it was completed. They were absolutely thrilled at this idea.

While we'd been at the hotel in West Warwick, I happened to make audio recordings of both Andrew and Sandra's interviews, simply so I could enjoy listening to them later on. While driving home that afternoon, Sandra and I were listening to my recording of her interview and I heard my own voice jokingly telling her, "If necessary, I'll hold your hand."I deleted this because it was redundant and takes away from the giggle factor of the recount.

And then unexpectedly, Sandra and I both heard a female voice on the recording say, "How sad."

"That's strange," I said to Sandra. "I don't recall Kathleen or anyone else saying that. And Kathleen was in the room, seated nearby to me."

Sandra said, "I don't remember anyone saying that either. Joann was in the next room, and I think I would've remembered if she'd said 'How sad.' She certainly wasn't anywhere close to your tape recorder."

After I'd rewound the tape and played the recording of a woman's voice saying "How sad" a few more times, Sandra commented, "That's definitely not Kathleen saying that. In fact, I can hear her softly laughing at what you said, and the voice saying 'How sad' sounds as though it's being spoken directly into the tape recorder. It seems you've caught a genuine EVP there."

"But I wasn't even trying to record EVP; I was simply recording your interview with Michael," I reminded Sandra.

Sandra said, "Well, it looks like you came away with an added bonus."

And indeed it seemed that I had. The voice was very clear, and it obviously sounded like that of an adult female. And as Sandra had said, the voice did sound as though it had spoken very close to the microphone of the tape recorder, yet the phrase "How sad" was definitely not spoken by anyone present in the room, at least not by anyone that could be seen.

Almost immediately following my discovery of the apparent EVP, I e-mailed Michael Baker and told him what I'd found on my audio tape. Michael in turn told me that he'd check his camera recordings.

When Michael got back to me after having reviewed his footage of the interviews, he confirmed that the female voice saying "How sad" could also be heard on his camera audio. He also confirmed that no one had been near enough to the camera for it to have been picked up that clearly.

Michael told me, "That's truly fascinating! Thanks so much for bringing it to my attention, Keith. I might never have noticed it otherwise, since it was recorded just before Sandra's interview began. And on the video, you can see the position of everyone in the room, which rules out anyone who was there saying ' How sad.'" Michael and his team later tried to replicate the phenomena under identical conditions, but were unable.

What both Michael and I unintentionally recorded does seem to be a genuine example of Electronic Voice Phenomena, meaning, of course, that it was not heard audibly by anyone in the room at the time of the recording. Also, the fact that my analogue tape recorder and Michael Baker's camera audio had picked up the same voice, would define this as "coupling." We were of course lucky to have made this catch, since neither of us had been actually trying to capture any evidence of paranormal phenomena at the time.

As to why I captured this particular EVP in a hotel room, I can only speculate that this may have been an example of the "Law of Attraction." Since our main topic of discussion as well as the interviews that afternoon had all been about spirit phenomena, a spirit may well have been attracted into responding in the form of EVP.

As to the identity of the voice, we haven't a clue. At the time we were there, the Comfort Suites in West Warwick was a relatively new building, and I seem to recall the area being a vacant lot just before it was built. The voice itself had an expressive, decidedly feminine quality to it. We do not know what possible connection, if any, this female voice may have had to room number 425 in this particular hotel, which again was less than two years old at the time. To our knowledge no one ever met with tragedy in this room. Then again, a great many people stay for brief periods of time in hotel rooms each year, and perhaps they leave some residual energy behind when they leave. Sandra and I have known other investigators, including some members of our own organization, who have captured multiple examples of EVP while staying in hotel rooms that were not even known to be haunted.

Or perhaps it was a spirit simply passing though, that was momentarily drawn into our conversation. However, in my personal opinion, it may also have been a spirit that was keeping tabs on the entire documentary project, and may perhaps have decided to comment at that particular moment.

The paranormal investigation documentary '14 Degrees' by New Gravity Media, written and directed by Michael J. Baker, produced by Anthony Z. Monti and co-produced by Joann Harritos was released October of 2007, and was an impressive addition to the list of documentaries that take a serious approach to paranormal research.

Michael has since gone on to found The New England Center for Advancement of Paranormal Science (necaps.org.), and is much in demand as a lecturer and presenter on the advanced theories of paranormal/scientific equipment and research. Michael made a guest spot as a paranormal researcher on the SyFy's Channel's hit TV show "Ghost Hunters" during an investigation of The Colonial House Inn in Yarmouthport, MA, and has appeared multiple times on "Ghosts R N.E.A.R."

Michael's latest film release is "Museum of the Paranormal," documenting John Zaffis' personal museum of haunted objects and collectibles.

**Keith and Sandra appear at the Portsmouth, NH ParaCon**

# Chapter 18

### "The Exorcist" vs. Reality

As is now generally well-known, "The Exorcist" is actually based on a true incident that took place in St. Louis in 1949. The true events involved the alleged demonic possession of a 14-year-old boy, which supposedly began after the boy had toyed with a Ouija board with an aunt. Shortly after his aunt's death, the boy's family began hearing strange scratching and knocking sounds in the walls that could not be accounted for. The boy himself eventually began experiencing some rather frightening and bizarre phenomena, including painful, burning physical assaults to his body, and even raised welts appearing on his chest and abdomen, seemingly in the form of letters. The boy's parents consulted with their Lutheran pastor who, while visiting with the family, observed the terrified boy being dragged across his bedroom floor by unseen hands. The Lutheran minister explained to the family that this was beyond anything he'd ever experienced, and in turn referred the family to the Catholic clergy. The Catholic Church responded by launching a full investigation into the case, eventually resulting in the Rite of Exorcism being performed over the boy by assigned Catholic priests. According to all accounts regarding this case, the exorcism eventually proved successful in ridding the afflicted boy of his demonic possession and the boy went on to live a normal life. While the only actual casualty during the exorcism was experienced by one of the attending Catholic priests, who suffered a broken nose, the entire ordeal lasted for several weeks, and it took an incredible emotional and physical toll on all who were involved.

Having heard of this true story while at Georgetown University, author William Peter Blatty wrote "The Exorcist" in 1971, loosely based on the actual events. In his book, Mr. Blatty updated the story to the present, and substituted a 12-year-old girl, Regan Theresa MacNeil, for the 14-year-old boy. The book soon became widely popular, and it seemed only natural that "The Exorcist" should eventually be made into a full-length movie.

Following a series of delays, the highly anticipated film version of "The Exorcist" premiered in December of 1973. The film was an instant success, rapidly taking its place among horror movie classics. It grossed $402,500,000 worldwide, and received ten Academy Award nominations, winning for Best Adapted Screenplay and Best Sound. While audience reactions varied, it seemed that the public in general was not really prepared for such a cinematic treatment of the subject matter. A movie that so graphically portrayed the phenomena supposedly associated with demonic possession was indeed a new experience. A great many people were genuinely terrified by the movie. In fact, some members of the viewing audience were even emotionally traumatized by the graphic nature of the film. One somewhat amusing story I personally recall took place when I went with my family to see the movie for the first time. My sister Cynthia and her boyfriend were with us, and upon first hearing the voice of the demon, performed by actress Mercedes McCambridge, Cynthia tightly buried her face against her boyfriend's shoulder. As a result, one of her pierced earrings became caught in his sweater. When the film was over, we finally had to ask for assistance from the theater manager, who readily came to the rescue with a pair of scissors and carefully cut a small hole in Cynthia's boyfriend's sweater.

After we'd thanked the theater manager for freeing my sister's ear, he was extremely amused by the incident and commented, "This has certainly been a first." It is not difficult to imagine the theater manager going home and relating this incident to his family. Perhaps he even mentions it at family gatherings right up to this very day.

Up until this time, it was one thing to see a movie about "ghosts," or spirits of the deceased, haunting a house or a family; but somehow, seeing a film depicting a 12-year-old girl being taken over by a demonic spirit while her mother watches helplessly was something almost entirely different. In a way, it was akin to the deep psychological thrillers of Alfred Hitchcock. Suddenly some people were being affected to the point of becoming paranoid.

After seeing the film, people were starting to wonder, "Could something like this possibly happen to me? Am I in danger of being possessed by a demon?" It was similar to the reaction many had to the movie "Jaws" came out a year and a half later, when people were suddenly afraid to go back into the water.

Shortly after the release and subsequent box office success of "The Exorcist," rumors began to abound about a series of mysterious mishaps and deaths surrounding the production, suggesting that the film may actually have been "cursed" because of the subject matter. Such reports were especially popular among the tabloid publications. I vividly recall the front page of one such tabloid of that time, dramatically announcing: "'Curse of 'The Exorcist!' Two dead! One Insane!" To illustrate the point, the front cover also published photos of Max Von Sydow and Jason Miller, who portrayed the two exorcist priests in the movie, making intense emotional expressions during the exorcism scenes, suggesting that they'd both been real-life victims of the "curse." These rumors also served as somewhat of a promo-gimmick for the movie, reminiscent of such films as "Mark of the Devil" (1972), in which paper "vomit bags" had been distributed to patrons as they entered the theater.

While most of these curse stories surrounding the production are largely fabricated, it is also true that that Rev. Thomas Birmingham, the religious technical consultant for the movie, was asked to bless the set on at least one occasion.

Another intentional lure of "The Exorcist" at the time of its release was the mystique surrounding it. No photos of Linda Blair in her demonic make-up were allowed to be published, and no footage publicly shown, until over a year after the film's release. The promo for the movie showed very little, although it was appropriately atmospheric. It simply displayed a fog-enshrouded nighttime shot of Father Merrin, wearing a long black cloak and a wide-brimmed Fedora hat, arriving at the Georgetown residence for the exorcism. The shot was illuminated by a single streetlight as Merrin, shown from behind, stands still, holding a briefcase and glancing up at the house. Also, when the full scene of Father Merrin's arrival at the MacNeil home was shown on television during the Academy Awards, only a brief out-of-focus glimpse of the possessed Regan was shown, from a distance, in a darkened bedroom.

"The Exorcist" also opened doors to other classic horror movies of the kind, such as "The Amityville Horror" – another thriller which people were lined up around the block to see, largely because it was billed as a true story – and later, the movie "Poltergeist." Incidentally, the original soundtrack for "The Exorcist," composed by Lalo Schifirn, was rejected. Instead, a haunting instrumental melody called "Tubular Bells" by Mike Oldfield was used as the main theme. Lalo Schifim's score was later revived and used as the soundtrack for "The Amityville Horror."

The story of "The Exorcist" is a compelling one. A kindly, scholarly Catholic priest named Lankester Merrin, (Max Von Sydow) who is advanced in years, accidentally uncovers a small likeness of the Assyrian demon Pazuzu, while working on an archeological dig in Nineveh. Father Merrin has apparently fought Pazuzu some years before, and it readily becomes apparent that he takes this archeological find as an omen that he must soon face this demon once again. In the film, before this beginning segment concludes, Father Merrin travels to another archeological site where an ancient, full-sized statue of the Assyrian demon Pazuzu happens to stand. Two dogs are fighting viciously in the background, as Father Merrin dramatically faces the statue.

This foreign, rather primitive setting then switches over to modern-day Georgetown, where actress Chris MacNeil (Ellen Burstyn) is filming a movie on location. Staying with her at a rented house is her 11-year-old daughter Regan (Linda Blair), along with Chris' secretary Sharon Spencer (Kitty Winn) and her two Swiss servants, Karl and Willie. Before long, some subtle haunting phenomena occur in the rented house, such as strange scraping noises in the attic and Regan's bed beginning to shake. It is also revealed that Regan has been playing with a Ouija board, and that she has an imaginary friend named "Captain Howdy." Chris suspects her imaginary friend may be an emotional substitute for Regan's estranged father, Howard, who fails to call his daughter on her 12th birthday. Regan's personality soon begins to alter, and she exhibits some bizarre and erratic behavior. The bed shaking becomes more violent, and Regan is also physically assaulted while being forced to masturbate with a crucifix. As her personality continues to be taken over, Regan's physiognomy also dramatically begins to deteriorate, until she is almost unrecognizable as the sweet, innocent little girl she once was. Desperately seeking help for her daughter, Chris MacNeil enlists the aid of a team of doctors, during which Regan is put through a series of grueling medical tests and procedures. Unfortunately the efforts of Chris and the medical team are frustrated at every turn. They then turn to psychiatric help, which proves equally fruitless. It is actually the medical team that suggests exorcism for Regan, as a possible psychosomatic remedy, because of the victim's supposed belief in possession.

While all this is going on, Father Damian Karras (Jason Miller), a Jesuit priest and resident psychiatrist at Georgetown University, has been dealing with personal loss of faith combined with guilt over the recent death of his mother, who had been living in near poverty conditions. Lieutenant Detective William F. Kinderman (Lee J. Cobb) has also been consulting with Father Karras about the recent, possibly ritual-style homicide of Burke Dennings (Jack MacGowran), who was the director of the film Chris MacNeil is starring in.

Through a mutual friend, Father Joe Dyer (Rev. William O'Malley), Chris MacNeil arranges a consultation with Father Karras, who subsequently agrees to become involved with Regan's case from a purely psychiatric view. Upon their first encounter, Regan – or rather, the demon – claims to be the Devil himself, in an apparent ploy to mislead Karras. Despite some of the incredibly bizarre phenomena Karras experiences with Regan (including the inexplicable movement of objects, telepathy akin to mind reading, Regan speaking in reverse English, raised letters spontaneously appearing on Regan's abdomen spelling out "help me," and her spewing him with green projectile vomit), he persistently refuses to believe the cause could be anything of a preternatural nature. Karras even learns from Chris that Regan, while under possession, was quite likely directly responsible for the death of Burke Dennings.

After weeks of involvement with the case, Father Karras eventually agrees that an exorcism might be beneficial, if only as a psychological shock. He presents his evidence to his superiors, and the exorcism is sanctioned. Father Lankester Merrin is assigned as the exorcist because of his prior "experience," although the church authorities have no way of knowing that Merrin will be confronting the same demon he's dealt with years before.

Father Merrin (who we have not seen since the beginning of the story, but whose name has once been mentioned by the demon) promptly arrives at the MacNeil household. Shortly after he has briefly advised Karras on how they should proceed, Merrin begins the Rite of Exorcism over Regan, with Father Karras assisting. It is a grueling ordeal within a small bedroom in which the temperature is arctic. Puffs of vapor issue from everyone's mouths, as an almost constant barrage of profanities and other verbal abuse is leveled against the two priests. Along with the verbal assaults, Father Merrin and Father Karras endure terrifying preternatural phenomena during the exorcism, such as Regan's body grotesquely distorting, her spewing copious amounts of greenish bile, terrifying apparitions appearing, and even earthquake-like tremors within the small bedroom. At one point, Regan temporarily rips out of her bonds while levitating, and later manages to deal a Herculean blow to Karras' back, sending him sprawling.

After the two priests have taken a brief respite in the exorcism, Father Karras returns to the bedroom to check on Regan. As a result of the demon's mocking attempts to impersonate his deceased mother, Karras becomes emotionally overwhelmed. Father Merrin compassionately sends the younger priest from the room, and begins to continue the Rite of Exorcism by himself. A short time later, Karras again returns to the bedroom, only to find that Regan has again managed to break free of her restraints, and that Father Merrin has collapsed and died, apparently of heart failure. When the possessed Regan mockingly giggles at Karras' unsuccessful attempts to revive Merrin, Karras instantly flies into a rage and attacks her, challenging the demon to leave Regan and come into him. The demon does so, and Karras, by a supreme force of willpower, manages to suppress the demon's control over him long enough to hurl himself through a nearby bedroom window with terrific force. Part of the fall down the steep steps leading to M Street is seen in the movie through Karras' perspective. Father Dyer arrives on the scene in time to tearfully administer the Last Rites over his friend. Regan is now freed from possession as the result of Father Karras' sacrifice, and she remembers nothing of the entire experience. However, in the final scene, as the MacNeils are moving out of their Georgetown residence, Regan is briefly introduced to Father Dyer. Regan glances at Father Dyer's Roman Catholic collar and on impulse, reaches up and kisses him on the cheek before she leaves.

The question is often asked of paranormal investigators, and especially to those of us who are also actively involved in the realm of demonology: Just how accurate are the events portrayed in both the book and the film version of "The Exorcist"? First, let's take the use of a Ouija board. Early on in the story of "The Exorcist," Regan has been playing with a "Talking board," or Ouija board. While doing so, she has also made the acquaintance of an imaginary friend named "Captain Howdy." It is soon made evident that Captain Howdy is very possessive of Regan's attention, in that he refuses to communicate with Regan's mother. As mentioned, Chris is initially concerned that Captain Howdy may represent Regan's father, Howard, from whom Chris is separated and who Regan misses quietly. In the context of the story, what Regan seems to have done, is to have innocently "invited" Captain Howdy into their home. It is only later that we realize that Captain Howdy is in fact the demon Pazuzu.

This, I feel, is a realistic portrayal of how a demonic spirit may unwittingly be invited in through the use of a Ouija board, or any similar device used for the summoning of spirits. A true demonic entity will often masquerade as a harmless, even friendly spirit, in an effort to be permitted further access. A demonic entity will also not hesitate to take advantage of someone's loneliness, or their grief over the loss of a loved one. By using a Ouija board, you are opening up your psyche and consciously surrendering a certain amount of your motor control to something which is unseen. You are allowing an unknown and unseen presence to momentarily take over some of your conscious function, just enough to enable it to move the planchette through your fingertips. The same thing, of course, holds true for automatic writing, as well as "channeling" a spirit.

Incidentally, on a recent episode of Coast to Coast AM, host George Noory was slated to attempt spirit communication through the use of a Ouija board while broadcasting live, near the end of the program, with author and guest Rosemary Ellen Guiley assisting him. However, Mr. Noory made a prudent decision not to go through with the experiment, sighting simply too many people in the listening audience might possibly be negatively influenced. Personally, I commended his conviction to ultimately make what he felt to be the correct decision, as opposed to what might have been the more popular approach.

Another aspect of demonic activity that is fairly accurately portrayed in "The Exorcist" is what is referred to as "oppression". This is a strategy used by the demonic to systematically wear down the emotional and psychological resistance of those who are under attack. For example, in the context of the story, the spirit initially known as Captain Howdy gains Regan's trust and begins to infiltrate her personal life. Once he has established a foothold, it is not long before he starts becoming dominant and controlling. He is soon able to begin taking over Regan's personality, although initially it is only for limited periods of time, known as "transient" possession. All the haunting phenomena thus far, such as the bed violently shaking, the scratching in the walls, the flickering of lights, have been done with this objective in mind. Once the demon has taken over Regan's personality completely, the psychological attack becomes focused on others such as Regan's mother and Father Karras, and ultimately on Father Merrin.

In both the book and the film versions of "The Exorcist," excerpts from the official Catholic Rite of Exorcism, known as the Rituale Romanum, were used. The Rituale, which is the only formal rite of exorcism sanctioned by the Roman Catholic Church, was originally written in 1614 under Pope Paul V. When first published in the 17th Century, the Rituale cautioned priests against too readily believing that a person may be possessed. And, with the increased advancement of medical science, which more proficiently defined medical illnesses, true possession, both demonic and spiritual, became more difficult to determine.

The exorcist rarely works by himself, but is usually assisted by at least three other people. The first is generally a younger priest, who is being trained or is trained in the performance of exorcism. His main duty is the continuance of the exorcism, and he will be required to take over if the exorcist is unable to continue. The second person is usually someone medically training who is able to assist the exorcist with the victim from a medical standpoint. In "The Exorcist," Father Karras serves both as assisting priest and attending physician. The third person assists with physically restraining the victim if this becomes necessary, and is often a member of the victim's family. If the victim is a female, then this third person is also usually a female to avoid scandal.

Of course, some of the more bizarre phenomena presented in "The Exorcist" is an exaggeration of what usually takes place during an actual case of demonic possession. For example, in the movie, Regan's personality is eventually taken over completely, and she then remains is a state of complete possession until the very end. It is basically the same situation in the book, except one instant when the demon allows Karras to get a momentary glimpse of Regan. This would mean that Regan would have been in a constant state of possession for at least three weeks, prior to the expulsion, if not longer. In reality, most victims of demonic possession undergo transitory states of possession, meaning that most of the time their own personality is dominant. They will usually suffer periodic spates of possession, and then return to their normal, lucid state of consciousness. However, depending upon the severity of the demonic possession, the "host," or victim, will gradually begin to deteriorate both physically and psychologically. This is often the result of malnutrition and sleep deprivation.

An extremely rare condition, "perfect possession," coined by the late Malachi Martin, indicates a state of possession where the invading entity is so ingrained into the individual's own personality, it is nearly impossible to ascertain when that person is undergoing a spate of possession, and when he or she is not. In these rare instances, the individual is perhaps under possession – or at least under the direct influence of the demonic entity – for the majority of the time.

Some of the other phenomena portrayed in the story, such as Regan's twisting her body into seemingly impossible contortions, and abnormal strength, are actually not uncommon in authentic cases of possession. The possessed individual will often exhibit accelerated motor function, enabling that person to perform physical actions which he or she would normally be incapable of. The same is of course true for some individuals who are suffering from extreme pathological states, a fact that is discussed in "The Exorcist" by members of the medical team attending Regan. Unlike extreme pathological states, however, actual cases of possession will also often be accompanied by external psychokinetic activity. Some examples of this activity may be objects moving seemingly by themselves within the room, heavy rumblings or poundings in the wall, ceiling or floor, individuals in the room being assaulted by something unseen, as well as a sudden noticeable fluctuation in the room temperature and/or atmosphere. My brother Carl and I have both experienced all of these phenomena taking place, while in the same room with an individual whom had suddenly gone into a state of possession.

Regan's head turning around to face backwards while mocking the death of director Burke Dennings, and later turning around a complete 360-degrees during the main exorcism scene was included merely for shock value. However, in both the book and the movie screenplay, William Peter Blatty may not have intended the head-turning scenes to be taken literally. Instead, he may have intended these as examples of telekinesis…in other words, an image projected into the minds of the viewers who are present. Other examples of this in the context of the story include when Lt. Detective Kinderman is parked outside of the MacNeil residence at night, and he glimpses an eerie silhouette of what appears to be Regan floating about her room. Since Regan is supposedly restrained to her bed at the time, this would suggest that what Lt. Kinderman is seeing, is an astral projection or a telepathically projected image, rather than an actual levitation. There are also "subliminal" flashes of Captain Howdy as a ghostly death's head throughout the film, with more shots included in the recently released version that contains additional footage.

At one point during the exorcism scene, when both Father Karras and Father Merrin are sent sprawling onto the floor by a violent tremor within the room, they glance up and see a vision of Regan, kneeling upright on her bed having torn free of her restraints. Directly in back of her the statue of Pazuzu appears which Father Merrin had confronted at the beginning of the film. A moment later we again see Regan lying upon the bed, struggling to free herself of her wrist restraints, once again securely intact. This indicates what the two priests had just witnessed was actually a psychically projected image, rather than something tangible. And again, during a break in the exorcism, Father Karras returns to the bedroom to check on Regan's vital signs. Instead of seeing Regan when he enters the room, Karras momentarily glimpses his deceased mother sitting up on the bed, mournfully gazing at him. Then, as Karras approaches the bed, the illusion has ended, and he once again sees that it is Regan lying upon the bed.

Another significant factor in this scene is that Regan then begins addressing Karras in his mother's voice, in a ploy for sympathy. The demon is manipulating him by using his emotional vulnerability against him, eventually causing Karras to cry out in anguish, "You're not my mother!" This is actually very typical of the strategy a demonic entity will use during an exorcism. It is essentially a delay tactic on the part of the invading spirit, in an effort to avoid expulsion from its host. A demon will certainly have no reservations against using a person's emotional weaknesses against him or her, and it will often drag up painful, hurtful memories in an attempt to get that person to back off. This is one of the reasons that such a situation should not be entered into lightly, or without taking proper defensive precautions beforehand.

Father Merrin's word rings true when he tells Father Karras just prior to the exorcism, "The demon is a liar. He will lie to confuse us. But he will also mix lies with the truth." Merrin also advises Karras, "The attack is psychological, but powerful. So don't listen."

Interestingly, while Regan is under possession, she exhibits four distinct personalities: the Demon (which is the dominant one), the Dennings personality, the Gibberish personality, and later, Mary Karras. However, Father Merrin tells Father Karras that in reality only one personality, the Demon, exists and the others are merely deceptions.


A well-known scene in the film takes place during the exorcism where Regan rips free of her wrist restraints and, with her arms spread out in a mocking crucifixion pose, begins to levitate upward. She then remains suspended several feet over the bed, as Father Karras and Father Merrin both throw holy water on her, while repeating over and over, "The power of Christ compels you!" This eventually proves effective, as Regan's suspended body slowly begins to drift back downward onto the bed.

This type of levitation by demonically possessed persons is extremely rare, although not entirely unheard of. Interestingly, what is more commonly reported is the levitation of individuals who are in a state of religious ecstasy, or mystics who are in a deep state of meditation. Saint Francis of Assisi was said to have levitated at times. There are also more modern examples of "holy" levitation on record, with Padre Pio being one, as well as certain Hindu mystics. As for levitation during exorcisms, it is much more common for objects in the room to be momentarily levitated, rather than the possessed individual. Instances of people who are performing or assisting in exorcisms, being "lifted" by something unseen, perhaps an inch or so above ground level, and then being violently flung or shoved backwards have also been documented. But again, this is an extremely rare phenomenon.

Also presented in both the book and the film version of "The Exorcist" is Regan, while under possession, speaking in languages she has never known or studied. This is certainly a true aspect of diabolical possession, and it is one of the criteria that the Catholic Church will accept as evidence of actual possession. In "The Exorcist," however, while Regan is manifesting the "Gibberish" personality, Father Karras records the gibberish and has it analyzed by the language department at Georgetown University, where it is eventually revealed that she's actually speaking English in reverse. The book delves into more thorough detail on this topic than the film does. Personally, I've never known of a case where a possessed individual spoke a language in reverse, although speaking in another language during possession which is foreign to the individual has, indeed, been repeatedly documented. Some victims of demonic possession have been known to speak in Classic languages such as Latin, or occasionally even Aramaic (the Hebrew dialect which Jesus spoke), without having previously studied these languages.

Despite some of the exaggeration and sensationalism, in many ways the story of "The Exorcist" rings true to authentic cases of possession and exorcism. It is, after all, at least loosely based on an actual account of possession, and the subsequent exorcism that took place. In both the true account as well as the fictionalized story of "The Exorcist", the afflicted individual was successfully delivered of demonic possession.

For many years, exorcism and demonic possession were relegated to a back burner, owing largely to the increased advancement in the medial diagnosis of pathological states such as epilepsy, schizophrenia, Multiple Personality Disorder, Gilles de la Tourette Syndrome, etc. Today in modern 21st Century America, a general resurgence of belief in spirit possession seems to be taking place. Exorcisms are also gaining more notoriety, and are reportedly being performed not only by the Catholic clergy, but also by every major religious denomination in the country. One can even turn on the TV and see publicly televised exorcisms being performed by popular deliverance ministers, such as evangelists Bob Larson and Tom Brown.

Some modern exorcisms performed in America today have a darker, more abusive side. This involves privately conducted "home-done" exorcisms, which are more frequently being reported. One such example of this recently occurred in Phoenix, Arizona, when a 48-year-old man grappled with police who were trying to restrain him from "exorcising" a demon from his 3-year-old granddaughter by choking her. Also inside the room was the girl's 19-year-old mother who was naked, smeared with blood, and continually chanting. Officers used a Tazer stun gun on the man twice in an effort to subdue him. The girl's grandfather was handcuffed and began to recover, but soon afterward, he stopped breathing and died.

"The Exorcist" remains a familiar icon within our culture, even to many people who have never even seen the film version or read the book by William Peter Blatty. Over the last thirty-four years since the film's release, a great number of movies and TV shows have been influenced by "The Exorcist," including an episode of the TV show "Hercules: The Legendary Journeys," and the movie "Repossessed," in which Linda Blair parodied her original role. And it is possible that the recently re-released DVD version of "The Exorcist" may indeed have had at least a partial influence in the renewed interest in demon possession and exorcism, as a new generation has become acquainted with the film.

Two final notes of caution, however. Firstly, exorcism is not a game, nor is it something to be taken lightly or attempted alone. Serious potential dangers exist in performing an exorcism, to both the exorcist and the person who is the subject of deliverance. Before exorcism is even attempted, professionals should medically and psychologically evaluate the condition of the allegedly possessed individual. And even those who are experienced in performing exorcisms should certainly not attempt it without capable assistance.

Secondly, under no circumstance should anyone ever challenge a demonic spirit to "come into me," as Father Karras does in one of the final scenes of "The Exorcist". A true demonic spirit can and will take this as an open invitation to invade that person. The person issuing this challenge will have given legal permission for the demonic entity to infiltrate his or her conscious will. At the very worst, spontaneous possession may occur... if not right then, more probably sooner than later. At the very least, the demonic spirit may begin seriously oppressing that person. This type of situation will be extremely difficult to resolve. When all is said and done, it is best not to tempt fate, by tempting the demonic.

So sit back, and enjoy watching "The Exorcist" if you are inclined to do so. However, because of the subject matter, viewer discretion is advisable, especially to those who are easily upset or impressionable to such a graphic presentation. Also keep in mind that while it is a work of fiction, the reality behind the story is something which should be taken seriously.

Recommended related reading:

"The Exorcist" by William Peter Blatty

"Hostage to the Devil" by Malachi Martin

"The Demonologist" by Gerald Brittle

"Shadows of the Dark" by John Zaffis & Brian McIntyre

"Deliverance from Evil Spirits" by Francis MacNutt

# Chapter 19

## The Lighthouse Inn

"There are few homes in America more attractively situated than the property of Mrs. Charles S. Guthrie in New London, Connecticut. This is the embodiment of the ideas of what a house should be." – American Homes and Gardens, September 1912.

$B$uilt in the year 1902 as the grand summer home of steel magnate Charles S. Guthrie, the Lighthouse Inn in New London, Connecticut was originally known as Meadow Court, due to the wildflowers that surrounded it. Famed Boston architect William Emerson designed the mansion itself, while the landscape was the brainchild of Frederick Law Olmstead, also noted for having designed Central Park. The mansion also commanded a magnificent view of Long Island Sound. In the year 1906, Charles S. Guthrie died at the relatively young age of 46. In 1925, Mrs. Guthrie sold the property, and in 1927 Meadow Court reopened as the Lighthouse Inn, renamed after its close proximity to the New London Harbor Light. In time, the Lighthouse Inn became a popular resort for many and was even frequented by such film stars as Bette Davis, Joan Crawford and William Bendix. It was during a stay at the Inn that songwriter Roger Williams wrote the popular song "Autumn Leaves" in 1951.

In the year 1979, a fire broke out on the 3rd floor of the mansion. Although apparently no deaths or serious injuries resulted from this fire, the 3rd floor area was heavily damaged. The entire inn was shut down for extensive repairs and renovations, reopening again in 1981. In 1996, the Lighthouse Inn was officially declared a National Historic Landmark, at which a lavish dedication ceremony was held. Then, in 2001, the inn came into the possession of Jim and Marylis McGrath. The following year the McGraths celebrated the inn's 100th birthday as a building, and its 75th anniversary as an inn.

The Lighthouse Inn is also supposedly haunted by at least two ghosts, although the identities of these two ghosts have yet to be determined. Sometime in the 1930's, a young bride supposedly tripped and tumbled to her death on the main staircase on her wedding day. Although this tragic story has never been verified, her spirit is believed to be one of the two ghosts that haunt the Inn. Also, the spirit of a little girl has reportedly been seen in one of the 2nd floor rooms. As is the case with the bride, this little girl's true identity and the reason she would be haunting this particular room remain unknown. It is theorized by some that the spirit haunting this room is that of a little girl who was left unattended in the bathtub, and subsequently drowned.

Some may of course recall the Lighthouse Inn being featured in an episode from Season 1 of Ghost Hunters. The TAPS crew arrived early on a September evening, and set up video monitors and other recording devices, such as wireless audio, throughout various places inside the inn. While investigating that evening with other members of TAPS, my brother Carl and I conducted an EVP session on the first floor staircase. This of course was the very same staircase upon which the bride allegedly fell to her untimely death several decades ago.

At one point during the EVP session, while I was recording with a small hand held analog recorder, Carl asked, "Did you die here on the stairs?" When I played back the recording, a distinctively male voice answered with an emphatic "No."

Later that same evening, in the basement tunnel of the Lighthouse Inn, TAPS investigator Steve Gonsalves felt as though he'd been touched on his shoulder. Understandably, Steve was more than a little uncomfortable at being touched by an unseen presence. Also that evening, a loud clattering noise emanated from the deserted kitchen area while Grant Wilson was passing by. This sound was caught on our recording devices as well. Although Grant tried to simulate the sound by dropping pans and other kitchen utensils, he was unable to reproduce the exact sound. The source of this sound remained unexplained when we left that night, as did the incident of Steve being touched by an unseen presence while in the basement tunnel.

On May 20th, 2006, the organization 'Ghost Images' founded by Judi Giramonti held its first annual conference at the Lighthouse Inn. Sandra and I, along with Andrew Graham of NEAR/TAPS and John Zaffis of PRSNE were the guest speakers.

Andrew spoke first, his topic being "String Theory and the Paranormal." During the Q&A portion of Andrew's lecture, I posed a question about time displacements, or perhaps more accurately, event displacements, regarding 'The Philadelphia Experiment,' and its possible relation to String Theory. This experiment, from the summer of 1943 at the Philadelphia Naval Yard, involved the USS Eldridge, and was intended to develop a 'cloaking device' for American Naval ships to avoid being detected by radar. Although no reliable eyewitness accounts, there were unconfirmed reports that the experiment resulted in some of the crewmen being partially embedded in the steel hull of the ship, as well as some completely irrational behavior by the crew.

When Andrew finished speaking, we all took a break with entertainment provided by a teenage Country and Western singer named Brittany Leigh, a family friend of our host Judi Giramonti, and the youngest member of Ghost Images. Brittany Leigh wowed us with three live upbeat songs.

When the lectures resumed, I spoke of the topic of true, historic vampire cases in New England. The premise of my presentation centered on the common thread of these renowned cases. Throughout the 18th and 19th Centuries, families throughout rural New England communities would often turn to folklore to combat diseases such as tuberculosis, referred to at the time as "consumption." This folklore practice involved disinterring recently deceased family members, looking for a corpse that had not properly decayed, and then disrupting the corpse in some manner, usually by cutting out the heart and burning it upon a nearby rock. In some cases, the ashes from the heart were fed to ailing family members as a possible remedy.

The next lecture was given by John Zaffis on the topic of haunted objects. This was indeed intriguing as John spoke about various cases he had been involved with where inanimate objects had somehow acquired spirit attachments. For example, a haunted doll was found in an attic, and mysteriously kept coming back no matter how many times the homeowners attempted to get rid of it. John also shared stories of Ouija boards, and explained that these conjuring boards were often more than just a game. As John explained, sometimes a spirit will come through masquerading as a human spirit, when in reality it may be an entity that has never walked the Earth in human form.

After the lectures were finished, I took a few moments to listen to some of the audio that I recorded from the lectures. It was during Andrew Graham's lecture, when he was mentioning about 'The Philadelphia Experiment' that I suddenly heard a voice on the recording saying "No!" Certainly no one in the room had said this at the time. I rewound the recording and replayed it, and sure enough, there was the low voice clearly saying "No!"

Although I had merely been recording the lecture for content, it turned out that I had inadvertently captured an EVP. And I had to wonder if there was any connection to this EVP, and the similar one that I had recorded with my brother Carl during our investigation with TAPS.

After the lectures completed, the host group and the speakers in the 2nd floor area undertook an investigation. Although Sandra, Andrew and I hadn't known an investigation would be included in the conference, we had fortunately at least brought along with us a couple of analog tape recorders and cameras, just in case!

We were all upstairs in the 2nd floor bedroom, where alleged sightings of the little girl's spirit have been reported, Room #14. Sandra decided to do an EVP session by herself for a few moments in the bathroom adjacent to the bedroom. She then rejoined the group in the bedroom for an EVP session in that room. After the second session, we decided to listen to some of her recording. It turned out that, just as she was entering the bathroom to begin her EVP session, a male voice was recorded, "Get ooouut."

We were later joined in the bedroom by a sensitive, who was giving readings to participants of the conference. Upon stepping into the bathroom, she commented that she could sense some sort of portal or "cylinder" in the same location where Sandra recorded the EVP. Now, I don't exactly know what to make of the sensitive's claim, I was intrigued she made this remark in the same area where Sandra recorded the EVP, without yet knowing about the EVP. And although this certainly could be a coincidence, I do consider it worth mentioning. Strangely, the EVP did have a hollow sound to it, as if it was recorded in a hollow space like a tunnel.

While we were in Room # 14, I continued my audio recording while Brittany Leigh, the youngest member of Ghost Images, happened to briefly mention an investigation she'd recently attended in Pennsylvania. Somehow this seemed to cause a reaction. Shortly after she'd finished speaking, John Zaffis bolted upright and suddenly announced that he was getting the distinct impression of an unseen presence in the room with us. Judy, Brittany and the psychic were also getting the distinct impression that there was some sort of unseen presence in the room with us. Although it did not last long, it did leave some people in the room visibly shaken.

I then rewound the audio tape and began playing it back. Just before Brittany Leigh finished speaking about the Pennsylvania case, a low male voice on the tape could be heard saying, "Heeeelp heeeer."

Although we did not verify the actual identities of any of the alleged spirits haunting The Lighthouse Inn, I do personally feel that we did, collectively, experience sufficient phenomena to prove something of a paranormal nature exists. We do believe The Lighthouse Inn to be haunted by more than one intelligent entity. Room # 14 of course seemed to be quite active. Subsequent research failed to verify any actual tragedy having historically taken place in this room, any more than we were able to verify that a bride had fallen to her death on the staircase out in the hallway. But then again a tragic event is not always necessary for paranormal activity to take place at a certain location. It would certainly have been interesting, if time had permitted, to have investigated some of the other individual rooms, to see if similar results might have been obtained.

Unfortunately, the Lighthouse Inn has since gone out of business and has subsequently been acquired by the city of New London. Hopefully, the existence of this once splendid hotel will be allowed to continue, for future generations to appreciate.... and perhaps also to respectfully investigate. We who did actually investigate there feel that we have only scratched the surface of the mysteries hidden within the Lighthouse Inn.

**Sandra Johnson, John Zaffis and Andrew Graham at The Lighthouse Inn.**

# Chapter 20

### An Interview With Houdini... Aron, That Is

**S**andra and I first had the pleasure of meeting Aron Houdini at Mid-South Paranormal Convention, held in Louisville, KY in October of 2009. This convention was of course the brainchild of the "Paranormal Rocker" himself, Keith Age. We found Aron to be quite an affable fellow, rather unassuming in appearance and soft-spoken with a slight Southern inflection to his speech. In fact, it was only his last name – and the fact that he was billed as "The Only Living Houdini" - that caused this polite gentleman with the stocky build and laid back Southern accent to stand out.

Yes, Aron was indeed directly related to the legendary magician and escape artist Harry Houdini (born Erik Weisz; March 24, 1874 – died October 31, 1926). In fact, he was the master's great-great nephew. Aron also casually informed us that he had followed his celebrated ancestor's footsteps, performing magic for over 15 years. Aron had been voted Entertainer of the Year, awarded 2 National Magic Championships, earned the title of Straight Jacket World Champion (would I have guessed that such a title even existed?) and a Guinness World Record. Aron told us he would be honored to have us attend his upcoming performance within the hour. Sandra and I assured him that the honor would be all ours; we were psyched about attending his performance.

Approximately an hour later, Sandra and I were seated among the audience in a room filled with eager spectators, watching as Aron performed a variety of fascinating magic tricks and illusions, interspersed with his witty brand of humor. It was apparent that once Aron was performing for a live audience, his normally laid-back personality became imbued with charisma and high energy.

It then came time for Aron's escape from a straightjacket, which has been most everyone's favorite escape stunt ever since Harry Houdini originally made the Straightjacket Escape famous. As an assistant was snugly fitting Aron into the jacket and tightly securing the various latches, Aron explained to the audience that unlike the type of jacket many magicians use, this is not a fake, but an authentic straightjacket. Aron explained that ownership of the authentic ones require a prescription issued by a physician. He added that the only way he can successfully escape from a fully secured straightjacket is to completely dislocate his shoulder, which he was about to do. And the only way he could accomplish this was to forcibly bang his shoulder against a solid wall.

"Say, what??" I thought to myself.

Aron stood silently in front of the audience for perhaps four or five seconds, psychologically preparing himself while taking a few deep breaths. He then made a running start before hurling himself against the nearest wall with a loud THUD, causing many of the audience members to gasp in shock. But apparently this initial impact had not done the trick. Aron then backed up a few paces, before again running and hurling his left shoulder against the wall a second time. This time, the thud was also accompanied by an audible, somewhat sickening-sounding POP... meaning that the second impact had been sufficient to dislocate his left shoulder from the socket.

Although Aron was obviously in considerable pain once his shoulder had been properly dislocated, he then set about the task of struggling out of the confines of his straightjacket. Sandra later recalled that his face was beet red from the incredible exertion. After several minutes of what appeared to be a painful-yet-determined effort, Aron Houdini did successfully manage to slip out of the straightjacket! While still red-faced and catching his breath, he held the empty jacket up and took his bows to a well-deserved round of cheers and applause from the audience. He then leaned his left arm against a nearby table to reinsert the joint properly back into the socket (this time with an audible CRUNCH), while speaking casually to the audience about the experience.

After the performance had ended, Sandra and I approached Aron and enthusiastically told him just how impressed we were, especially with the straightjacket escape.

Sandra said, "I could tell that you were in a considerable amount of pain after dislocating your shoulder!" Despite the discomfort he was obviously still in, Aron managed to laugh and told her it was just something he had to endure. He thanked us so much for being there, and for lending our support. Before Sandra and I left, I also told Aron that I would very much enjoy doing a full interview with him some day when time permitted, to which he responded that he'd be honored.

The opportunity for me to interview Aron Houdini finally came in March of 2011, when Sandra and I were invited to participate in Phenomenology103, a paranormal convention held in Gettysburg, PA, organized by Dana Steward Wingard of N.E.P.I. (North Eastern Paranormal Investigations). As luck would have it, our pal Aron attended the convention as well, teaming up with the Kling Brothers of Ghost Lab fame. Accompanying Aron was his significant other, a pretty, petite young woman named Bridget Lynn Brady. It was late on Saturday afternoon that I finally found time to sit down with Aron and conduct my anticipated interview with him, to which he cordially agreed.

Once again, Aron's black-rimmed glasses and down-to-earth demeanor belied the fact that this was an actual blood relation to the great Harry Houdini, who carried on his celebrated ancestor's tradition of performing daring escape acts that required incredible skill and stamina... not to mention pure guts. After some casual conversation, Aron, Bridget and I sat down at a table in one of the quieter sections of the convention hall, and the interview commenced.

K: "Aron, could you explain exactly how you are related to the great Harry Houdini?"

A: "Yeah. Houdini's brother Theodore married my great-grandma's sister Elsie. So Houdini would literally be my great-great uncle."

K: "Now, many people who are descended from famous people don't necessarily carry in their footsteps. What made you decide to carry on in your famous ancestor's tradition?"

A: "Growing up, when I'd hear people talk about Houdini, I'd always want to do magic tricks, and Houdini was the best, and I always wanted to be the best. I started learning to do basic magic tricks and began performing at birthday parties and various other functions. And when people started paying me for it, I soon realized that this was what I wanted to do. It was when I turned eighteen that I took on the straightjacket, and many of the other crazy escapes."

K: "Aron, how did you acquire these skills? Obviously it took a great deal of practice, but did you have any manuals or personal notes left from Harry Houdini himself?"

A: "Yeah, I've got a lot of personal notes, and I've also got a few books and manuals. But much of it's also self-taught. Another magician and escape artist, Lance Burton also taught me a lot of the magic tricks. You just take an old trick, try to change it around and make it new."

K: "Now, what are the specifications for the straightjackets that you yourself personally use?"

A: "Well, first it's got to be a real straightjacket. A lot of magicians use the fake straightjacket."

K: "Well, that's not really fair."

A: "No. They're gonna be an entertainer, and that's fine. But they need to call it a magic trick, and not an escape. The actual escapes, they're dangerous and you can end up getting really hurt. I've been hurt several times getting out of the straightjacket."

K: "Which is why they're illegal, right?"

A: "Exactly. So first you've got to dislocate your shoulder to get out, which I do. And once you do that, you can get out of the sleeve. The next step is to get that crotch strap off, and then get the jacket off of your head. But there's a great deal of dedication involved in the process. You have to be able to commit to being in pain, to get out of the thing."

K: "Now, how did you learn to dislocate your shoulder for this escape?"

A: "The same doctor who wrote me the prescription for my first straightjacket also took on the challenge of helping me out. He and a local chiropractor in my hometown worked extensively with me, and stretched my arm and taught me how to dislocate my shoulder."

K: "That's amazing!" I was glad that Aron did not notice that I was probably turning a slight shade of green at this point! "Now, would anybody be required to dislocate their shoulder? Is that a prerequisite to getting out of a straightjacket?"

A: "There's no way whatsoever to get out of one without dislocating your shoulder. Not a real straightjacket."

K: Is there a difference between the jackets you use, and the ones used in asylums?"

A: "Not really any difference, no. The ones I use are made by Posey. That's the only company in the world that makes the real straightjacket; nobody else makes one. Most of the hospitals that use them are federal hospitals. A lot of state hospitals aren't even allowed to use them. I don't know how it is overseas, but Posey is the only way to get the kind I use. And these are the same ones used in hospitals and asylums or wherever. Same exact ones."

K: "You in a way have taken up where Harry Houdini left off, correct? I mean there's some things he did and you are taking it a step further, right?"

A: "Yeah, I try to. Houdini was Jewish. He spoke Russian, Hebrew and English. When I attended University, I took Russian and Hebrew for three years. Mentally those are the two hardest classes; people there couldn't believe I took both of them at the same time! I went that far and I take on the paranormal. I work with paranormal investigators and psychics, trying to understand or find evidence. To date I've been unlucky. I've heard things that I can't explain, but I've not seen anything that I couldn't explain. So, every avenue Houdini took, I've tried to take as well, or have my sights on taking."

K: "So, you go into the spiritual realm as Houdini did as well, from a practical standpoint, right?"

A: "Yes, with an open mind. Anything's possible. And I go in looking to be the one to find the evidence, or to be there if something happens. And I've been to over four hundred locations, and just not had any luck as yet. Hopefully one day!"

K: "Now, Houdini seemed to have somewhat of a vendetta into debunking spiritualists and psychics, which of course were rampant during his time. People made a good living from supposed spirit contact, and that's what he seemed to be diametrically opposed to. How do you feel about that?"

A: "Same way Houdini did. A lot of people who depend on psychics go to psychics because they want to hear good news. They want to talk to loved ones. They want to know what the future has for them, and who's visiting them. They pay these psychics or spiritualists money to find these things out. It becomes an emotional bondage, and I don't think it's fair to take advantage of people. If you go to the door and it says, 'This is for entertainment purposes only,' that's a different thing. When you go in there believing what you're paying someone to tell you and you're being lied to, to me it's a form of fraud. That's where I kinda like step in. You know, I'm no one to prove anything to, but before you get my personal approval, you're gonna have to convince me. And you better believe, once you do, I'm gonna promote you. All it needs is, sit down with me, and a little proof. Every day I have people ask me, 'Can you recommend a real psychic? I needed to talk to somebody.' Sadly, nobody's ever taken the time to sit down with me. A lot of psychics come by my table. They'll get to all the tables; they get to my table and they walk around me."

K: "Is it the reputation of the name Houdini?"

A: "Yes, that's one-hundred percent the reason why. They think I'm gonna call them out, so they steer clear."

K: "Would you classify yourself more as a magician, an escape artist, an investigator, or is it pretty much equal?"

A: "You know, I love the escapes more. But, I would say I'm a magician, an escape artist, illusionist and paranormal investigator."

K: "All around good guy, too."

A: (laughs) "Thanks! I don't know if you need to limit it into one category. These are things I'm passionate about. I want to prove that there's nobody out there that can get out of the things that I can get out of, or willing to put themselves through what I do, to get out of 'em. And then when I get into the paranormal, I want to find evidence. I want to believe. I want to be able to say, 'I don't care what you believe, I KNOW that there's something; I've seen it.' And then to do magic. I want to be an entertainer. I want to entertain people, make 'em laugh. And leave them with a little something they didn't have before they've seen my show."

K: "Now, would you classify yourself as any kind of extremist? I know there are of course some stage magicians, without naming names who will test their limits by exposing themselves to deprivations, such as being buried alive, extreme temperatures, or confinement without food or water for extended periods of time. Do you ever perform any sort of extreme stunts like that?"

A: "Sometimes. In Waverly Hills, for example, I spent two days in the freezer, locked in the mortuary for two days. I've spent forty-five minutes locked in a coffin sealed with no air. Things like that. I've been locked in a box in a straightjacket, with a copper head snake. So I've done some of the extreme, crazy things, and I just do 'em as they come. I'm saving some for maybe a TV show or something down the road."

K: "Speaking of extreme, Aron, could you describe, from your personal perspective, exactly what it's like to be in a straightjacket, hoisted upside-down... how high up were you?"

A: "Thirty feet, last week."

K: "Okay, thirty feet, and getting out of a straightjacket while dangling upside-down. How would you describe that?"

A: "The fastest way, 'painful.' As I've explained, the only way to get out of a real straightjacket is to dislocate your shoulder. So once I have a rope on to be hoisted up by the crane, I don't use any safety things, just a rope tied to my bare legs and ankles. And right before I go upside-down, I dislocate my shoulder. When I'm upside-down, all my weight's reversed, and the pressure is all on my knees and ankles. I weigh two-fifteen, so that's two hundred-fifteen pounds pulling on my knees and ankles. I also got rope burn. I was bleeding, because it was pulling on my skin like that. So it's painful. It's exciting, seeing everybody looking up like that, and I'm looking down at them. It's a whole different perspective, and it's definitely an attention-getter. It's a lot of fun!"

K: "How do you avoid going into panic mode while you're performing some of these extreme escape stunts?"

A: "A lot of times I used to. I'd panic and I'd almost mess up. I'd hurt myself in some way. But you've got to accept what you're about to do, and accept the consequences of what could happen. Prepare, and be extra cautious. Hope for the best."

K: "Now if you could actually describe yourself, who is Aron Houdini? What drives you?"

A: "You know, I'd like to say that at some point in my life, I'd be the greatest escape artist ever. Nobody has to know me. Nobody has to remember me. Just if I had one thing, that's what I'd want. And I know it's a long shot, because I've got another Houdini in my way. But, you know, his ideas and ways have led me down the path I'm on, looking at those dreams."

K: "Now in a spiritual sense, do you ever feel you're being personally guided by Harry Houdini?"

A: "A lot of times I do, yeah. I think, what would he say? What would he do? What would go wrong here for me to do it this way or that way?

You know, I look at it from all views. And a lot of times, Houdini was the greatest showman of all time... off the stage more than on. He could promote his show, show up in town an hour before, and sell the theater out, just by word of mouth. He was the best at that. And I look at it that way too."

K: "Talking to you, you seem like a very average, everyday nice guy. You wouldn't notice anything unusual about you on the street. So, how do people react when they find out who you are and what you do?"

A: "Exactly like you just said. A lot of times they're like, 'You don't look like you do what you do!' But for me, I'm in my jeans and tee shirt, and that's all I need. I'll put a straightjacket on whether I'm in jeans and a tee shirt, shorts and flip flops, or wearing a tuxedo and dress shoes. It don't matter to me. This is who I am, so this is the way I go with it."

K: "Now, of course I assume your advice to the average lay person would be, 'Don't try this at home.' What would you advise other people who are getting into escaping or stage magic? What would be your basic advice to them?"

A: "With magic, I would say just keep going and do it. Don't give up. The escapes, I would advise against it. I'd probably even say, if I went back fifteen years, I wouldn't do it. Not for what I had to go through: emergencies, laying on heating pads and icy-hot pads and pain medication all the time just 'cause I hurt. And it's just the price you have to pay. So far I've always gotten out. I don't guarantee I'm not gonna get hurt, but I always get out. So of course, there's always a few maniacs that are gonna do it. But concerning magic and illusions, I'd say be yourself. Never try to copy, or be what you think somebody wants you to be. I tried to do that. I'd show up at these conventions wearing black pants, a black shirt, a completely dark look, but it just wasn't me. So be yourself. If you're a serious type, perform the real prestige type magic. If you're a goofy guy, you can do the goofy magic. It may take you a few performances, but eventually you'll know what's right for you."

K: "One saying Harry Houdini helped to make famous was of course, 'Ladies and gentlemen, as you can see, I have nothing up my sleeve.'"

A: "With the whole sleeve thing in general, you can do the greatest magic trick in the world, and maybe you got one shot at it. And if you come out you've got sleeves, you may win everybody in the audience except for one person, because they say it went up your sleeve. It's devastating. You work to win the entire audience and you got all but one, because you wore the sleeves. So I never wear sleeves when I'm performing. If I have a jacket on, the sleeves are up, I roll 'em up, which is exactly what Houdini did."

K: "Would you describe yourself as a contortionist?"

A: "I don't know. When I graduated high school I weighed about one hundred-twenty pounds. Ran track, I was a little-bitty stick and bones. Then I left and went into the army, and was marching and running and eating constantly. And I went straight up to two-hundred pounds. And it immediately made it more difficult for me to get out of my escapes. I had to get a bigger straightjacket. And because I wasn't as flexible, it hurt me to do this. So, I'm not much of a contortionist. I have no double joints. One time I was doing handcuff escapes, and I had a handcuff hung on my hand. I was so close to getting out, but I had to keep pushing my thumb until the handcuff came off, and my thumb broke. I had no choice but to break my thumb. And the handcuff came off, and the audience is clapping and cheering. And I ended up having surgery and stuff because of it. Mentally I'm a contortionist, but not physically."

K: "Now that's dedication, Aron! Would you say you have an abnormally high tolerance for physical pain?"

A: "Yeah, probably. I've also had a kidney stone blocked while performing. I think I'm mentally strong enough to hide the pain. So, you've got to ask yourself what's more important... living without this pain and discomfort, or being a professional escape artist going somewhere. For me, it's going somewhere."

K: "Do you practice any sort of meditation?"

A: "No, I don't. No meditation, just discipline. You know, at night when I'm going to sleep, or while on the computer, I'm sitting there and thinking, 'Well, what way will this technique work, or that work?' But I never sit and meditate, or sit backstage for five minutes of quiet before I go on, because I'm a go-go-go person. I'd rather put my shoes on and run straight out to the stage. I always stay prepared, though. So when I'm ready, everything's right there where it needs to be. Same thing with everyday life, as with my magic and escape tricks."

K: "So, you don't place yourself in any kind of a trance, or self-hypnosis?"A: "Nope, never. I looked into it once, about people who do that and I found out quickly it wasn't for me."

K: "Do you do any sort of hypnosis as part of your act?"

A: "I do a little comedy bit of hypnosis, but it's not actual hypnosis. The original Houdini did though, as part of his act. His audience members would claim they didn't remember seeing the show. He'd hypnotize them on the first trick. A lot of times they'd look at their watch and two hours just went by, but they wouldn't remember seeing anything; they couldn't remember anything in between. They'd want their money back. Lots of writings out there about that."

K: "That's something I've never heard about him."

A: "He was a very smart guy, and he knew how to put 'em in the seats."

K: "What do you think of the way Harry Houdini died? I mean, was it because he didn't seek medical attention and just went on with the show as is often portrayed, even though he was suffering from acute appendicitis?"

A: "Yeah, he was a little headstrong. If he had gone to the doctor immediately instead of performing three more days, he would have lived and went on, and who knows what he would have accomplished? But what a loss, because he went way, way too early. That's a hard thing for me to swallow, because I think there's a part of me that wants to believe that he never did die. Nearly a century after his death, he's still the most talked about person in magic."

K: "Aron, how would you feel if you were eventually compared to Harry Houdini to the point of people saying, 'Houdini returns! Here we have Houdini again!' How would that make you feel?"

A: "Extremely honored. You know, I'd like to see the headlines, 'Aron Houdini equals feat of Harry Houdini!' I don't want it to say better. Equal is good. Just being compared with him would be amazing. He's the greatest of all time, no one even close."

K: "How would you compare yourself with Evel Knievel?"

A: (Laughs) "I wouldn't. His was not escapes, his was stunts, where you gotta practice and ride the bike, and jump so many cars. There's also a lot of practice required in escaping. It's like, if you don't get outta here, you're dead. Or it really hurts. Two different things, both dangerous. Both with a certain result if you fail. But, he was an interesting guy, too."

K: "So, what is ahead for you, Aron?"

A: "I'm doing a lot of paranormal events, where we go out just like Houdini done, and search for answers. A lot of magic shows are coming up. I do magic at all the Ghost Lab events, every event they have. We have an investigation one night. We go out and have a party the next night, and I do magic and entertain. And I'm also working on doing a TV show. Maybe everybody can see a lot more of me. Hopefully. And then hopefully we'll go from there to Vegas. That would be great."

K: "What types of extraordinary escapes might we be seeing you perform on a TV series, Aron?"

A: "Well, we've got lots of ideas for a television show. Our goal is a hundred different escapes. That means a minimum of twenty a season. We'll split it up into two a show. We've come up with all kinds of crazy things. Pretty much we looked at what Houdini had done, and I plan to redo them. And some of them are totally original... one being me locked in a box, in a straightjacket, with a dangerous snake. Another would be me going over Niagara Falls in a barrel, tied to something, and having just so much time to get out of it. I'd be hooked onto like a zip line before I go over the Falls. That's certain death if it fails. So lots of ideas. But going over the Falls is one of them. We've looked at actually going back to my hometown, and having me go over a place there called Cumberland Falls. We'll definitively see where it goes."


K: "Great! Thank you very much for this interview, Aron Houdini. And Sandra and I are both hoping that you'll take a detour to Rhode Island some time, and appear on our show Ghosts R NEAR."

A: "Cool! I've love to do it."


K: (Turning to Bridget) "Any contributing words, Bridget?"

B: "I love him!!"

**Aron Houdini escaping a straightjacket, with his shoulder painfully dislocated.**

# Acknowledgments

**M**uch appreciation goes to my editor, Susan Soares, of SJS Comic Promotions for her input and help in shaping this edition of the Paranormal Realities series.

Many thanks, also, to Jeanine Calkin (Jeanine Calkin Photography) for her photographic submissions and assistance with cover design.

For lending me your expertise, you both have my (and Sandra's) admiration!

Keith Johnson Jr. collecting cemetery data.

## About the Author

Keith and Sandra Johnson are regularly called upon to assist individuals in dealing with alleged malevolent paranormal phenomena or potential inhuman infestation in their homes and together have over 40 years of experience as paranormal investigators.

Keith has had an interest in the paranormal since he was a teenager when he had phenomena occur in his own home. In the seventies, he was a member of the paranormal research group Parapsychology Investigation & Research Organization, out of RI College.

Keith has been featured on the SyFy Channel's Ghost Hunters, as a consulting demonologist, and both he and Sandra are former core members of The Atlantic Paranormal Society (TAPS).

They have been featured as demonology consultants in two first season episodes of the A&E series Paranormal State as well as assisting with documentaries dealing with the paranormal including New Gravity Media's '14 Degrees'.

The pair are co-founders of New England Anomalies Research and host a local TV talk show dealing with paranormal topics called Ghosts R N.E.A.R. which airs locally in Rhode Island and can also be seen online.

Keith is the author of the 'Paranormal Realities' book series that chronicle his experiences as a paranormal investigator.

You can learn more about them by visiting www.nearparanormal.com.

www.ingramcontent.com/pod-product-compliance
Lightning Source LLC
Chambersburg PA
CBHW030914090426
42737CB00007B/190